Hotel Development

PKF Consulting

Principal Authors

Bruce Baltin
Brian D. Bash
Thomas E. Callahan
John A. Fox
Karen Johnson
John M. Keeling
Corey Limbach
Patrick Quek
W. Martin Winfree, Jr.
Lynda Schrier Wirth

Contributing Authors

P. Peter Benudiz
James R. Butler, Jr.
Ronald J. Holecek
Walter A. Rutes
Ronald O. Van Pelt
Howard J. Wolff

Urban Land Institute

About ULI–the Urban Land Institute

ULI–the Urban Land Institute is a nonprofit education and research institute that is supported and directed by its members. Its mission is to provide responsible leadership in the use of land in order to enhance the total environment.

ULI sponsors educational programs and forums to encourage an open international exchange of ideas and sharing of experience; initiates research that anticipates emerging land use trends and issues and proposes creative solutions based on this research; provides advisory services; and publishes a wide variety of materials to disseminate information on land use and development.

Established in 1936, the Institute today has some 13,000 members and associates from more than 50 countries representing the entire spectrum of the land use and development disciplines. They include developers, builders, property owners, investors, architects, public officials, planners, real estate brokers, appraisers, attorneys, engineers, financiers, academics, students, and librarians. ULI members contribute to higher standards of land use by sharing their knowledge and experience. The Institute has long been recognized as one of America's most respected and widely quoted sources of objective information on urban planning, growth, and development.

Richard M. Rosan
Executive Vice President

Recommended bibliographic listing:
PFK Consulting. *Hotel Development*. Washington, D.C.: ULI–the Urban Land Institute, 1996.

ULI Catalog Number: H06
International Standard Book Number: 0-87420-798-3
Library of Congress Catalog Card Number: 96-61398

Copyright © 1996 by ULI–the Urban Land Institute
1025 Thomas Jefferson Street, N.W.
Suite 500 West
Washington, D.C. 20007-5201

Printed in the United States of America. All rights reserved. No part of this book may be reproduced in any form or by any means, electronic or mechanical, including photocopying, recording, or by any information storage and retrieval system, without written permission of the publisher.

Project Staff

Senior Vice President, Research, Education, and Publications
Rachelle L. Levitt

Vice President/Publisher and *Project Director*
Frank H. Spink, Jr.

Managing Editor
Nancy H. Stewart

Manuscript Editor
Libby Howland

Book Design/Layout
Helene Y. Redmond/HYR Graphics

Production Manager
Diann Stanley-Austin

Word Processing
Maria-Rose Cain
Joanne Nanez

Review Committee for *Hotel Development*

Gregory R. Dillon
Vice Chairman Emeritus and Director
Hilton Hotels Corporation
Beverly Hills, California
with Vladimir Sanda, Architecture and Construction; and
James L. Philon, Senior Vice President, Development (retired)

Ronald Eastman
Group Vice President, Lodging Development
Marriott Corporation
Washington, D.C.

Lee G. Lyles
President/COO
Canizaro Lyles Development Company
Charlotte, North Carolina

Charles H. Shaw
Chairman
The Shaw Company
Chicago, Illinois

Alan L. Tallis
Executive Vice President, Development
Red Roof Inns
Hillard, Ohio

About the Authors

PKF Consulting is a national hotel and real estate consulting firm with offices in major U.S. cities. As a member of the Pannell Kerr Forster International Association, PKF/C is networked with one of the world's largest accounting and consulting firms, which has 340 offices in 90 countries. PKF Consulting owns and maintains the database for *Trends in the Hotel Industry*, an annual statistical review of U.S. hotel operations that first appeared in 1935. The firm provides advisory services to assist hospitality practitioners in planning, managing, financing, appraising, valuing, and administering assets; improving operations; and buying and selling properties.

Bruce Baltin, CPA, is a senior vice president in charge of PKF Consulting's Los Angeles office. He has more than 25 years of diverse experience in economic, financial, and operational analyses, including market demand and development consulting for the hospitality and real estate industries. Before joining PKF, he was a corporate operations analyst for the Sheraton Hotel Corporation and a member of the hotel administration faculty at the University of Nevada–Las Vegas. He holds a bachelor's of science degree in hotel administration from Cornell University.

Brian D. Bash, CRE, is a vice president in the Philadelphia office of PKF Consulting. His specialties include advisory services for structuring large-scale real estate developments and complex financial analyses. He is experienced with public/private partnerships and with residential and hotel/retail mixed-use projects and conference centers. He holds a bachelor's of arts degree from Texas Christian University and a master's of arts degree from Pennsylvania State University, both in economics. He holds a Counselor of Real Estate designation and is a member of the International Association of Conference Centers.

Thomas E. Callahan, CPA, CRE, MAI, is an executive vice president of PKF Consulting and based in its San Francisco office. He formerly headed the PKF management advisory practices in Boston, Houston, and Los Angeles. His areas of expertise include market and feasibility studies, appraisals, hotel acquisition and disposition analysis, and real estate development planning. He has overseen masterplan studies for multiuse real estate projects in the United States and Asia, and has performed large, multihotel appraisal projects for a number of major banks. He holds a bachelor's of business administration degree in accounting and hotel and restaurant administration from Washington State University.

John A. Fox is a senior vice president in charge of PKF Consulting's New York office. His experience extends to market studies, due diligence, and financial consulting for hotel owners and lenders. No stranger to the courtroom, he appears regularly as an expert witness in business litigation matters and serves as a commercial arbitrator. He holds a bachelor's of science degree in hotel administration from Cornell University and is on the Panel of Arbitrators of the American Arbitration Association. He is a frequent contributor of articles to various hotel trade journals and is regularly quoted on hotel and travel issues in the national press.

Karen Johnson is a vice president in the Los Angeles office of PKF Consulting. A former regional director of hotel development planning for Marriott Hotels, she is experienced in multiproperty and portfolio analysis and with franchise and management contracts. She has performed feasibility and operational analyses in Europe and the United States. She holds a bachelor's of science degree, with honors, in hotel and restaurant administration from Michigan State University.

John M. Keeling is a senior vice president in charge of the PKF Consulting office in Houston. He has produced numerous market and positioning studies for hotels in the United States and Mexico and provides real estate advisory services to developers, financial institutions, and government agencies in the south central United States. Keeling was formerly a partner with Laventhol & Horwath. He received his master's of business administration degree from Michigan State University.

Corey Limbach is a vice president in the San Francisco office of PKF Consulting. He has headed engagements to provide market and financial consulting for hotels, resorts, casinos, and related hospitality enterprises on the West Coast and in Asia, particularly Southeast Asia and Polynesia. He holds a bachelor's of arts degree from the University of California–Berkeley in anthropology and is a member of the Pacific Asia Travel Association and the California Redevelopment Association.

Patrick Quek is president and CEO of PKF Consulting, headquartered in San Francisco. Before founding PKF Consulting in 1992, he was national director of management advisory services for Pannell Kerr Forster and chairman of its International Consulting Committee. He is a member of the board of directors of PKF Worldwide. He has more than 25 years of experience in tourism master-plan studies, economic and financial modeling, and portfolio management consulting. He has extensive experience in managing projects throughout the Pacific Rim, from Chile to Canada to China, Singapore, and Malaysia. He holds a bachelor's of business administration degree and master's of business administration degree from the University of Hawaii.

W. Martin Winfree, Jr., MAI, is a vice president in the San Francisco office of PKF Consulting. He is an experienced real estate appraiser who has completed engagements across the United States, particularly in the Southeast, the New York metropolitan area, and California. He holds a bachelor's of science degree in applied mathematics from North Carolina State University. He is a member of the Appraisal Institute, where he has served on its Regional Ethics and Counseling Panel.

Lynda Schrier Wirth is a vice president in the New York office of PKF Consulting. Her experience includes feasibility analysis and appraisals of hotels. She is a state certified general appraiser and holds a bachelor's of science degree in hotel administration from Cornell University. She is a past president of the Cornell Society of Hotelmen and an adjunct faculty member of New York University.

Contributing authors **James R. Butler, Jr.,** and **P. Peter Benudiz** are partners with the law firm of Jeffer, Mangels, Butler & Marmaro. **Butler** is chair of the firm's Real Estate and Lodging & Leisure Group. He is a graduate of the University of California–Berkeley and the Bolt School of Law. **Benudiz** is a member of the firm's Real Estate and Lodging & Leisure Group and a graduate of the University of California–Berkeley and Harvard Law School. With 100 attorneys and offices in Los Angeles and San Francisco, JMB&M offers a full-service business law practice. Its real estate and lodging group provides a full range of advisory services for the leisure industry, including workouts, acquisitions, sales, syndication, and financing.

Contributing authors **Howard J. Wolff, Ronald J. Holecek, AIA,** and **Ronald O. Van Pelt, AIA,** are principals with Wimberly Allison Tong & Goo, Architects and Planners. **Wolff** is vice president and corporate managing principal, responsible for spearheading the firm's worldwide strategic planning and business development. He is a graduate of Rensselaer Polytechnic Institute with degrees in both architecture and communication and is a frequent speaker and author on the subject of hospitality design trends. **Holecek** is president and CEO. A graduate of the University of Washington, he has been with WAT&G since 1972 and has been responsible for the design of over two dozen completed hotel and resort projects throughout the United States and Asia. **Van Pelt** is vice president and director of WAT&G's London office. He is a graduate of California Polytechnic State University–San Luis Obispo. He has taught a course on hotel projects for the Cornell University Essec Graduate Hotel Program in Paris, and has been responsible for the design of hotels and resorts in India, Spain, England, the Middle East, the United States, and the Caribbean. Wimberly Allison Tong & Goo is recognized as one of the world's leading architectural firms specializing in hotel and resort planning and design.

Contributing author **Walter A. Rutes, FAIA,** is chairman of 9 Tek Ltd., Development Consultants, and was vice president and director of architecture at such major hotel companies as InterContinental, Sheraton, Ramada, and Holiday Corporation. His projects include the design of the initial all-suites prototype for Embassy Suites. He spent two decades as associate partner with Skidmore, Owings & Merrill. He is a visiting professor at the Cornell University Essec Graduate Hotel Program in Paris and coauthor of interactive software systems used in planning hotels and resorts.

Contents

Foreword and Acknowledgments viii

Preface ix
Patrick Quek

Chapter 1. Historical Perspective 1
W. Martin Winfree, Jr.

Chapter 2. Market Segmentation and Analysis 11
Lynda Schrier Wirth

Chapter 3. Products and Their Markets 21
John A. Fox

Chapter 4. The Development Process 29
Brian D. Bash

Chapter 5. Acquisition as a Development Tactic 45
Bruce Baltin, James R. Butler, Jr., and P. Peter Benudiz

Chapter 6. Financing 55
John M. Keeling

Chapter 7. Management Contracts 61
Karen Johnson

Chapter 8. Trends in Hotel Development 69
Thomas E. Callahan

Chapter 9. Hotel Development around the World 77
Corey Limbach and Patrick Quek

Chapter 10. Architecture and Design 85
Howard J. Wolff, Ronald J. Holecek, and Ronald O. Van Pelt

Chapter 11. The Construction Process 101
Walter A. Rutes

Chapter 12. Development Profiles 107

Luxury Resort 108
Arizona Biltmore Hotel and Resort, Phoenix, Arizona
Restoration and expansion of a hotel and condominium resort, and its repositioning under independent management.

Downtown 112
Chateau Sonesta, New Orleans, Louisiana
Adaptive use of the 1849 D.H. Holmes Department Store and its 1919 warehouse as a hotel and apartment building on the edge of the city's French Quarter, by means of a public/private development process.

International Market 116
Conrad International Hong Kong
A deluxe but conservative hotel catering to overseas business travelers and, to a lesser extent, upscale leisure travelers, and located within a mixed-use complex that includes three hotels.

Resort/Convention 120
Walt Disney World Dolphin and Swan Hotels, Orlando, Florida
Two convention hotels within Walt Disney World with shared recreational amenities and special design themes.

Downtown, All-Suite 125
Doubletree Guest Suites/New York City, New York, New York
The performance of an all-suite hotel in a highly competitive market, through a renovation process and brand-name changes.

Mid-Market, Commercial 129
Hilton Garden Inns, Prototype Design
A prototype of a hotel chain's second generation mid-price hotel targeted to business travelers.

Economy 132
Holiday Inn Express/Strathclyde Country Park, Strathclyde, Scotland
A hotel chain's own development and management of a franchise brand hotel in a new market, in order to introduce the hotel concept to potential investors.

Downtown, Conference 134
Hotel Roanoke and Conference Center, Roanoke, Virginia
The renovation of a historic railroad hotel and the development of a conference center, under the auspices of a public/private team that included the city, a university, and a civic association.

Themed Resort **138**
Hyatt Regency Hill Country Resort, San Antonio, Texas
A luxury resort on a 200-acre, wooded ranch, using a regional theme.

Convention **143**
Loews Miami Beach Hotel, Miami Beach, Florida
Public/private construction of a 17-story tower and renovation of a 100-room historic art deco style hotel, to provide an 800-room hotel to support the city's convention center.

Suburban, Economy **145**
Red Roof Inn/Alamo Downs, San Antonio, Texas
An owner-operated hotel in a suburban business corridor.

Nonmetropolitan **149**
Sheraton Great Valley Hotel, Chester County, Pennsylvania
A full-service hotel outside a metropolitan area, catering to business travelers and tourists.

Appendices 153

Appendix 1. Leading Hotel Chains 154

Appendix 2. Glossary of Hotel Terms 161

Appendix 3. Sample Project Brief for a Five-Star Hotel with 350 Keys 164

Foreword and Acknowledgments

When ULI's first book on hotels, *Hotel/Motel Development*, was published in 1984, it provided information that until that time had been most difficult to find. The manuscript had been prepared by Laventhol & Horwath, and John Keeling, one of the principal authors, later became associated with PKF Consulting.

When ULI decided that a new edition of the hotel development book was needed, Patrick Quek, president of PKF Consulting, stepped forward and offered to assemble a team to write it. This team has produced a totally new book. Rooted in an understanding of the skills required for success, it provides the best information available on the process of hotel development.

Over the last decade, the hotel industry has evolved a dramatically different and larger range of product. Hotel guests have gone from demanding simply a clean bed and a wholesome meal to expecting a variety of business services and recreational amenities. The industry will continue to evolve as the expectations of the marketplace change. No doubt *Hotel Development* too will be followed by newer editions, but much of what it has to say is of timeless value. The best vision of the future is usually achieved by observation of the best of the past and present, and this book seeks to provide that quality of perspective.

The authors' contributions to this book are readily apparent. But to complete any book project like this after the manuscript has been submitted to the publisher and the authors are winded, the work of collecting materials and tracking down information must continue. The book manuscript was reviewed by seven ULI members or their associates. Their comments along with those of the ULI project staff were sent back to the authors for response. Gary Carr of PKF Consulting spent many hours with the various authors, dealing with editorial queries and confirming or correcting matters of fact.

Many contributors not included among the list of authors provided development profiles so that *Hotel Development* could cover a wide range of hotel types in its case studies chapter. Special thanks for contributing hotel development profiles go to Patrick Wong, Conrad International Hotels Asia project director, for the Conrad International Hong Kong; Gregory Dillon, vice chairman emeritus of Hilton Hotel Corporation, for the Hilton Garden Inn prototype hotel; Alan Tallis, president of Red Roof Inns, for the Red Roof Inn/Alamo Downs; Greg O'Stean, corporate real estate director, and David Sinyard, senior vice president of Holiday Inn Worldwide, for Holiday Inn Express/Strathclyde Country Park; Jenny Little and Chris Watson of Doubletree Hotels for Doubletree Guest Suites/New York City; and Debra Kelman for Loews Miami Beach Hotel.

In addition, a book on hotel development needs a broad base of photo examples to illustrate various types of hotels and specific elements of hotels. For supplying or helping to supply the photographs that enrich this book, I am grateful to the following firms—RTKL; Wimberly Allison Tong & Goo; Helman Hurley Charvat Peacock/Architects; Turner Steiner International; Thompson, Ventulett, Stainback & Associates; Brennan Beer Gorman/Architects; and Daniel, Mann, Johnson & Mendenhall—and to the following individuals—Susanne Pelt of South of the Border; Kerri Wrightman of Holiday Inn Worldwide for the image of the first Holiday Inn; and Stasi Tsirkas of the Radisson Plaza Hotel at Mark Center for giving me access to photograph the hotel's back-of-house.

Frank H. Spink, Jr.
Vice President/Publisher
Project Director, *Hotel Development*

Preface

Owning, developing, or acquiring a hotel is a dynamic process similar to kiteflying. Sometimes when the wind is favorable, we let out the string a little and the kite soars higher. Sometimes when the wind is too rough, we have to pull it in a little and the kite can get caught in the trees. The principal purpose of this handbook is to help the development community to stay out of the trees.

Many participants in the hotel industry consider hotels to be highly complex real estate projects that involve great risk and often consume far too much time, energy, and capital. We tend to forget that hotels are in fact an unusual type of business formula that combines a form of real estate with an ongoing service-oriented business. Most investors strive to keep their exposure to a minimum and hope to prosper. Notwithstanding investor wariness, the distinction of owning a hotel continues to attract investors seduced by the status and glamour they can bestow as well as the potential for tremendous gain.

This book has been written for real estate practitioners who have an interest in the lodging industry. We have structured the book to cater to needs ranging from the development of a new project to the acquisition of an existing property. We hope to provide readers with the basic information they will need to plan successful lodging projects.

We realize that the order of steps will change from project to project, but the methods and process used for evaluating lodging investments will be the same from one project to another. It is our intention that the first-time hotel investor will find this book easy to use and that the experienced investor will find in it valuable insights. We hope that this book will be a useful reference tool for anyone planning or assembling a hotel deal.

Patrick Quek

Chapter 1
A Historical Perspective

W. Martin Winfree, Jr.

While the origins of hostelries are lost in the mists of ancient history, fulfilling the food and shelter needs of travelers is as old a function as travel itself. An early reference to tavernkeeping can be found in the Code of Hammurabi, of about 1800 B.C.E. The Romans established an extensive system of paved roads with way stations and inns at set distances along them. During the European Middle Ages, when religious pilgrimages were why most people traveled, charitable institutions and religious orders provided the primary lodging services.

With the emergence by the 15th century of many European cities as centers of commerce and culture, innkeeping for profit was born. The development of a network of stagecoach routes connecting these cities set off the first hotel building boom. This would be only the first of many transportation innovations, among them railroads, streetcars, automobiles, and airplanes, that would transform the hospitality industry.

The Birth of the Hotel

Inns and taverns were an important focus of activity in the American colonies in the 17th and 18th centuries. They were patterned after English country and city inns, which were designed to fit into their communities as unobtrusively as possible. Boston's (and perhaps the Colonies') first tavern, Coles Ordinary, was founded by Samuel Coles in 1630. The term "ordinary" referred to the midday meal or supper served as part of an overnight stay, an arrangement which hoteliers today call the American plan. By the time George Washington toured the new nation shortly after his election as president, inns were everywhere—many of them soon advertising: "George Washington Slept Here."

A remarkable number of these early inns and taverns survive, particularly in New England and Pennsylvania. A few contain sizable modern hotels within their colonial exteriors, such as the Red Lion Inn in Stockbridge, Massachusetts, and the Nassau Inn in Princeton, New Jersey.

Another survivor of sorts is the concept of the ordinary, as carried on by the modern bed-and-breakfast. B&Bs began to appear in the United States in the mid-1960s, and grew strongly in the late 1970s and 1980s as an alternative to commercialized hotels. B&Bs tend to be located in restored 18th and 19th century homes or (less frequently) historic inns. Ideally, they are situated in residential neighborhoods that also feel historic. The room count is often less than ten and usually under 30. They offer a continental breakfast that typically features homebaked breads and muffins. The development of B&Bs has waned along with the rest of the hotel industry in the 1990s, but many individuals regard operating a B&B as an ideal way of life, and their enthusiasm should keep the concept alive.

By the beginning of the 19th century, the term "hotel" had come into vogue, used to describe establishments that were more commercial than inns. Hotels offered food and drink, as well as lodging.

Perhaps the earliest of the new breed of hotel was the six-story City Hotel built in Baltimore in 1826 and containing 200 rooms. Many of these early hotels were designed by New England architect Isaiah Rogers, beginning with the Tremont House in Boston in 1829. Rogers designed the first of the great hotels built by the Astor family in New York City. The luxurious Park Hotel (renamed the Astor

Red Lion Inn, Stockbridge, Massachusetts.

House as soon as its success was assured) opened in May 1836 with 18 high-class shops, 300 bedrooms, and an unheard-of 17 bathrooms. Rogers designed similarly elegant properties in Bangor, Charleston, Richmond, Cincinnati, New Orleans, Mobile, Louisville, and Nashville.

Many hotels of the era became social and commercial centers in their communities. Civic and fraternal groups used them as meeting places. Hotels housed the first merchant exchanges, hotel guests often brought news from afar, and the first presidential preference polls were conducted in hotels.

Hotel Growth and Diversification

In the latter half of the 19th century, sumptuous grand hotels catering to a new café society were appearing in Europe—the Grand Hotel in Rome, the Paris Ritz, the Savoy of London, and gracious hotels adorning the newly fashionable Riviera. At the same time, the hotels being built in America were more utilitarian in nature. On the west side of the Atlantic, they were nicknamed Palaces of the Public or People's Palaces. Desiring to bring European elegance to America, William Waldorf Astor erected the Waldorf Hotel on the site of the family mansion on Fifth Avenue. It opened in March 1893 and grossed $4.5 million in its first year, a staggering sum for that time.

Not to be outdone, his cousin John Jacob Astor soon afterward built the much larger and just as luxurious Astoria Hotel on the site of an adjoining mansion, from which Caroline Astor had reigned as the undisputed head of New York society in the 1870s and 1880s. The 400 couples who could comfortably fit into her ballroom gave rise to the term "the Four Hundred" for the New York upper crust. The Astoria Hotel upped the ante by providing a ballroom for 600 couples. In 1897, the rival hotels were linked by interior corridors to become the 1,300-room Waldorf=Astoria Hotel, the world's largest hotel. The Waldorf=Astoria Hotel, with its "=" and its luxury intact, was rebuilt on Park Avenue in the 1930s. The Empire State Building stands on its old site.

Another notable project, the Astor Hotel, opened on Times Square (then known as Longacre Square) in 1904. Only half its floor space was devoted to sleeping rooms. Its dining rooms were said to offer the best eating in the city. Its lobby became one of the world's most famous meeting places. Its meeting rooms and its roof garden were other distinctive elements. Crowds packed the hotel during the annual Thanksgiving Day Macy's parade and on every New Year's Eve, to this day.

The grand hotel soon made its way across the country, in cities and resorts alike. In time, every city and town had a more or less ostentatious edifice to offer the traveling public. Hotels cropped up in places that were scarcely more than minor crossroads. Rural folks with urban pretensions saw the establishment of a major hotel as a sign that they—and their town—had arrived. Hotels scraped the sky long before office towers came into being. In smaller towns and cities, the hotel was usually the tallest building in town. The largest hotels were often built near the town's railroad station. Sadly, most of the grander hotels of the 1800s and early 1900s have fallen to the wrecking ball, because they were usually well located but could not be adapted easily to changing times.

Hoteliers in the 19th and early 20th centuries introduced or perfected building components that would be widely adopted in the hotel industry. Isaiah Rogers's Astor House introduced indoor plumbing above the ground floors. Mount Vernon Hotel in Cape May, New Jersey, which opened in 1853, gave each room not only running water but also a bathtub. Rooms with private baths would not become standard in the industry until after 1908, the year in which Ellsworth M. Statler opened the Statler Hotel in Buffalo, New York, with the catchphrase: A bed and a bath for a buck and a half. Other innovations introduced or perfected by the hospitality industry included central heat via radiators, elevators, gas and electric lighting, telephone exchanges and switchboards, and even spring mattresses.

Two major hotel chains that have survived to the present —Hilton and Sheraton—were founded between the world wars. Conrad Hilton entered the hotel business in 1919 with the 40-unit Mobley Hotel in Cisco, Texas. He had acquired eight hotels by 1929, and by means of heroic cost-cutting measures he managed to retain five through the early years of the depression. By 1935, Hilton had used oil profits to buy control of a number of high-profile hotels, including the Plaza and Roosevelt hotels in New York, the Stevens in Chicago, the Town House in Los Angeles, and the Sir Francis Drake in San Francisco. The Hilton hotel empire grew with the continued absorption of smaller hotel chains and distressed independent hotels, culminating in Hilton's purchase of the Statler chain in 1954. Ernest Henderson, who founded Sheraton, was more of an investor than a hotelier. He acquired four hotels in the late years of the depression, beginning with the Stonehaven Hotel in Springfield, Massachusetts, and he took the name of the chain from one of these, the Sheraton Boston Hotel.

Before streetcar and subway systems became widespread around the turn of the century, there was a need for hotels in every urban commercial district and in many residential areas as well. Nearly every corner seemed to have a hotel. They kept their height and shrank their other dimensions to narrow slices. The guest rooms became tiny and jumbled to fit into restricted floor plates.

These small commercial hotels continued to be built into the Roaring Twenties. Later, they often were converted into apartment houses or rooming houses or, in less fashionable neighborhoods, welfare hotels. In the 1980s, many of the better located of these were converted into luxury boutique hotels. Boutique hotels typically have 40 to 100 rooms. They generally de-emphasize food and beverage operations, and stress personalized service and a striking decor. These hotels often are marketed to business travelers or tourists from a particular country or region. Alternatively, other commercial hotels built early in the century have been well maintained without a major rehabilitation, and they are marketed today as an affordable alternative to new hotels. San Francisco in particular has hundreds of small hotels, supplying about 30,000 rooms in formats that run the gamut from the most affordable to the most prestigious.

Other hotel forms began to appear in the 1920s as the industry diversified. Apartment hotels were built, catering to people to whom hotel style living appealed. Tourist courts came into being as people opened their homes to travelers or built additions with a handful of rooms. A few roadside hotels

The grand lobby of the Chicago Hilton Hotel and Towers, after its renovation and restoration in 1985. The old Stevens hotel was built in 1927 and acquired by Conrad Hilton in the 1930s.

built between major destinations to house people on long-distance trips spelled the beginning of the motel industry.

The heavily traveled vacation route down the eastern seaboard from New York to Miami provides a remarkable example of early motel development. The structures in one small area at the approximate halfway point in North Carolina along U.S. 301, which was the main highway before I-95 was begun in the 1960s, show the entire early history of the motel industry. The oldest buildings are little more than groups of cabins or shacks. Tourist courts and mom-and-pop motels soon followed. Few of these properties ever had a national or even regional affiliation. Most of their patrons must have seemed peculiar to the keepers of these hotels, which, even where they skirted sizable communities like Fayetteville, Rocky Mount, or Wilson, were a world apart.

One of the properties along the New York to Miami highway route is South of the Border, a full-blown resort celebrating nothing so much as an exit from the Old North State. North Carolina was one of the driest states in the country when the roadside motel opened in the 1940s, just inches over the line into South Carolina, a state that was more forgiving about liquid refreshment (not to mention fireworks). With a schlock Mexican theme and a string of preposterous billboards proclaiming itself from as far away as 200 miles, South of the Border covers 100 acres and is a popular tourist trap and honeymoon spot. It boasts 302 guest rooms, two enormous gift stores, numerous restaurants and "cantinas" (none serving Mexican food until the mid-1970s), including a revolving restaurant atop a sombrero tower, and one of the most garish neon lighting displays east of the Mississippi.

While independents can capture demand that has few options, the trend in the industry in the second half of the 20th century has been to provide a wide variety of national and regional chains. The dramatic changes in the hotel industry beginning in the 1950s find their roots in the state of the hotel industry just after the end of World War II.

In 1948, hotels with fewer than 50 rooms dominated the industry. They represented about 85 percent of all hotel establishments and over 40 percent of the number of rooms. Almost all hotels were independently owned and operated properties. Not even 5 percent belonged to a hotel chain. The major chains were Sheraton and Hilton.

Approximately one-fourth of the hotels and over one-third of the rooms in the country were concentrated in the eight states of the Middle Atlantic and East North Central regions—Illinois, Indiana, Maryland, Michigan, New York,

From one motel in 1940, South of the Border has evolved into a sprawling tourist mecca on I-95 in South Carolina.

Ohio, Pennsylvania, and Wisconsin. These states contained 40 percent of the nation's population and a fair number of its largest trade centers, including New York City, Philadelphia, Cleveland, Detroit, Chicago, and Milwaukee.

Hotels were concentrated in population and trade centers. The typical hotel was in an urban setting, usually in a downtown business district and often near a railroad terminal. Business travelers constituted the primary source of room demand. What resorts there were served primarily wealthy individuals. Many were seasonal operations, near a body of water or in the mountains.

In the late 1940s, standardization of hotel product, amenities, or services was limited. Rooms were typically small. Some lacked private bathrooms. Most rooms had no telephone. Swimming pools were uncommon. Only larger facilities usually could support restaurants and bars. The average room rate in 1948 was $3.75.

As businesses expanded to supply the rebuilding of Europe and pent-up and expanding domestic demand for consumer and durable goods, hotels began to experience occupancies in excess of 80 percent. Thus was brought about a significant amount of updating, replacing, and building of hotels, after years of neglect through the depression and the war.

With automobile ownership burgeoning by the early 1950s, hotels began to move outside traditional urban districts. The first motels also ran the gamut in terms of amenities and services offered. With more people traveling to more locations, visitors often would be unfamiliar with the hotels they planned to use. Clearly, the time was ripe for the development of standards for hotels.

Kemmons Wilson's founding of Holiday Inn in 1952 revolutionized the industry. From four motels in the Memphis area, the chain grew to an unprecedented 100 properties across the country by 1960, featuring a reliable standard of quality for guest rooms and considerable similarities in restaurant menus—all at an inexpensive price. Children under 12 traveling with their parents were offered free lodging.

The company has continued to be innovative, developing, for example, the Holidome enclosed recreational center, essentially a glass dome covering the swimming pool and part of the atrium. Holiday Inn became Holiday Corporation after it brought Harrah's Casinos in the early 1980s. It then created a series of new products: Embassy Suites in 1983, Hampton Inn in 1984, and Homewood Suites in 1988. In 1990, Holiday Inn was sold for $2.1 billion. The remaining pieces—Harrah's Casinos, Hampton Inn, Homewood Suites, and Embassy Suites—became the Promus Companies.

Lodging is a multidimensional industry. Its growth and diversification in the United States since 1950 have been phenomenal, and eight key trends have been most influential: population growth and migration, household formations, rising incomes, increased leisure time, construction of the interstate highway system, business development in the suburbs, airport construction and growing air service, and convention center construction.

The first Holiday Inn, Memphis, Tennessee.

Population grew rapidly from 1950 through 1980, at a rate of 1.35 percent compounded annually. The populations of the South Atlantic, West South Central, Mountain, and Pacific regions increased significantly faster than populations in the New England, Middle Atlantic, North Central, and East South Central regions. Population strongly shifted toward the Sunbelt and western states; toward Florida, Texas, Colorado, Arizona, and California.

The population not only expanded, but also grew older and more disposed to form households. Dispersed families needed to travel more frequently, and increased leisure time and improved family incomes made more travel possible.

The construction of the interstate highway system provided the family's primary means of travel and created a demand for lodgings in new locations. Congress authorized a 42,500-mile interstate system in 1944, and its funding in 1956. The system would eventually connect most of the nation's cities having populations of 50,000 or more, and would offer an irresistible opportunity for exploring the country.

The number of vehicles registered in the United States rose rapidly in tandem with the population, and disposable income increased. Travel by automobile was convenient and affordable. It spurred the development of motor hotels along interstate highways.

The interstate system also eased travel within metropolitan areas and aided the development of residential neighborhoods in the suburbs. The residential base attracted shopping centers, office buildings, and recreational and entertainment facilities, as well as hotels, to suburban locations.

After 1945, a growing number of travelers flew. Air travel both inhibited and encouraged hotel development. On the one hand, it reduced travel times and therefore made short stays away from home—especially for business trips—more feasible. On the other hand, jet speeds encouraged business concerns to bring people together for meetings and training sessions more frequently. And access by air opened up many new destinations for pleasure travel.

The development and expansion of airports created business centers outside the downtown. By the early 1980s, more than 700 U.S. airports were certified by the FAA for scheduled passenger service. This included 120 large, medium, and small hub airports, which accommodated the vast majority of U.S. air passengers.

Economic growth, which was accompanied by an expansion in the number and size of professional and fraternal associations, created a strong market for conventions, while improvements in ground and air transportation brought more regions of the country into consideration for conventions and meetings. Some larger cities began by marketing their civic centers and auditoriums as facilities for conventions and trade shows. Although the convention facilities themselves might operate at a loss, the host cities received important economic benefits. Many smaller cities began to construct convention centers to accommodate state and regional groups.

The growth in demand for hotel rooms from the group/convention segment was strong during the 1960s and 1970s. Facilities like McCormick Place in Chicago, the Georgia World Congress Center in Atlanta, the Coliseum in New York, and the Gateway Convention Center in St. Louis generated a need for large hotels to house convention delegates. In many cases, large new hotels were included in urban mixed-use developments that also housed office, retail, recreational, and other types of space.

Lodging chains such as Holiday Inn, Ramada, Howard Johnson, and Travelodge emerged in the 1950s to seize the opportunities for hotel development at new locations. Later, in order to grow faster, many chains became franchisers as well as developers and operators of company-owned facilities. By the early 1990s, about 70 percent of hotel rooms and 40 percent of properties in the United States were affiliated with a chain, franchise, or referral organization.

Hotel chains established their own standard designs, specific development parameters, management structures and systems, operating efficiencies, and advance reservation and referral networks. Easy recognition by the traveling public was an end, the means to which included uniformity of design and distinctive signs, emblems, and slogans for use in chains' advertising programs and sales promotions.

Independent hotels found it increasingly necessary to improve their marketing efforts. Thus, referral organizations like Best Western International, Friendship Inns, and Superior Motels, Inc., evolved to unite the efforts and resources of independent operators. Referral organizations are nonprofit groups that are owned and controlled by their members. They provide reservation referrals, sales promotions, and other advantages of hotel chain operations without causing operators to lose control of their properties.

During the 1950s and 1960s, mature chains such as Sheraton and Hilton needed to develop roadside and suburban hotels in order to compete with the newer chains, but they were unwilling to divert significant capital from their large projects in downtown and resort areas. The solution they came up with was franchising.

All this competition enlarged the range of amenities and services that hotels offered, to include indoor and outdoor swimming pools, restaurants, lounges, meeting and banquet rooms, valet service, complimentary limousine service, live entertainment, saunas, whirlpools, and in-room movies. Hotels that had been developed mainly to provide sleeping accommodations were turned into entertainment, dining, and meeting complexes resembling earlier grand hotels. Intense hotel competition—and the fact that travelers were gaining in sophistication—forced hotels to become more specialized.

Then during the 1970s, high inflation shrank the purchasing power of the dollar and room rates at most full-service hotels climbed to record levels. Perhaps, hotel chains reasoned, less expensive limited-service hotels could serve a market niche. They developed them and by the 1990s they were well patronized. Leisure travelers realized they did not always use the facilities provided by full-service hotels, such as meeting rooms, recreational amenities, restaurants, and lounges. And recession-weary businesses had begun to evaluate more closely their travel expenditures.

The budget or economy hotel chain made its first appearance in the 1960s, and began to grow quickly in the early 1970s. By getting back to basics and eliminating ancillary facilities, budget operators could charge a lower room rate.

Current Conditions and Trends

Different hotel products arose to meet the needs of different travelers. The differences involved five salient hotel traits: prices, amenities and facilities provided, location, traveler markets served, and distinctiveness of style. Marketing

■ **Figure 1-1**

U.S. Lodging Properties, 1948–1993

	1948	1958	1963	1967	1972	1977	1981	1987	1993
Establishments	55,569	70,535	64,276	65,579	58,688	51,861	54,135	44,500	45,000
Rooms Available per Day	1,854,044	2,118,777	2,385,930	2,101,500	2,223,600	2,198,700	2,497,700	2,730,000	3,300,000
Rooms Occupied per Day	1,575,669	1,437,553	1,448,630	1,297,800	1,317,500	1,451,200	1,570,700	1,692,600	2,277,000
Occupancy	85.0%	68.0%	62.0%	62.0%	59.0%	66.0%	63.0%	62.0%	69.0%

Sources: American Hotel & Motel Association; and PKF Consulting.

strategies gained in importance as a way of targeting specific traveler needs.

As Figure 1-1 shows, between 1948 and 1993, the inventory of hotel rooms in the United States increased by about 1.4 million. During the same period, however, the number of properties decreased by about 10,600, as smaller hotels gave place to larger ones. Figure 1-2 shows the distribution of U.S. lodging properties by hotel size categories in 1993.

The number of rooms demanded failed to keep pace with the growing supply, and occupancy decreased. That the 85 percent occupancy rate achieved in 1948 has never been repeated is not surprising; in 1948, outside factors were holding hotel room supply at an artificially low level. Annual occupancies in the range of 60 percent have been the norm for the industry in recent years.

Between 1948 and 1993, the South Atlantic replaced the Middle Atlantic as the top U.S. region for number of guest rooms. Major expansion of the guest room inventory occurred also in the East South Central and Mountain/Pacific regions. The number of rooms in the New England and West North Central regions grew minimally, while the number of rooms available in the Middle Atlantic and East North Central regions declined. (Figure 1-3 shows properties and room inventories by major U.S. region in 1987.)

The 1980s were an era of incredible excess in the hotel industry. The resulting pain was largely self-inflicted. Although the decade saw some innovations—all-suite hotels, extended-stay hotels, and dedicated conference centers—the segmentation frenzy mainly involved splitting hairs, mostly between hotels offering a luxury version of budget and hotels offering a budget version of luxury. A bewildering array of brands were launched, some totally new and others the entry of local or regional chains on the national scene. The success of these efforts generally was spotty. Hampton Inn, for instance, became a phenomenon in the Southeast, while it never really took hold in the West. In the South, Best Western came to describe hotels of last resort, while in the West, the brand was attached to upper-end and high-rise hotels. Potential confusion grew as re-flagging became commonplace later in the decade. This practice took bizarre turns at times, with a Holiday Inn and a Ramada Inn, for example, simultaneously exchanging affiliations, or a high-rise Sheraton Hotel becoming a Days Inn overnight.

The industry leaders survived the 1980s the best, though not without scars. Two of the most successful new flags were launched by Holiday Inn Worldwide: Embassy Suites was the best designed all-suite chain, and Hampton Inn offered a pleasant room with a free muffin-and-juice breakfast. Marriott mastered the segmentation game with four brands: Fairfield Inn, a stick-built budget product with a fixed price; Courtyard by Marriott, a hybrid full-service hotel carefully designed to meet the needs of people traveling on business; Residence Inn, an extended-stay hotel that offered miniature apartments; and JW Marriott, a luxurious hotel.

Both Holiday Inn and Marriott, however, began to have problems with their flagship brands. Aging Holiday Inn properties seemed out of step with their time, and the separation of the new brands from the older hotels with the creation of Promus Corporation in 1986 seemed to exacerbate the problem. Marriott Hotels remained the premier commercial hotel through the 1980s, but the company's attempts to introduce all-suite and downsized Marriotts met only sporadic

■ Figure 1-2

U.S. Lodging Properties by Hotel Size Category, 1993

Size Category	Properties Number	Percent of Total	Rooms Number	Percent of Total
Under 75 Rooms	30,600	68.0%	871,200	26.4%
75 to 149 Rooms	9,495	21.1	1,148,400	34.8
150 to 299 Rooms	3,915	8.7	867,900	26.3
Over 300 Rooms	990	2.2	412,500	12.5
Total	45,000	100.0	3,300,000	100.0

Source: American Hotel & Motel Association.

■ Figure 1-3

U.S. Lodging Properties by Region, 1987

	Properties Number	Percent of Total	Rooms Number	Percent of Total
New England/ Middle Atlantic	7,151	17.7%	454,011	16.2%
North Central	8,438	20.8	520,497	18.5
South Atlantic	8,070	20.0	628,467	22.4
South Central	5,864	14.5	433,508	15.5
Mountain/Pacific	10,901	27.0	769,173	27.4
Total	40,424	100.0	2,805,656	100.0

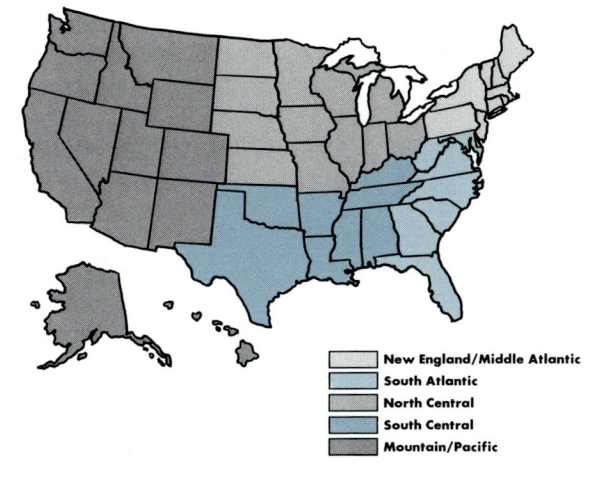

Source: U.S. Department of Commerce.

Clarion Plaza Hotel, Orlando, Florida.

success, with some of the planned products barely leaving the prototype stage. Marriott Hotels also faced formidable competition from the brands Marriott itself created.

Halfway through the decade, Choice Hotels International, a unit of Manor Care, Inc., is the one success story of the 1990s. Its founders, Robert C. Hazard and Gerald W. Pettit, had revitalized Best Western in the 1970s. Neither man is from the hospitality field, but they are wizards in franchising and segmentation. Choice Hotels has grown to 3,300 franchised hotels. It started in 1981 with a moribund chain of 339 hotels, having the by-then ironic name of Quality Inns. Three brands were added: Clarion, Comfort Inns, and Sleep Inns. And the rights to three other brands were bought: Rodeway Inns, EconoLodges, and Friendship Inns. All seven brands crowded toward the budget end of the hospitality field, each supposedly marketing to a slightly different segment of guests. In view of the hotel industry's overbuilding, this degree of segmentation is at best debatable, but Choice, unlike all other hotel companies, grew unchecked throughout the 1990s. The company established exacting standards that tend to favor only new or nearly new properties. Many hotels have been dropped from the Choice Hotels system.

Many chains face the problem of properties growing old and wearing out. Best Western has a no-nonsense inspection policy that is among the toughest in the industry. Unlike, say, Hilton or Sheraton, Best Western has no national policy of wanting to cover major markets to a certain level. Its standards, while less restrictive than those of most chains, must be met in order to retain the affiliation. By contrast, many higher-end chains—in order to keep their presence in a particular city—are more likely to overlook problems with standards at strategically located properties. To reflect the effects of aging and inconsistency among its properties, in 1994 Days Inn introduced a rating system ranging from one to three stars for its affiliated hotels. Other chains are sure to follow suit.

The use of variations on the same basic name for segmented brands poses another problem for many chains. This is less of a problem if the similarly named brands are generally similar hotels, like Knights Inn, Knights Lodge, and Knights Stop—all of which are economy flags. But the differences between a Radisson Inn and a Radisson Plaza Hotel or between a Sheraton Inn and a Sheraton Hotel can be monumental. Often the aging hulk of a lower-end flag is only a short drive from a luxurious high-rise convention hotel with the other flag. In 1995, Sheraton addressed this problem by renaming its franchised Sheraton Inns. The new name is Four Points Hotels.

Modern hotels are now sufficiently old for an accurate determination of their economic life to be made. The modern version of the grand hotel and most well-designed convention hotels and downtown hotels are experiencing no serious functional or physical inadequacies. With good upkeep and periodic renovation, many hotels, including hotels built in the 1920s, should be able to celebrate their 100th anniversaries in great shape. Recent stem-to-stern renovations of some major hotels like New York's Sheraton Hotel and Essex House suggest, however, that keeping older hotels competitive can be expensive.

The picture for other types of hotels is much different. Hotels of 1950s vintage have not been generally competitive with newer suburban hotels for about 20 years. A significant shakeout of hotels dating from the mid-1960s has taken place in the past few years, suggesting that the kind of full-service hotel typified by a suburban Holiday Inn has an economic life of about 30 years. The economy motels dating from the early 1970s seem to be nearing the end of their useful lives, and the end may be in sight for lower-end budget motels as well. Economic lives of 20 years or even 15 years may become the norm for these limited-service properties. Fully renovating budget hotels may not be economically competitive with the construction of new hotels in their stead.

As the 1990s come to a close, large segments of the hotel industry with short economic lives are aging out simultaneously. The limited reuse potential of many hotels may hasten the elimination of thousands of hotel rooms. As one wag commented: the problem with the hotel industry is not overdevelopment, but underdemolition.

While travelers have recently demonstrated a willingness to trade up to a better room, even sophisticated guests may perceive a new Courtyard to offer more value than a 12-year-old Marriott. Obsolescence has begun to affect the marketability of 1980s vintage full-service hotels. Hotels that once had as many as a half-dozen food and beverage outlets are typically down to one or two, while space cannot be found for a proper health club. Their competition is the many mid-range and low-end properties that provide a range of recreational amenities and such guest room appointments as coffeemakers, hairdryers, videocassette players, refrigerators, microwave ovens, minibars, and in-room movies.

Many property types likely will not be represented among the hotels built in the near future. Few convention hotels, for instance, are on the drawing boards. Their potential developers face not only oversupply in most U.S. markets, but also the possibility that not enough corporate and leisure business will materialize to subsidize the meeting space and group business. Travelers who decide to upgrade from budget hotels may be unwilling to share their travel time with boisterous conventioneers. In the near future, public incentives may not be enough to bring in hotels to support downtown convention centers. The hotels as well as the convention centers may have to be built with public money, with tax revenues subsidizing the chronic net income shortfalls of the hotels.

Traditional full-service hotels may be going the way of full-service gasoline stations, although they may not become

Loews Miami Beach Hotel in Florida is scheduled to open in 1998 with 800 rooms, of which 700 will be in a new 17-story tower and 100 in the landmark St. Moritz Hotel, which will be returned to its art deco splendor.

as scarce. Like drivers who no longer depend on one-stop shopping to fill their automotive needs, using instead self-service stations for their gas and freestanding repair shops for their oil change, lube, transmission, muffler, and other car needs, travelers also have an expanded array of options for satisfying their needs away from home. The traveling public has become more inclined to explore the community for dining and entertainment options. Most corporate and leisure guests limit their hotel dining to breakfast. Fast-food chains have captured even the breakfast business of many travelers. Hotel lounge entertainment is often only a last resort for travelers too tired to venture from the hotel. The nightclub and comedy club operations at hotels are usually more geared to the general public than to guests.

The U.S. hotel industry has changed greatly over the last several decades, becoming more diverse and complicated. Anyone considering the development of a hotel should understand hotel supply and demand trends, as well as the hotel development process and alternative approaches to financing and structuring hotel projects. The remaining chapters of this book deal with these issues.

Chapter 2
Market Segmentation and Analysis

Lynda Schrier Wirth

A developer's success in the hospitality industry depends on knowing how economic cycles and social trends affect demand. In the lodging market, demand is a moving target. But taking its measure is crucial to the development and operation of a hotel.

Hotel Demand Segments

In measuring lodging demand 20 or 30 years ago, analysts considered that people made trips for only two purposes, either for business or for pleasure. Later, more sophisticated market research and a growing awareness of distinct travel market segments led marketers to identify more specific purposes for travel. Many questions were raised along the way. Is the business traveler on his own or attending a conference? Is the conference a training meeting or an executive retreat? Is the business traveler attending a trade show or convention? Is the traveler's business purpose related to the government or the military? Is the pleasure traveler part of a tour group or traveling independently? Is the visitor from the United States or abroad? Is this stop the final destination or part of a more extended trip? The responses to such questions help define the distinct demand segments available to a hotel in a certain market area.

Figure 2-1 summarizes the travel market's basic segments. At the bottom of the chart are examples of a representative type of guest for each segment. The figure shows three key variables in the general composition of hotel room demand: the trip's purpose, the mode of travel (independent or group), and the guest's status (in transit or at the trip's destination). Segmentation can, of course, be taken further.

San Francisco's Marriott Hotel can house large conventions itself and it also serves the nearby Moscone Convention Center.

Figure 2-1
Hotel Market Segments

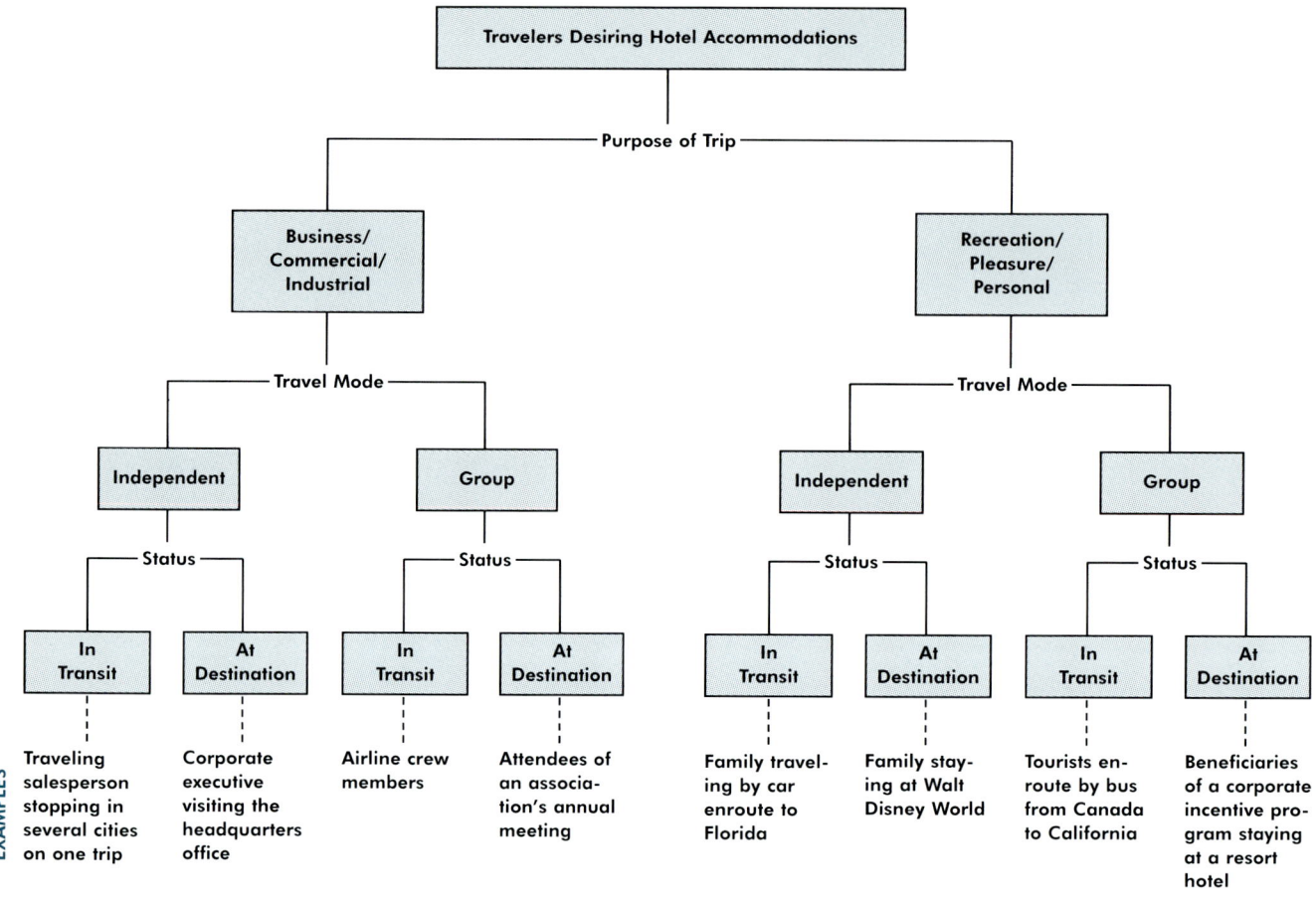

A destination resort hotel might, for instance, target both independent and group travelers with special interests, such as golf, tennis, or skiing. Or, a hotel targeting association meetings would have to subdivide this market by size of group, according to its capacity to accommodate groups.

The major demand segments for hotels are described in the following list.

- *Corporate/Commercial Individuals.* This demand segment consists of individuals whose purpose for traveling is related solely or predominantly to their jobs or businesses. Its peak days of demand are Monday through Thursday.
- *Corporate Groups.* The purpose of travel for this demand segment is also business. This segment is distinguished from the corporate individual segment by virtue of its booking of rooms on a block basis. The specific purpose of travel is likely to be a company-sponsored meeting in the hotel or at a nearby location.
- *Convention and Association Groups.* Conventions and association meetings can have thousands of attendees, many of whom travel as corporate groups or book rooms on a block basis through the sponsoring organization.
- *Tourists and Leisure Travelers.* This demand segment encompasses most pleasure travelers and includes many family groups. Double (or higher) occupancy of rooms is common. Travel tends to occur at peak periods of demand. Room rates are infrequently discounted for tourists. Lengths of stay vary widely from one-night stopovers a day's drive from home to vacations lasting a week or longer at a resort thousands of miles from home.
- *Long-Term Guests.* Hotels can serve as temporary residences for executives, members of the armed forces, or government employees who have relocated to an area and need lodging until they can make permanent living arrangements, or for consultants, auditors, or engineers working on projects lasting several months. Typically, these travelers need a suite or efficiency unit with some limited cooking facilities. Family members quite often accompany relocating employees.
- *Contract Demand.* Airlines contract with hotels for crew lodging and emergency housing for travelers stranded

because of weather or flight conditions. They typically block multiple rooms for this purpose and obtain a very low rate. Businesses with employees who travel to perform low-budget jobs also frequently negotiate contract rates with hotels, which usually are heavily discounted. Construction crews, disaster relief workers, and truck drivers are typical kinds of contract guests.

- *Government and Military Personnel.* Government workers and members of the military travel with generallly modest per diems and thus tend to strongly prefer low-rate rooms. They gravitate to establishments that offer special discounts to government and military personnel.
- *Getaway Guests.* Downtown and suburban hotels catering to (weekday) corporate guests pioneered the getaway concept to bolster sagging weekend occupancies. The practice has been adopted by virtually all nonresort hotels. Typically, guests are offered a package plan that includes the room, some meals, entertainment of some sort, and other perks. Rates often are discounted substantially; in some cases they are as low as half the typical rack rate.

The Lansdowne Conference Center near Washington, D.C., markets a weekend getaway package that includes golf, use of the health club, and deluxe dining.

■ Figure 2-2

Typical Profiles for Four Hotel Demand Segments

	Corporate Individual Traveler	Corporate Group Traveler	Leisure Individual Traveler	Leisure Group Traveler
Seasonality	None	Fall and spring are peak	Summer and winter are popular	Varies with destination
Day of Week	Weekday (Wednesday and Thursday are peak)	Weekday (Monday arrival and Thursday departure are popular)	Friday arrival and Sunday departure are peak	Stays are usually for a week or encompass both weekdays and weekends
Double Occupancy	Limited	Rare	Frequent	Always
Price Sensitivity	Varies, but not extremely sensitive	Varies, but not extremely sensitive	Often sensitive, but varies	Very price sensitive, commissions paid
Average Length of Stay	2 nights	2.5 to 3 nights	2 to 6 nights	3 to 6 nights
Facilities/Amenities Needs and Preferences	Business center, modems, room service, video checkout	Recreational facilities, breakout rooms, audiovisual equipment	Recreational facilities, variety of restaurants and nearby amenities	Double/double rooms, on-premises restaurant, large lobby
Repeat Patronage	Often	Often	Occasionally	Repeat tour operators
Source	Travel agents, corporate travel departments, individual secretaries	Corporate meeting planners	Travel agents, self-booking	Travel agents, tour operators

The Little Nell is a luxury, ski-oriented resort hotel in Aspen, Colorado, that attracts a year-round market.

Each type of hotel guest shown in the examples in Figure 2-1 is a segment of demand with a distinct profile. The profile of a demand segment might include such considerations as the following:

- Fluctuations in demand by day of week and by month of year;
- Occupancy preferences (one, two, or more guests per room);
- Length of stay;
- Needs and preferences for facilities and services (meeting space, restaurants, recreational amenities, and the like);
- Price sensitivity;
- Extent of repeat patronage;
- Origins (city, state, region, or county); and
- Reasons for visiting (which local companies, attractions, institutions, and events attract this type of visitor to the area).

The uninitiated developer might not recognize the need to understand market segmentation before moving ahead with a hotel project. But the demand for hotel rooms is not a generic one. Understanding this fact and determining the specific market potential for a proposed hotel through a detailed market study can prove to be crucial to the suc-

■ Figure 2-3

Sample of Economic Indicators Used in Hotel Market Analysis: Oregon Metropolitan Areas, 1994

	Eugene-Springfield	Medford-Ashland	Portland-Vancouver	Salem
Population				
Total (Thousands)	299.3	159.5	1,656.1	303.1
Percent of U.S. Population	.1153%	.0615%	.6379%	.1168%
Median Age	35.0	37.5	34.7	34.8
By Age Group (Percent)				
18–24	10.8	7.8	8.5	9.2
25–34	14.4	12.7	16.0	14.4
35–49	24.5	24.0	25.5	22.8
50 and Over	25.5	30.2	23.9	26.9
Households (Thousands)	117.8	62.7	642.5	110.3
Retail Sales by Store Group (Thousands of Dollars)				
Total	2,713,015	1,795,205	15,362,788	2,357,612
Food	533,297	267,622	2,485,881	454,490
Eating and Drinking Places	238,284	125,737	1,443,071	206,144
General Merchandise	357,136	280,001	2,869,070	366,766
Furniture/Furnishings and Appliances	112,034	66,018	932,431	109,718
Automotive	717,999	364,815	3,417,843	547,864
Drug	64,537	33,136	319,180	83,849

Source: Survey of Buying Power: 1994 (Sales and Marketing Management).

cessful operation of that hotel. The market segments to be served should form the primary focus for the design, marketing, and operation of the new hotel. Figure 2-2 summarizes typical profiles for four demand segments of destination travelers. It shows that particular demand characteristics can vary widely from one segment to another, and sometimes they can vary within a single segment.

Fluctuations in Demand

Of all demand characteristics, fluctuation in demand is the one most frequently overlooked by inexperienced hotel developers. In a sense, the guest rooms and space that a hotel offers are perishable commodities. One day's nonsales cannot be made up at a later date. A careful analysis of demand

■ Figure 2-4

Sample of Travel Indicators Used in Hotel Market Analysis: United States, 1993–1994

			Percent Change From...		
	Month	Monthly Value[1]	Previous Month	Year Ago	Year to Date
Establishment Receipts or Retail Sales					
Hotels, Motels, and Other Lodging Places (1)	July	$6,830	–10.3%	7.9%	7.7%
Eating and Drinking Places (2)	July	$19,002	1.3	7.8	5.8
Gasoline Service Stations (2)	July	$11,277	–0.5	1.5	–0.3
Commercial Lodging Demand					
Hotel/Motel Occupancy Rates (3)	July	64.7%	0.2	1.1	3.0
Real Demand for Commercial Lodging (4)	July	78.8	–0.4	3.3	4.2
Airline Passenger Traffic (5)					
Domestic Revenue Passenger-Miles	July	34,200	7.1	6.3	4.4
International Revenue Passenger-Miles	July	13,800	8.7	3.8	2.7
Highway Traffic Volume (6)					
Rural Arterial Vehicle-Miles	June	52,931	2.2	4.3	4.0
Rail Passenger Traffic (7)					
Amtrak Passenger-Miles	July	528	5.3	–5.5	–3.5
Travel Price Index (8)					
(1982–1984=100)	July	160.1	1.2	2.4	2.7
Visitor Volume at National Park Service Areas (9)					
Visits	July	42,449	29.1	2.6	–0.4
Overnight Stays	July	3,540	22.7	1.0	2.0
Foreign Arrivals in the U.S.					
From Overseas (10)	February	1,216	–3.3	–6.0	–2.9
	March	1,520	25.5	13.1	2.7
From Canada (11)	February	873	–11.3	–12.8	–12.3
	March	1,436	64.6	–9.5	–11.1
From Mexico (10)	February	96	–9.2	–12.9	–4.4
	March	153	58.3	57.6	15.0
Domestic Demand for Motor Gasoline (12)					
Barrels Per Day	June	7,926	4.4	2.9	1.6
	July	7,665	–3.3	–1.5	1.1

[1]All monthly values in millions, except occupancy rates (3) and price index (8).
Sources: (1) Smith Travel Research, seasonally adjusted; (2) U.S. Census Bureau, preliminary, revised monthly; (3) Smith Travel Research, seasonally adjusted; (4) Smith Travel Research, unadjusted room nights sold; (5) Air Transportation Association, preliminary; and U.S. scheduled-service air carriers; (6) Federal Highway Administration, preliminary, revised monthly; (7) National Railroad Passenger Corporation (Amtrak); (8) U.S. Travel Data Center; and U.S. Bureau of Labor Statistics; (9) National Park Service, preliminary, unadjusted for differences in reporting units; (10) U.S. Travel and Tourism Administration; Mexican data reflect arrivals on I-94 only; (11) *Statistics Canada*; and (12) U.S. Department of Energy, preliminary.

Figure 2-5

Travel Price Index and Components, July 1994

	Monthly Percent Change (June 1994–July 1994)	Annual Percent Change (July 1993–July 1994)
Transportation	1.7%	2.6%
Airline Fares	1.3	2.8
Intracity Public Transportation	0.0	1.3
Other Intracity Transportation	–0.2	0.3
Motor Fuel	2.3	2.4
Lodging	2.3	2.8
Food and Beverages Away from Home	0.1	1.6
Entertainment	0.6	5.3
Travel Price Index	1.2	2.4
Comsumer Price Index	0.3	2.8

Source: U. S. Travel Data Center.

trends for each segment of the market for a specific project permits a realistic projection of annual occupancy.

Commercial travel remains relatively consistent throughout the year, while the volume of pleasure travel changes with the seasons. Pleasure travel peaks in the summer quarter, when children are out of school and families take vacations.

In the United States overall, August is the month of peak hotel demand. June is usually second, followed by October, a popular month for meetings and conventions. The demand for rooms reaches its lowest point in December, when business travel declines around the Christmas holidays. Thanksgiving week is usually not a good time for room demand from U.S. nationals, and some resorts in the Sunbelt target Canadian group meetings to fill this time.

Seasonal profiles for particular geographic areas tend to be weather related. The seasonal fluctuations in demand in some resort destinations are so extreme that some hotels stay open for only part of the year. Florida beach resorts, Rocky Mountain ski lodges, and New England shore resorts are highly seasonal.

Seasonality can play havoc with a resort's operations. Most service personnel need and want to work year-round, so it is difficult to keep good employees. Turning off the air conditioning or heating for an extended period can cause harm to interior finishes and furnishings. The operators of seasonal resorts must exercise careful control over budgets and cash flow, especially during periods when little revenue is coming in but many costs, like debt service, remain fixed.

For such reasons, the purely seasonal resort has become a rarity. Some resorts have made the transition from seasonal to year-round operations successfully, by identifying market segments that could be attracted to them in their off-seasons. For example, ski resorts have added recreational amenities like mountain biking to attract summer tourists. Others have pursued group meetings business for the non-ski season.

Measuring Demand

While knowing the seasonal patterns for the travel segments currently demanding rooms in a given market area helps a developer evaluate the potential for a new hotel, a forward-looking analysis does not rely on current visitor statistics alone. It must also identify and analyze the travel group comprising the visitors who may come to the area because of population growth, new commercial or industrial development, new tourist attractions or recreational development, changes in transportation networks, or even new lodging facilities.

The link between new commercial, industrial, recreation, or transportation development in an area and an increased demand for hotel rooms is direct and easy to understand. Developers may find it more difficult to grasp the idea of supply-induced (or latent) demand, which is the new room demand that can emerge simply because a new lodging facility opens. Room demand is affected not only by local, regional, and sometimes national economic trends, but also by hotel marketing strategies and changes in the competitive supply of hotel rooms.

Business and leisure travel are tied closely to the health of the economy. When projecting lodging demand and income potential, analysts look at a market's economic and demographic trends. A review of various economic and demographic data can provide evidence on whether the

The Willard Hotel in Washington, D.C., has become a preferred choice of dignitaries and foreign visitors to the nation's capital.

Figure 2-6

Food and Beverage Sales by Food Service Industry, 1992–1995

	Food and Beverage Sales (Thousands of Dollars)			Percent Change		
	1992 Estimated	1994 Projected	1995 Projected	1994–1995	1994–1995 Real Growth	1992–1995 Compound Annual Rate
Commercial Food Service[1]						
Eating and Drinking Places	$175,174,812	$191,593,984	$201,046,357	4.9%	2.7%	4.7%
Food Contractors	15,400,171	16,357,679	17,110,593	4.6	2.1	3.6
Lodging Places	15,053,254	16,218,902	16,932,534	4.4	2.2	4.0
Total[2]	226,140,546	246,114,005	258,004,292	4.8	2.6	4.5
Institutional Food Service[3]						
Total	27,856,700	29,532,764	30,574,524	3.5	1.4	3.2
Military Food Service[4]						
Total	1,115,188	1,102,043	1,097,617	–0.4	–2.6	–0.5
All Food and Beverage Sales	255,112,434	276,748,812	289,676,433	4.7	2.4	4.3

[1] Data given only for establishments with payroll.
[2] Includes some commercial food service categories not shown.
[3] Business, educational, governmental, or institutional.
[4] Continental United States only.
Source: NRA Trend Book (National Restaurant Association).

economy of a specific market area will grow, stabilize, or decline.

Federal and state agencies are the primary source for most of the economic and demographic data used by hotel market analysts. The economic indicators shown in Figure 2-3 are illustrative of the kinds of economic and social data that are available and useful for the analysis of lodging demand. There follows a list of typical types of economic data used by hotel market analysts.

- *Employment.* The characteristics of an area's work force and employment data by establishments provide an indication of the performance of the local economy and of the type and amount of room demand it may generate.
- *Office and Industrial Space.* Data on the amount, vacancy rates, and rental rates of a market's office and industrial space are useful measures of its potential. This kind of information is collected by real estate agents, trade associations, and major consulting firms.
- *Income.* A market's income levels are a good indicator of its demand potential. The amount of disposable income available determines how much spending can be devoted to leisure travel. Private organizations as well as state and federal agencies publish this kind of information.
- *Retail Sales.* Analysts use retail sales data to gauge the purchasing power of both visitors and residents. Data on net sales for establishments engaged primarily in retail trade can be obtained from local trade associations, real estate agencies, and chambers of commerce. The effective buying power of both visitors and residents is important to the hospitality community. Hotels and associated restaurants located in areas offering shopping, entertainment, or sports attractions can draw locals to spend a night on the town (and considerable money). Regional outlet malls, as well, have become a significant draw for suburban or roadside room nights.

Travel industry trends are also a clue to future lodging demand. The travel indicators shown in Figure 2-4 are illustrative of the kinds of data that are available and useful for the analysis of travel trends. There follows a list of travel data series and typical types of travel data used by hotel market analysts.

- *Travel Price Index.* Formerly produced by the U.S. Travel Data Center, the travel research department of the U.S. Department of Commerce, the travel price index is a composite price index that provides a snapshot of the performance of a variety of segments of the travel industry (see Figure 2-5). The index is now published by the Travel Industry Association of America, an association based in Washington, D.C.
- *Food and Beverage Sales.* While not a direct indicator of lodging demand, food and beverage sales data incorporate such sales for lodging places (see Figure 2-6) and also provide hotel analysts with information on consumption levels and consumer preferences. Such data are collected by various private and public institutions and categorized in various ways.

Figure 2-7

U.S. Hotel Occupancy and Rate Trends by City, 1993–1995

	Occupancy			Average Daily Rate		
	1993 Actual	1994 Estimated	1995 Projected	1993 Actual	1994 Estimated	1995 Projected
New England/Middle Atlantic						
Atlantic City, New Jersey (Noncasino)	55.0%	50.0%	53.0%	$73.50	$73.00	$74.00
Boston, Massachusetts	75.4	77.0	78.0	120.57	122.00	126.00
New York, New York	70.1	72.0	73.0	137.64	143.00	150.00
Philadelphia, Pennsylvania	65.0	70.0	68.0	90.00	96.00	97.00
TOTAL	70.2	72.1	72.9	127.07	131.41	137.02
North Central						
Chicago, Illinois	64.4	67.0	68.5	88.10	91.60	95.25
Kansas City, Missouri	60.2	61.6	63.0	62.27	64.00	66.00
Minneapolis, Minnesota	64.2	66.2	68.5	65.83	68.75	71.75
St. Louis, Missouri	61.5	63.0	66.0	67.60	68.75	70.50
Wichita, Kansas	74.8	75.0	75.0	57.35	59.50	61.90
TOTAL	64.1	66.2	67.9	77.83	80.85	83.93
South Atlantic						
Atlanta, Georgia	67.4	70.5	72.0	61.97	65.00	67.00
Charlotte, North Carolina	54.0	61.0	67.0	49.00	52.00	55.00
Daytona Beach, Florida	61.7	62.0	63.0	62.98	63.00	65.00
Florida Keys, Florida	75.9	72.0	73.0	141.09	147.00	150.00
Fort Lauderdale, Florida	71.6	70.0	71.0	87.88	90.50	92.50
Fort Myers, Florida	69.9	68.0	68.0	120.28	122.00	125.00
Jacksonville, Florida	64.7	68.0	69.0	63.07	65.00	67.00
Miami, Florida	75.6	72.0	73.0	86.96	84.00	85.50
Naples, Florida	65.8	68.0	68.0	136.36	140.00	144.00
Orlando, Florida	74.6	72.0	72.0	64.63	65.00	66.00
Palm Beach, Florida	66.2	67.0	68.0	130.24	134.00	136.00
Panhandle, Florida	67.5	70.0	70.0	64.70	66.00	68.00
Raleigh, North Carolina	61.0	65.0	67.5	58.00	56.25	58.00
Tampa Bay, Florida	64.3	67.0	68.0	67.42	70.00	71.50
Washington, D.C.	73.2	70.7	72.5	122.34	119.74	122.47
TOTAL	69.7	69.6	70.7	77.76	78.41	80.12
South Central						
Austin, Texas	71.5	72.5	73.0	58.61	60.25	62.00
Baton Rouge, Louisiana	66.8	67.0	67.5	48.70	49.75	51.25
Birmingham, Alabama	65.0	67.0	68.0	44.00	46.00	48.00
Corpus Christi, Texas	63.2	63.0	64.0	53.86	54.50	55.00
Dallas/Fort Worth, Texas	64.0	67.0	67.5	67.53	69.50	71.00
El Paso, Texas	74.0	74.0	74.0	43.26	43.50	45.00
Houston, Texas	62.5	63.5	64.0	65.53	66.25	68.00
Jackson, Mississippi	64.2	68.0	69.5	45.50	48.50	50.50
Knoxville, Tennessee	64.0	64.2	64.5	52.30	55.00	56.00
Little Rock, Arkansas	62.5	63.7	64.2	44.00	45.00	46.00
Memphis, Tennessee	65.5	70.0	71.5	56.75	60.50	63.00
Nashville, Tennessee	72.0	75.0	77.3	86.67	88.50	89.25
New Orleans, Louisiana	70.7	73.0	74.0	83.69	85.50	88.00
Oklahoma City, Oklahoma	56.3	59.0	60.0	50.50	51.00	51.50
San Antonio, Texas	69.5	74.0	74.0	62.02	62.50	64.25
Tulsa, Oklahoma	63.2	65.0	66.7	52.26	52.50	53.00
TOTAL	65.8	68.0	68.7	65.63	67.15	68.86
Mountain/Pacific						
Albuquerque, New Mexico	73.4	75.0	76.2	58.74	60.25	61.00
Billings, Montana	66.8	67.0	68.3	45.65	46.00	46.75
Boise, Idaho	73.4	75.0	75.0	53.74	57.00	59.00
Colorado Springs, Colorado	60.9	63.4	64.0	61.10	63.50	64.75
Denver, Colorado	73.4	75.3	78.6	70.70	72.25	75.00
Great Falls, Montana	64.3	65.8	66.9	46.47	47.25	48.50
Honolulu, Hawaii	76.4	81.0	82.0	96.16	94.00	95.00
Los Angeles, California	61.9	64.3	63.0	78.11	80.00	80.00
Orange County, California	66.9	65.0	66.0	76.18	78.50	79.00
Phoenix, Arizona	70.9	73.6	74.0	87.50	90.50	92.25
Portland, Oregon	73.5	73.0	73.0	81.66	84.00	87.00
Salt Lake City, Utah	78.3	81.5	82.0	55.36	56.75	58.50
San Diego County, California	63.0	66.5	67.5	79.64	81.00	83.00
San Francisco, California	69.9	70.7	71.2	103.00	104.00	106.50
Santa Fe, New Mexico	72.4	72.5	72.7	99.85	100.25	101.00
Scottsdale, Arizona	70.4	73.7	74.1	107.30	110.00	114.00
Seattle, Washington	71.5	73.0	73.0	98.47	100.00	103.00
Tucson, Arizona	71.0	73.0	74.0	68.20	70.75	73.00
TOTAL	69.0	71.4	72.0	82.65	83.87	85.30
All Cities	68.0	69.7	70.6	81.73	83.39	85.54
U.S. Average[1]	66.9	68.5	69.5	79.30	80.84	83.03

[1] The average property size is 210 rooms.
Source: PKF Consulting.

The Peninsula Hotel, Bangkok, Thailand, illustrates the dramatic growth of hotels outside the United States serving the international business and travel markets.

- *Attendance at Major Attractions.* Attendance figures—historic and projected—by the local or out-of-town origin of the visitors for such demand generators as theme parks, convention centers, and natural attractions are valuable in determining potential demand for lodging services. Sources for such data include the National Park Service, local Chambers of Commerce, and state and city tourism offices.
- *Arrivals of Foreign Visitors.* In many markets, foreign visitors can be an important component of hotel demand. Foreign travel depends, to a large degree, on the relative strength of foreign currencies in terms of the U.S. dollar. In general, the weaker the U.S. dollar, the more likely are foreign visitors to come to the United States to take advantage of travel bargains. Sources for data on foreign visitors include the U.S. Department of Commerce, the U.S. Travel Data Center, and local visitors bureaus.
- *Airport Activity.* Reflecting both local business activity and the overall economic health of a market, airport passenger volumes and other data on airport activity can be good indicators of current and potential lodging demand.
- *Hotel Operating Trends.* Hotel operating statistics—historic and projected—are clearly an important market indicator. PKF Consulting maintains a database of U.S. hotel operations and publishes the annual *Trends in the Hotel Industry* covering major U.S. cities and various hotel market segments (see Figure 2-7).

■ **Figure 2-8**

Domestic Traveler Expenditures in Top Five Travel Spending States, 1992

	Travel Spending		
	Amount (Billions)	Percent Change 1991–1992	Share of Total U.S. Travel Spending (Percent)
California	$41.4	–0.4%	13.6%
Florida	27.1	4.2	8.9
New York	19.0	1.4	6.2
Texas	18.8	5.7	6.2
Illinois	12.8	6.7	4.2

Sources: U.S. Travel Data Center; and U.S. Travel and Tourism Administration.

■ **Figure 2-9**

Domestic Traveler Expenditures in Top Five Travel Spending Growth States, 1992

	Travel Spending	
	Amount (Billions)	Percent Change 1991–1992
Georgia	$8.4	8.7%
Arkansas	2.6	8.5
Illinois	12.8	6.7
Louisiana	4.7	6.6
New Mexico	2.5	6.5

Sources: U.S. Travel Data Center; and U.S. Travel and Tourism Administration.

■ **Figure 2-10**

Domestic Travel Employment in Top Five States, 1992

	Travel Employment	
	Employees (Thousands)	Share of Total U.S. Travel Employment (Percent)
California	581.0	11.4%
Florida	433.7	8.5
Texas	363.5	7.1
New York	258.8	5.1
Nevada	241.4	4.7

Sources: U.S. Travel Data Center; and U.S. Travel and Tourism Administration.

Figure 2-8
Travel Spending, 1988–1993[1]

	1988	1989	1990	1991	1992	1993 Projected
Spending within the United States						
Domestic	$258.0	$272.9	$290.5	$296.2	$305.3	$322.5
International	$29.4	$36.2	$43.0	$48.4	$54.3	$57.6
Total	$287.4	$309.1	$333.5	$344.6	$359.6	$380.1
International Payments to U.S. Carriers	$9.0	$10.7	$15.3	$15.9	$17.0	$16.6
Total Travel Spending	$296.4	$319.8	$348.8	$360.5	$376.6	$396.7
Percent Change in Total Travel Spending	11.6%	7.9%	9.1%	3.4%	4.4%	5.4%
Percent Change in U.S. GDP[2]	7.9%	7.2%	5.6%	3.2%	5.5%	5.6%

[1]Dollar figures in billions.
[2]Gross domestic product.
Source: U.S. Travel Data Center; and U.S. Travel and Tourism Administration.

- *Travel Spending.* Expenditures for travel (including airlines, trains, and rental cars) are another good indicator of current and potential room demand. Figures 2-8, 2-9, 2-10, and 2-11 illustrate the kinds of travel spending data that are available. Sources of travel expenditures data include the U.S. Travel Data Center, chambers of commerce, the U.S. Department of Commerce, and various trade associations.

A focus on the customer is critical in today's crowded and complicated marketplace. Travelers are more diverse and sophisticated in their demands than ever. The demand for hotel rooms will continue to be cyclical. Occupancies and average room rates will continue to fluctuate. However, hotel industry has become more sophisticated as well, and its better understanding of markets can help to mitigate the potential effects of the next downcycle.

Chapter 3
Products and Their Markets

John A. Fox

In general, hotel development has followed paths taken by other types of commercial real estate in the United States. In the first half of the 20th century, most hotel development occurred in center city downtown areas, where most office and retail development was also taking place. Then, new highways, particularly interstate highway systems and major expressways that wound through and around major cities, sparked the development of suburban areas. Demand for hotel rooms accompanied the outward movement of offices, stores and people.

Hotel product geared toward highway locations and other suburban sites differed significantly in character from center city hotels, which were typically high rises, primarily because less expensive land allowed for low-rise construction. In addition, suburban hotels and motels provided extensive parking, because their guests generally arrived by automobile.

Beginning in the 1970s, hotel product segmentation was carried to great lengths as developers and operators attempted to define their potential markets more narrowly and to develop facilities targeted at those markets.

The two principal methods of classifying hotels are by location and by market served.

- **Location.** The primary locational distinction is downtown hotel versus suburban hotel. Other frequently used categories include airport hotels (hotels located on airport grounds or near airports) and highway hotels, (hotels not in city limits and not in what generally is considered a suburban location). Classifiers sometimes include "resort" as a locational category, but more often the term "resort" in resort hotel refers to the facility's amenities—on site or nearby—rather than its location. Resort hotels can be located almost anywhere. However, the vast majority are found in either waterfront or mountain locations.
- **Market Served.** Categorizations of hotels on the basis of the niche or segment of the market they target have evolved. It is probably more accurate to describe hotels on the basis of markets served rather than by distinctions between locations, which have become somewhat blurred due to urban sprawl.

Hyatt Regency Aruba, a resort hotel and casino in the Netherlands Antilles.

Figure 3-1

Types of Hotels by Five Development Criteria[1]

Price	Function	Location	Particular Market Served	Distinctiveness of Style or Offerings
Budget/Economy Hotels Rooms-only operations; little or no public space; no food and beverage facilities; room rates 20 to 50 percent below the average for the market area.	**Convention Hotels** Large; 500 or more guest rooms; extensive meeting space, several restaurants and lounges; sometimes adjacent to convention centers.	**Downtown Hotels** High-rise structures with attached or covered parking; pricing and market orientation determine number of guest rooms and mix of facilities and amenities.	**Executive Conference Centers** Located in secluded settings; fewer than 300 rooms; a variety of well-planned small meeting rooms and classrooms; modern audiovisual equipment; meals and the use of athletic facilities included in the quoted daily room rate.	**All-Suite Hotels** Larger-than-normal guest rooms; living/parlor area separate from sleeping area; cooking and refrigeration equipment; residential feel in public spaces; cater to long-term guests.
Middle-Market Hotels Wide range of facilities and amenities; room rates equal to or slightly above market-area average.	**Commercial Hotels** Comfortable, functional guest rooms with ample work areas; small meeting and conference rooms; limited recreational amenities.	**Suburban Hotels** Low- to mid-rise structures with surface parking; interior corridors; recreational amenities; meeting and banquet facilities.	**Health Spas** Catering to specific needs of guests (losing weight, reducing stress, or breaking a habit); usually have professional staffs (dietitians, therapists, physicians, or counselors).	**Historic Conversions** Historic hotels or other buildings refurbished to their original splendor and elegance; classic hotels.
Luxury Hotels Upscale decor and furnishings; concierge service; a limited amount of high-quality public space; a high ratio of employees to guest rooms; room rates substantially above market-area average.		**Highway/Interstate Hotels** Low-rise structures with surface parking; exterior corridors; some food and beverage facilities; minimal banquet space; outdoor swimming pool. **Airport Hotels** Location and size of the airport determine number of guest rooms and mix of facilities and amenities.	**Resort Hotels** Emphasis on recreational amenities, food and beverage outlets, and meeting and banquet space; typically located in picturesque settings.	**Hotels in MXDs** The focus of large mixed-use developments; architecturally significant; inward facing.

[1] Many types of hotel can be defined by more than one development criterion; for example, a resort hotel can be defined by market, location, or style and offerings.
Source: PKF Consulting.

Two hotel classification schemes based on market served are presented in Figure 3-1 and Figure 3-2. The generic classification in Figure 3-1 sorts hotels according to five development criteria: price, function, location, special market served, and distinctiveness of style or offering. Figure 3-2 shows the market niches for which certain hotel chains have developed brand name products.

Kinds of Hotels

Some major niche hotel categories are described in the following sections. However, many hotels appeal to more than one market niche.

Convention Hotels

Probably the best-known hotel, the downtown convention hotel generally contains 400 to 500 rooms and considerable banquet and meeting space. In many cases, convention hotels are physically connected with or adjacent to large convention centers. They usually contain several food and beverage outlets in different styles and price ranges. Many also include substantial amounts of retail space.

Convention hotels also have large lobbies to handle the check-in and checkout functions that occur in a concentrated period at the beginning and end of every convention. It is common for up to 10 percent of the guest rooms to be suites. Guests use the living rooms of the suites as hospital-

Figure 3-2

Chain Brand-Name Hotels by Market Segment

	Lower-Range Economy	Upper-Range Economy	Middle-Range Full-Service	Upper-Range Full-Service	Luxury	All-Suite	Other
Choice Hotels	■ Sleep Inns ■ Econo Lodges ■ Friendship Inns	■ Comfort Inns ■ Rodeway Inns	■ Quality Inns	■ Clarion Hotels		■ Comfort Suites ■ Quality Suites ■ Clarion Suites	
Doubletree			■ Doubletree Club	■ Doubletree Hotels		■ Guest Quarters	
Forte Hotels	■ Thriftlodge	■ Travelodge	■ Travelodge Hotels	■ Exclusive Hotels		■ Travelodge Suites	
Hilton Hotels Corporation			■ Hilton Garden Inns	■ Hilton Hotels		■ Hilton Suites	
Holiday Inns, Worldwide		■ Holiday Inn Express	■ Holiday Inns	■ Crowne Plaza ■ Holiday Inn Select			■ Sunspree Resorts ■ Crowne Plaza Resorts
Hospitality Franchise Systems	■ Super 8	■ Park Inns ■ Days Inns ■ Wingate Inns ■ HoJo Inns ■ Ramada Limited	■ Howard Johnson ■ Ramada Inns		■ Ameri-Suites		
Hyatt Hotels Corporation				■ Hyatt Regency	■ Grand Hyatt ■ Park Hyatt	■ Hyatt Suites	■ Hyatt Resorts ■ Hyatt Vacation Clubs
ITT Sheraton			■ Four Points	■ Sheraton Hotels	■ Luxury Collection	■ Sheraton Suites	
Marriott Corporation		■ Fairfield Inns	■ Courtyard by Marriott	■ Marriott Hotels	■ Marriott Marquis	■ Residence Inn by Marriott ■ Marriott Suites	■ Marriott ■ Marriott Timeshares
Promus Hotels		■ Hampton Inns				■ Embassy Suites ■ Homewood Suites	
Wyndham Hotels & Resorts			■ Wyndham Garden	■ Wyndham Hotels			■ Wyndham Resorts

Source: PKF Consulting.

ity rooms, or the hotel turns them into meeting spaces for small groups.

Wishing to overcome the perception that they cater solely to large groups, some convention hotels designate specific space for small group meetings or conferences. The Boston Sheraton and the Chicago Sheraton both offer this type of arrangement.

In addition, many convention hotels have set aside concierge floors. For a premium price, these concierge floors typically offer controlled access, separate check-in and check-out areas, a lobby or lounge area, extra in-room amenities, complimentary daily newspapers, and continental breakfasts. Often, their concierge services are separate from the normal concierge services of the hotel. The New York Hilton and the Chicago Sheraton both have a concierge section.

Figure 3-3 provides a profile of the operating characteristics of convention hotels. Descriptions of three representative convention hotels follow:

Spacious lobby of the Westin Century Plaza, Los Angeles, a convention hotel.

- *New York Hilton.* This hotel contains 2,042 rooms and suites, including 237 rooms and suites in the Tower (concierge section). It has 47 meeting rooms, the largest of which will seat nearly 3,000 for banquets, and a separate exhibition space of approximately 81,000 square feet.
- *The Sheraton Chicago Hotel and Towers.* This has 1,200 guest rooms, of which 96 are in the Towers (concierge section). The hotel also includes 36 meeting rooms, the largest of which can accommodate more than 3,000 people for banquets, and a 35,000-square-foot exhibition hall. The facility also contains newsstands, gift shops, and business service centers.
- *Century Plaza Hotel and Tower.* Located in Los Angeles, this is a 750-room hotel with an additional 320 rooms provided in the adjacent Century Plaza Tower. The hotel has 16 meeting rooms, the largest of which will seat nearly 2,000 for banquets, and a large shopping arcade. It is adjacent to a large and well-known shopping center that offers numerous specialty shops and theaters. Hotel amenities include two heated outdoor pools, a whirlpool, and two fully equipped fitness centers.

Commercial Hotels

Commercial hotels are generally considerably smaller. They offer from 100 to 500 guest rooms. While meetings may represent an important part of their business, the groups that are served generally are smaller than those using convention hotels. Compared with convention hotels, most commercial hotels provide less public space and a limited number of food and beverage outlets.

Figure 3-3 provides a profile of operating characteristics. Two examples of typical commercial hotels are the following:

- *Meridien Boston Hotel.* This hotel contains 326 guest rooms, including 22 suites. It has one formal restaurant open for lunch and dinner and a café that remains open throughout the day. Meeting rooms number eight, the

Doubletree at Concourse, Atlanta, a 371-room commercial hotel.

The lobby of the Ritz Carlton, a luxury hotel in Naples, Florida.

Figure 3-3

Revenue and Expense Components by Hotel Type, 1994

	Average Size, Occupancy, and Rates		
	Rooms	Occupancy	Daily Room Rate
Convention Hotels	1,142	70.0%	$103.86
Commercial Hotels	251	66.5	68.66
Luxury Hotels	323	65.5	196.62
Economy Hotels	108	65.5	44.88
All-Suite Hotels	186	74.4	84.87
Conference Centers	248	62.1	79.33

	Revenue Categories (Percent of Total Revenue)					
	Rooms	Rental and Other	Food	Beverage	Telephone	Other Operated Departments
Convention Hotels	58.0%	1.8%	22.5%	5.9%	2.5%	9.3%
Commercial Hotels	61.5	0.8	25.7	7.0	2.6	2.4
Luxury Hotels	55.4	3.1	24.8	7.1	2.7	6.9
Economy Hotels	95.8	0.7	0.0	0.0	2.4	1.1
All-Suite Hotels	86.4	1.2	5.5	1.6	2.9	2.4
Conference Centers	42.9	1.7	30.3	7.2	1.8	16.1

	Expense Categories (Percent of Total Expenses)								
	Rooms	Food and Beverage	Telephone	Other Operated Departments	Maintenance	Energy	Marketing	Administration and General	Operating Profit[1]
Convention Hotels	17.3%	23.0%	1.4%	2.4%	5.9%	3.9%	6.9%	9.0%	30.2%
Commercial Hotels	16.3	26.0	1.6	1.7	5.2	5.2	8.6	9.8	25.6
Luxury Hotels	17.2	28.9	1.8	5.3	5.9	3.6	6.9	9.4	21.1
Economy Hotels	21.6	0.0	1.6	0.5	6.1	5.9	7.3	9.2	47.8
All-Suite Hotels	22.3	5.9	1.4	1.8	5.1	4.5	9.8	8.8	40.4
Conference Centers	10.1	26.9	1.2	8.8	5.2	4.8	7.9	8.8	26.3

[1] Profit before all fixed charges.
Source: PKF Consulting.

largest of which can seat 220 people for banquets. An indoor swimming pool and health club and a gift shop are the major amenities.

- *Holiday Inn Cincinnati North.* This hotel contains 408 guest rooms, six meeting rooms totaling approximately 5,300 square feet, a 140-seat restaurant, and a cocktail lounge in a number of two- to four-story structures. A Holidome recreation area offers an indoor swimming pool, whirlpools, and game rooms.

Luxury Hotels

Luxury hotels tend to be located in large metropolitan areas, places visited frequently by persons who will pay a premium price for accommodations. Most have fewer than 300 rooms, and the few larger luxury hotels tend to cater more to corporate travelers and overseas visitors. These hotels are distinguished by high-quality furnishings, amenities, and services. Many house superior restaurants, although this is not a requirement. Their high ratio of employees to guest rooms affects the economics of operations. Although luxury hotels may accommodate some meeting and banquet business, they do so generally only for very small groups.

As shown in Figure 3-3, the operating profile for luxury hotels (defined as hotels achieving average rates for 1993 in excess of $200) differs significantly from the profile for convention hotels. Two examples follow:

- *Four Seasons Hotel.* This New York City hotel with 367 rooms, including 58 suites, is atypical of most luxury facilities in that it occupies 52 floors. Guest room amenities include minibars, two-line speaker phones, safes, terry cloth bathrobes, and superior furnishings; 23 guest rooms/suites have terraces. Although the hotel has 13 meeting and function rooms, the largest measures only 1,600 square feet. A restaurant seating 64, a cocktail lounge seating 80, a fitness center and spa, and a business center are among the amenities.

- **Lowell Hotel.** By contrast, New York's Lowell Hotel contains only 90 rooms and 62 suites. Its restaurant, a leased facility, is a landmark New York steakhouse. The Lowell also has a small tearoom for guests. Each suite is elegantly appointed and contains an extensive array of amenities. This type of boutique hotel usually depends to a large extent on return business from a loyal clientele.

Budget/Economy Facilities

Appearing at the opposite end of the spectrum are the economy hotels, which go by many names, including budget, hard budget, limited service, and economy.

They are a response to the emergence of more value-conscious travelers in the late 1970s and 1980s. With inflation heating up, many businesses became concerned about travel expenditures and began to control them much more carefully. At the same time, while tourist travel expanded rapidly, much of the growth came from a more price-sensitive portion of the market.

The economy hotel offers limited services and average room rates significantly below prevailing market rates, typically 20 to 50 percent below the rates of full-service facilities in the same area. These facilities usually do not have restaurants or banquet space, recreational facilities, or many other amenities found in more traditional hotels.

The first economy hotels were built along highways outside metropolitan areas, on relatively inexpensive land. They have since moved into suburban areas, airports, and, in some cases, even downtowns. The original economy properties were one- and two-story structures with exterior corridors. Generally, they contained 50 to 150 rooms. Motel 6 was the first budget hotel. It began operations in 1963 with, as the name applies, a room rate of $6 a night. Showers, but no bathtubs, were offered. Guests paid extra to use the television sets. Telephones were not available in the guest rooms.

The economy segment has expanded greatly. In 1970, half a dozen chains operated fewer than 200 hotels. Today, more than 40 chains operate over 9,200 budget properties. The segment has diversified as well, and now offers at least three separate tiers of product:

- **Upper Tier.** Hotels at the high end of the budget segment offer more upscale furnishings and decor, and generally charge rates much closer to market area averages. These hotels are generally larger—usually over 100 rooms. While the guest rooms are small, the level of quality is often much closer to that of commercial hotels.
- **Middle Tier.** Mid-economy hotels generally have 60 to 125 fully furnished rooms, and charge rates that are usually 25 to 40 percent below market. Their corridors can be either external or internal.
- **Lower Tier.** Economy hotels at the lower end have room rates that are about 50 percent below market. They generally have 50 to 125 bareboned rooms, and exterior corridors.

Economy properties operate at generally higher occupancy levels than do full-service hotels, and, as shown in Figure 3-3, achieve income ratios that are significantly higher. Their higher profits are the consequence of lower staff requirements and the lack of food and beverage facilities, which generally operate at fairly low profit margins.

All-Suite Hotels

All-suite hotels came into existence as a separate category in the 1970s. Their guest spaces are larger than normal (usually containing more than 500 square feet) and have a living area separate from the bedroom. Some all-suite facilities offer nearly full-size kitchen areas, some offer a small compact food preparation area (often called a pullman kitchen), and others offer no kitchen at all.

The all-suite hotel was developed to meet the needs of business travelers who spend a lot of time on the road and long-stay guests like corporate personnel who are relocating or consultants who are on a project that will last some time. Many leisure travelers, especially families, also find these facilities desirable.

This product category varies widely from property to property. Still, all-suite hotels generally take one of three basic forms:

- **Urban.** Urban all-suite hotels are usually mid- to high-rise structures containing 200 to 300 suites, a size generally considered small enough to retain a residential atmosphere and large enough to provide the desired level of service.

Embassy Suites, Chicago, an all-suite hotel.

Figure 3-4

Characteristics of Selected All-Suite Hotels, Atlanta, Georgia

	Guest Suites	Stories	Category	Dining Seats	Meeting Space (Square Feet)	Pool (✓ = yes)
Embassy Suites/Buckhead	328	16	Suburban	125	3,900	✓
Embassy Suites Hotel	261	9	Suburban	175	2,200	✓
Embassy Suites/Airport	233	5	Suburban	134	7,500	✓
Embassy Suites/Perimeter Center	241	7	Suburban	75	3,400	✓
French Quarter Suites	155	7	Suburban	80	3,750	✓
Homewood Suites	124	3	Suburban	0	400	✓
Hyatt Regency Suites	200	7	Suburban	70	7,000	✓
Marriott Midtown Suites	254	19	Urban	114	3,680	✓
Regency Suites Hotel	96	9	Urban	0	2,500	
Sheraton Suites	279	17	Suburban	134	4,000	✓
Summerfield Suites	122	3	Suburban	0	2,000	✓

Source: PKF Consulting.

- *Suburban.* Usually found in areas containing a concentration of office buildings, such as edge cities or built-up highway corridors, suburban all-suite hotels generally have four to eight stories.
- *Residential.* In contrast, residential all-suite hotels usually occupy two-story structures. They resemble apartment complexes more closely than they resemble hotels. Their guest spaces are large, with separate living and sleeping areas, full kitchens, exterior entrances, and a variety of amenities. Residential all-suite facilities usually attract guests who stay longer and, because of the higher occupancies and smaller staffing needs attributable to low guest turnover, they frequently are more profitable than regular hotels.

All-suite facilities have achieved occupancy levels well above average for the hotel industry. In most cases, they command significant rate premiums. Their operating profile is shown in Figure 3-3. Despite good performance, all-suite facilities constitute a relatively small proportion of the total number of rooms in the United States—around 4 percent.

The Atlanta region encompasses a wide variety of all-suite hotels, illustrating the diversity of hotels in this segment. Figure 3-4 lists the characteristics of selected all-suite hotels in Atlanta: some have restaurants, some do not; some have more meeting space, other less; some have a swimming pool, others do not.

Conference Centers

While many hotels market themselves as conference centers, truly dedicated conference centers are designed to provide a setting free of distractions for executive and professional meetings. Usually located in rural areas or in suburban office communities near major metropolitan areas, they combine meeting and conference facilities with lodging in a way that can accommodate groups in a self-contained learning environment.

Conference centers usually contain 200 to 400 guest rooms and a large number of dedicated conference and meeting rooms. They provide a carefully designed and more or less isolated learning environment, with comfortable seating, suitable lighting, audiovisual equipment, conference support services, and living and recreational facilities to occupy the hours when conferences are not in session. The food offered is typically of a sufficient quality and variety to make leaving the facility even for an occasional meal unnecessary. These centers offer recreational facilities that are more extensive than those in traditional hotels. In many, if

The Oxford Alexis, a boutique hotel in Denver.

Atrium of the San Antonio Hyatt.

not most cases, occupancy by transient guests is a relatively small part of the operations. A profile of conference center operations is provided in Figure 3-3.

Other Hotel Products

The catalog of hotel products contains some other noteworthy entries, which get only a one-sentence mention here. Ma-and-pa hotels usually are fairly small and old motels. B&Bs (bed-and-breakfasts) are usually small inns (fewer than 20 rooms) that are heavy on charm and provide breakfast as part of the package price. Boutique hotels are small hotels (usually fewer than 125 rooms) that cater to an upscale clientele desiring a high degree of luxury and personalized service. Condo hotels offer hotel services and amenities within a condominium ownership structure, usually a timeshare.

Design and Amenities

Over the past 30 years, the basic design of hotels has undergone significant changes. As facilities began to be developed outside of major urban areas, low-rise motel style products proliferated. Until the late 1970s, most of these facilities had fairly standard guest room layouts, as well as a standard overall design that included outside corridors. Interior corridors became popular for security reasons, but operators discovered that this design also helped lower energy use and labor costs.

The basic square footage of guest rooms can vary significantly, from under 200 square feet at the lower end of the budget segment to more than 600 square feet in some all-suite facilities.

The Hyatt Regency in Atlanta pioneered a now much-used design element: the central atrium around which the guest rooms are grouped. Besides providing a feeling of spaciousness in the public area, the atrium design gives the impression of security by opening all corridors to the central atrium. Atriums were put in everywhere in the late 1970s and early 1980s, but by the 1990s few hotels were being designed with a central atrium.

The swimming pool, perhaps the hotel's most common amenity, was the signature of facilities built in the 1950s. Hotel chain competition has often taken the form of a battle of differentiation by amenities—from better grades of soap to marble bathtubs. Among the more common amenities found today in hotel guest rooms are safes, refrigerators and minibars, irons and ironing boards, coffee makers, entertainment centers (pay TV and movies and, often, video games), and business facilities (fax machines, telephones with dataports, and oversized desks).

While many of these features are not critical to the design of a hotel room, all must be considered in basic planning. Market demand and competition will determine the mix of amenities that a hotel offers, just as the market will determine the hotel product itself—luxury or economy, all-suite or conference center.

Chapter 4

The Development Process

Brian D. Bash

The development process for a lodging facility is complicated and requires a great deal of planning and coordination. The developer plays multiple roles: visionary, entrepreneur, risktaker, coordinator of the various disciplines involved, and ultimate decision maker. The developer is the arbitrator between the hotel project concept and the realities of the marketplace.

Taking a global view of the disciplines that developing the hotel will require, the developer selects a team that attends to the nuts and bolts of planning and implementation. Various specialists must be included in the initial planning process as well as the implementation stage. The developer must thoroughly understand the development process, know when to seek professional advice, and be able to bring experts in various disciplines into an effective, integrated development team.

The development of a hotel takes many months and sometimes years. It should be market driven, based on the principle that hotels meet the development objectives of investors and owners by providing the type and quality of products and services that the market desires. The development process, therefore, links the investor/owner, the developer, and the operator with the public to be served.

Great uncertainty, an extensive and ever-shifting array of market segments, and high expectations on the part of the parties involved frequently make hotel development more challenging and exciting than other kinds of real estate development. A hotel development is both a real estate venture and the creation of a new business establishment. The successful developer will understand this essential duality of a hotel as both real estate and business.

Development planning for the reuse of the D.H. Holmes Department Store and warehouse as the Chateau Sonesta hotel in New Orleans began in 1989, and the hotel opened in 1995.

The development process—regardless of the hotel's type, size, location, or market orientation—requires five distinct and generally sequential phases: (1) development planning, (2) assembly of the development team, (3) feasibility analysis, (4) project implementation, and (5) initial marketing and operations. The remainder of this chapter discusses each of these phases in turn.

Development Planning

In the planning phase, key members of the development team work to accomplish four tasks:

- Establish financial, development, and operational objectives;
- Identify the major development issues;
- Formulate a preliminary development concept; and
- Hire a professional financial and development adviser and establish a timetable for the feasibility analysis.

Seasoned real estate professionals allocate a generous amount of time and resources for this phase. The objectives that they establish and the plans that they make at this time will serve as a framework by which they can measure the subsequent progress and success of the development process. In some cases, too little effort goes into the planning phase. Budgets are restricted, time is short, and the desire to get started is strong. But the result of cutting corners here is likely to be a hotel that performs poorly.

The first question a developer needs to answer is: "Why are we developing this property?" The reasons can range from pure economics to pure emotion—the lure of having a world-class place of one's own in which to entertain or be entertained. There are many strategic reasons for developing a hotel. Once having identified a compelling reason (vision) for a hotel's development, the developer must proceed to validate the vision. Finding a potential market, identifying a suitable product, and locating a site or existing facility are the necessary first steps.

The idea for a hotel project can originate from many quarters. Generally, one or more of the following parties initiates the development program: an equity investor, investment group, institutional investor, or investment fund; a property owner recognizing a development opportunity; a developer that is seeking an opportunity, interested in expanding its real estate portfolio, or needing a cash-producing investment; a developer needing a hotel as a component of a mixed-use development; a hotel development or management company seeking to expand its product into new markets; a local nonprofit, tax exempt development corporation; a public or quasi-public agency (such as a redevelopment authority, a planning department, a development corporation, or a tourism authority), citizens advisory committee, or special community task force; a special interest group, organization of local businesses, or merchants association; or the owner/developer of a sports or entertainment facility.

The Ritz Carlton, Pentagon City, as seen through the dome of the Fashion Center at Pentagon City. Pentagon City is a mixed-use development in northern Virginia comprising a shopping center, office building, and hotel. A subway connection provides easy transit access to Washington National Airport, nearby Crystal City (another large mixed-use development), and the nation's capital.

The original proposal may be fairly specific concerning the site, type of hotel, operator preferred, and many of its physical characteristics. Although a hotel may start out as a multiparty initiative, eventually one individual or group—typically the landowner, developer, or investor—emerges as the prime sponsor for its development.

Objectives

Development planning starts with setting overall objectives. The central problem with many unsuccessful hotels is that the inexperienced party's original inspiration is never solidified with sound business planning. Some developers and investors attempt a project without considering their level of commitment, their ability to finance the project, or their expectations of financial gain. Developers building a hotel in a mixed-use development often fail to make these critical assessments. Developers that perceive an overriding need for a hotel—for example, to generate economic development—often ignore good planning practices.

Answering the following questions will aid the initial development team in its effort to establish development objectives:

- *Financial Objectives.* Is long-term value appreciation an objective? Is the creation of an operating entity an objective? Are development profits being sought? What are the priorities of the developer regarding these goals? How much equity can be invested by the development partners? Can the developer obtain financing for a project of this magnitude? What return on investment will be acceptable to the developers and the potential financial partners? How much time, money, and resources can be committed by all parties involved?
- *Development Issues.* Does the site present development constraints? Development opportunities? Is the site free

of toxic contamination? Are the surrounding land uses—existing and proposed—compatible with a hotel? Who will serve as the developer? How familiar is the developer with the hotel development process? Is making a special statement—through distinctive design, for example—an objective? Do government policies encourage development of the site? Discourage it? Are appropriate public financing incentives available? How will the public react to the proposed development? How long will the necessary approval processes take?

- *Operational Considerations.* What type of hotel management will be best—franchise, affiliate, or owner/manager? Can the owner/developer manage the hotel, or will the services of a professional hotel operator be required? What level of owner/developer involvement in the hotel is desirable or even possible?

Development Issues

Objectives must mesh with real-world conditions. Thus, initial planning has to identify any conditions and activities that could have positive or negative impacts on the hotel's development. Important data must be assembled at this early stage and consultations initiated with experts and potential participants—public agency officials, lenders, developers, syndicators, bankers, hotel operators, and architects. Failure to do so will limit the developer's chances of putting together a development program that is economically feasible. The developer must obtain the answers to some detailed questions on development issues.

Will condemnation proceedings or the relocation of people or businesses be required for land assembly? If so, how will this affect the timing, cost, and public relations aspects of the project? Will public hearings be necessary? Are there active and influential groups in the community that might constrain development? Can the concerns that they are likely to have be remedied or mitigated? At what cost?

Can the developer exercise any control over the development of adjoining land parcels? Is there room for later expansion of the hotel?

The developer needs to understand the local political climate. Do certain political interests favor the development of the project? Is the community progrowth? Do local groups aggressively market the community to promote economic development and tourist visits? What contingency plans may be needed to weather changes in the political climate?

And the developer needs to understand also the local economic and investment climate. How stable are the major employers? What has been the basis for recent economic growth? How has the community fared during national or regional recessions?

Professional Adviser

For most hotel projects, it is important to obtain the services of a professional financial and development adviser—an individual or a firm—during the development planning phase. On complex projects, having such an adviser on board early is particularly important.

The responsibilities of the adviser at this stage depend somewhat on the sophistication and hotel development experience of the project initiator. The adviser cannot have a vested interest in obtaining future work from the project. The duties of this individual or firm include some or all of the following: identify other potential members of the development team; coordinate the preparation of the development objectives; liaise with other parties involved in the development process; set a timetable for market and feasibility analyses; identify similar hotel projects that have been developed and study the lessons to be learned from them; establish regular contacts with hotel operators, developers, architects, and other professionals in the lodging industry; establish the project's credibility within the financial community; and advise the developer to proceed as quickly or as slowly as the project requires.

The preliminary planning phase is complete when the initiator has a set of development objectives, a real-world awareness of the major opportunities and constraints facing the project, an initial development concept, a professional financial and development adviser hard at work, and a timetable for the feasibility analysis.

Assembly of a Development Team

Given a hotel property's dual nature as real estate and a business, a developer should be sure to secure the advice of professionals who are familiar with the lodging industry. Normally, a developer assembles a core team of about six professionals to help guide the overall development process, including, usually, an architect, an interior designer, a market and financial consultant, and an attorney or legal consultant, and other consultants depending on the nature of the project.

The architect interprets, reviews, and renders the concepts and specifications set forth by the developer, making sure that the proposed design fits the applicable state and local regulations. The architect usually assumes lead responsibility for the development team and coordinates the efforts of the design team.

The interior designer interprets the developer's concepts, plans and designs the interiors, and supervises their construction and installation. Generally, the architect and designer work together closely.

As has been noted, the market and financial consultant is generally hired early on to ascertain how a proposed property might perform. A market consultant evaluates market conditions, determines general development parameters, and prepares market projections. On the financial side, the consultant projects revenues and expenses and helps assemble the business plan. This firm or individual also might evaluate companies that potentially could manage the property.

International sources financed the development of the Hyatt Regency Hill Country, San Antonio.

Attorneys who specialize in hotel development work can help formulate a development strategy. Legal advice, generally, is needed to establish the terms and structure of transactions and to assist in regulatory matters, writing contracts, obtaining titles, preparing documents, drawing up the management or franchise contract, and dealing with real estate tax, corporate, and trademark issues.

Other types of consultants that may be brought in to work with the core team include but are not limited to the following: environmental consultant/engineer, marine consultant/engineer, government relations adviser, marketing consultant, management adviser, kitchen and food service consultant, structural engineer, land planner, landscape architect, cost estimator, electrical engineer, mechanical engineer, soils engineer, fire/life-safety engineer, financial adviser, public finance adviser, appraiser, accountant, and tax adviser.

Feasibility Analysis

Because of today's changeable climate for hotel development, a thorough examination of market potential must precede the go/no-go decision. Determining a project's feasibility is a two-step process. The first involves assessing the market feasibility of the project. The second is preparing an operating and development statement based on the market findings. At this point, preliminary development costs can be determined, the best financing structure identified, and preliminary operating and consolidated financial statements prepared. The ultimate aim of the feasibility analysis is to recommend a product that will meet the various expectations of the project's investors, developer, and operator.

The level of risk involved in the decision to proceed varies according to the nature of the project, the reliability of the database, the team's ability to control future events and conditions, and the expected level of financial gain and commitment.

The "go" decision rests on a set of assumptions, analyses, and expectations—that is, on beliefs regarding events that have not yet occurred. It requires an accurate assessment of current and future economic and market conditions, a development plan and business strategy that insulate the project from conditions outside the developer's control, a management group committed to maintaining the quality of the investment, and a feasibility study that is pragmatic, timely, and responsive to all potential influences on the hotel's performance.

The preliminary feasibility study helps maintain control of the project's pace and financial commitment. It may be conducted by experienced team members, a hotel operating company, or a consulting firm that specializes in hotel development. Conducting this analysis internally saves money initially. Developer analyses, however, usually lack the level of detail that most lenders require for funding consideration or that most hotel operators require to consider entering into a management or affiliation relationship. Asking a national hotel consulting firm to conduct the analysis is a bigger investment, but it can give the developer access to continuing financial and development advice, and thus save time and resources in the long run.

Assessing Market Feasibility

The feasibility of a hotel project today depends on a number of factors, only one of which is location. The other factors include: the size and origins of the travel market, competitive hotels, and the suitability of the site. Assessing market support requires much quantitative data. The analyst will need to develop a database that can serve as a reference point for making development recommendations and allow comparisons of the property's projected performance with actual results from similar existing properties. The development team should keep all information collected during the research process for future reference.

Location. The proposed hotel's market area—the geographic area from which its major sources of demand will originate—needs careful delineation. The distance from the proposed site to major visitor attractions such as office concentrations, convention centers, and recreational centers (theme parks, public parkland, ski slopes, major bodies of water, golf courses, tennis facilities, and the like) is an important locational element, as are the current and likely future size and segmentation of the market area's visitor population (see next paragraph). Employment trends and overall economic prospects in the region are a key factor. The analyst should meet with economic development officials and review employment statistics to assess economic trends.

Travel Market. The analyst must examine travel patterns and trends in the market area, by type of visitor—commercial, convention, or vacation traveler—as well as visitor spending patterns. Some good methods of collecting travel market and lodging demand data and information include the following:

- Interview representatives of local tourist and convention bureaus and chambers of commerce. Request data on the number, length of stay, expenditure patterns, typical group size, lodging demand, and seasonality of tourists and convention delegates. (Note that these agencies sometimes overstate visitor activity. Also, many fail to maintain a research program that adequately quantifies travel patterns.)
- Interview officials from car rental agencies, bus companies, and other major ground transportation firms to determine the sources and seasonality of their demand.
- Interview corporate travel officers, meeting planners, association executives, wholesale tour operators, travel agents, brokers specializing in group or corporate travel, incentive-travel organizers, and spokespersons for travel clubs in feeder cities. (Feeder cities can be identified by referring to American Express's annual *Lodging Market Analysis* and by questioning representatives of major air and ground transportation carriers and local hotel operators.) Determine their clients' lodging needs, perceptions of the area, frequency and seasonality of visits to the area, primary reasons for visiting, and typical group size. Find out how their clients rate the strength and weaknesses of existing hotel properties in the area; how they rate the strengths and weaknesses of other travel market areas; what services and amenities they seek; what is the size of their typical lodging budgets; what are their future travel plans; and how they perceive the need for additional lodging facilities in the market area.
- Interview the operators of comparable hotels to ascertain the number of guest rooms, average annual occupancy, average annual room rate, market mix of guests, and type and class of facilities. If no comparable properties exist in the market area, collect such data on similar facilities in nearby market areas, and adjust it for the location.
- Talk with representatives from local redevelopment agencies, planning departments, real estate brokerage firms, office leasing firms, and development companies to discover the existing and future supply of office space and the profile of incoming office tenants. Will these tenants generate demand for lodging facilities?
- Interview representatives of government agencies and public institutions such as colleges and universities to assess their current and likely future needs for lodging facilities. Are colleges and universities thinking of developing or sponsoring the development of a hotel to meet their needs?

The Hyatt Regency Waikola, built at the peak of Hawaii's resort development boom in 1980, boasts a waterway system and monorail.

A high-end art gallery may be a successful retail tenant for a luxury urban hotel, like this one located at the Georgetown Four Seasons Hotel in Washington, D.C.

- Obtain counts of how many cars per day, per month, and per year go past the site. Note any seasonal variations that imply increased pleasure travel.
- Assess the existing capacity and arrival/departure patterns at the major airport in the market area. Determine the mix, seasonality, and growth rate in the number of passengers.
- Identify major tourist attractions, planned special events, scheduled regional and state fairs or expositions, athletic contests, and the like, and interview their sponsors or organizers to determine their typical needs for lodging facilities.

The Competition. The location of competitive hotels and the origination of their major business by location and travel market segment are important feasibility factors for a proposed hotel. The analyst must seek to compile an inventory of existing and proposed competitive lodging supply in the market area. For each facility that because of its location, size, and room rate will compete with the proposed hotel, competitive strengths and weaknesses should be assessed. The following property data will need to be collected: number of rooms, whether it is an independent operation or affiliated with a chain, whether it is owned by the operator or leased out, its market orientation (convention delegates, business travelers, vacationers, or others), the types of amenities offered, average annual room rate, and average annual occupancy.

Suitability of the Site. The analyst must examine the competitive market strengths of the site to determine if the proposed hotel will capture its fair share of the market area's lodging demand. At this stage, however, it is not necessary to conduct engineering or environmental studies. The evaluation of the site's competitive strengths and weaknesses should look at accessibility from major highways and public transportation; existing zoning, including limits on allowable development and any regulations—like designation as a redevelopment area or historic district—that affect development potential; proximity to facilities that generate lodging demand; the extent of preparation that will be needed to make the site ready for building; infrastructure improvements on the site; the compatibility of a hotel use with surrounding land uses; room for expansion; and plans or proposals in the works that could modify the site, its surroundings, or its access. Any negative site characteristics should be considered in light of the development team's ability to mitigate them.

Recommendation for a Hotel Product. A market segmentation analysis using all the market data collected should yield information on demand and supply trends by market segment, by seasonality, and by day of the week. A projection of annual growth in demand and supply for a ten-year period by market segment should follow, reflecting all market factors including the opening or closing of major visitor attractions, regional economic trends, and an informed judgment on the probability that proposed lodging facilities will actually be built. From these analyses, the development team can determine the optimal size and the best choice of amenities for the hotel. The hotel must be properly sized if it is to satisfy the lodging needs of the available market segments, respond to the opportunities and constraints of the site, compete with other hotels, and take advantage of development opportunities. Figure 4-1 shows a typical range of hotel sizes by category of hotel.

Once a decision has been made on the hotel's size and amenities, occupancy levels can be projected. Although a number of methodologies are available, the one most endorsed by lenders is the fair share penetration technique.

■ Figure 4-1

Hotel Sizes by Type of Hotel

Type of Hotel	Number of Rooms
Downtown	500–700
Suburban	200–350
Highway	100–250
Airport	250–550
Resort	200–500
Convention	700–2,000
Casino	600–1,000
Luxury	150–400
First-Class	>100
Economy (Large)	350–600
Economy (Small)	150–350
Budget	75–150
Motor Hotel	100–150
Inn	<50

Source: PKF Consulting.

■ Figure 4-2

Penetration Rates (Percentage of Fair Share) for a Proposed 275-Room Hotel by Travel Segment, 1990–1995[1]

	In-Season Travelers				Off-Season Travelers				All Travelers			
	Commercial	Leisure	Group	Total	Commercial	Leisure	Group	Total	Commercial	Leisure	Group	Total
1990	100%	120%	165%	113%	100%	110%	180%	109%	100%	115%	175%	110%
1991	98	122	168	113	98	118	183	110	98	120	178	111
1992	95	126	170	114	95	128	185	111	95	130	180	112
1993	93	124	173	112	96	127	188	111	95	130	183	112
1994	90	120	173	109	97	125	191	112	95	130	185	110

[1] For a deluxe hotel in Texas. Estimated penetration rates are shown as a percentage of the hotel's fair share for each travel segment.
Source: PKF Consulting.

Fair share is the ratio of the hotel's available guest rooms to the total number of competitive rooms in the market area. A proposed 250-room hotel in a market with 1,400 existing competitive rooms and 200 more under construction would have a 14 percent fair share (250 ÷ (1,400 + 200 +250)). A hotel's fair share percentage remains constant until the competitive supply grows (or wanes).

According to a hotel's competitive strengths and weaknesses, it may capture more or less than its fair share of business. Taking into consideration the property's location, room rates, amenities, relation to competitive facilities, image among commercial travelers and leisure travelers, and affiliation—and remembering that it may take three to five years for a hotel's occupancy rate to stabilize, the development team with the aid of experienced hotel consultants and operators should perform sensitivity analyses to determine likely capture rates. Inexperienced analysts often overlook several important market dynamics affecting occupancy, for instance the ability of a hotel with a strong image to generate its own (supply-induced) demand. Figure 4-2 shows a five-year analysis of penetration by traveler segment for a proposed 275-room hotel in Texas.

Once the orientation of the hotel has been determined, room rates can be projected. The basis for setting rates typically incorporates published room rates at competitive properties, published room rates at similar projects in similar markets, discounts needed to attract price-sensitive guests, and any influences or events unique to the market area. Questionnaires can be useful in helping to set initial rates.

Preparing an Operating and Development Costs Statement

At this point, with the size and amenities of the hotel known, occupancy estimated, and room rates projected, analysts can proceed with the second part of the feasibility analysis, which is the operating and development costs statement. This generally involves four discrete elements: revenue projections, operating expense projections, an estimate of development cost, and financing considerations.

Revenue Projections. Revenue should be projected by department: guest rooms, food and beverage sales, telephone, other operated departments, and rental income. Figure 4-3 shows the sources of revenue for the U.S. lodging industry in 1993.

Representing the largest source of income for a hotel, room revenue is the single most important element in revenue projections. Accordingly, it should be analyzed carefully. Potential room revenue depends on the number of rooms, the annual occupancy, and the annual average

■ Figure 4-3

Sources and Disposition of the U.S. Hotel Industry Dollar, 1993

Sources of Revenue	Percent of Total Revenue
Rooms	63.7%
Food	21.0
Beverage	5.6
Rental and Other Income	1.5
Telephone	2.5
Other Operated Departments	5.7

Expense Categories	Percent of Total Expense
Salaries, Benefits, and Meals	35.2%
Operating Expenses	26.5
Cost of Sales	9.4
Energy Costs	0.1
All Taxes	3.7
Management Fees, Insurance, Rent, Interest, Depreciation, Amortization, and Other Additions and Deletions	25.1

Source: PKF Consulting.

Good locations near interstate highways are prized. This Comfort Inn, Hampton Court, and Hilton Hotel operate within a block of one another along an interstate, and a Holiday Express and Days Inn are located nearby.

room rate. A 300-room hotel with an annual occupancy of 70 percent and an average room rate of $70 would yield $5,365,500 in room revenue in a 365-day year.

Food and beverage sales can be as high as 30 to 35 percent of total hotel revenue. A hotel's restaurants, bars, coffee shops, and banquet facilities serve hotel guests and special events as well as walk-in trade. The types and mix of these facilities should be determined carefully to fit all these user markets.

Accurate projections of food and beverage sales require consideration of a number of factors, including the following: the hotel's location and market mix of guests; the quantity and quality of competitive food and beverage outlets; resources dedicated to marketing; the average cost of meals in each facility; the number of "turns" per seat that the restaurants can accommodate comfortably; and the size, quality, and versatility of the meeting and banquet rooms. Guests at a resort hotel, for example, may have no convenient restaurant choices outside the hotel. A downtown hotel may attract a high volume of walk-in dining trade as well as banquet business. A convention hotel generally draws a high volume of banquets. A commercial hotel tends to serve a lot of breakfast meals to business travelers.

Sources for data that can be useful in projecting food and beverage sales include comparable hotels, leading hotel firms' annual publications and special studies, national trade publications covering the restaurant and volume-feeding businesses, and local restaurant owners and operators.

Revenue from charges to guests for local and long-distance phone calls generally constitutes 2 to 3 percent of total revenue. Telephone revenue reflects the mix of hotel guests. Commercial travelers tend to use in-room telephones heavily to arrange meetings and confirm appointments.

Most mid-market and luxury hotels generate some income from a variety of services, such as a guest laundry, valet service, and in-room movies. If there will be operating departments that generate significant revenues, for example, a tennis or recreation club, a parking garage, or a golf course, their sales should be projected as separate line items.

Rental and other income generally provides 1.5 to 2.5 percent of a hotel's revenue. A determination of revenue from retail rents requires an estimate of the amount and type of retail space a hotel's operation will support. A newsstand and a gift shop are common in hotels. Other potentially viable retail outlets include clothing stores, souvenir shops, jewelry stores, travel agencies, air reservation desks, and car rental services. The hotel's revenue from leased space will depend on prevailing lease rates for such space at comparable facilities. Some hotel operators have been able to obtain rents based on a percentage of sales above a minimum base rent.

Other miscellaneous income that should be included in the revenue projections includes income from commissions on concession sales, interest income, and vending machine and game room income.

Operating Expense Projections. Figure 4-3 shows the use of funds by U.S. hotels in 1993. Projecting expenses requires an in-depth knowledge of how hotels operate, as no standard industry rules of thumb apply to all hotels.

Operating expenses are both fixed (meaning they do not vary with the rate of operations) and variable (meaning that they change in direct proportion to the rate of operations). A hotel's major fixed expenses include rent, property tax, insurance, and replacement cost for fixed assets. In financial projections, expenses should be divided into their fixed and variable components, according to the Uniform System of Accounts for Hotels.* Figure 4-4 shows the share of expenses that typically are fixed and variable by major expense categories.

Among the primary expense categories that should appear in the operating statement are cost of food sales, cost of beverage sales, cost of telephone calls, payroll and related expenses, and undistributed operating expenses.

The cost of food sales and the cost of beverage sales are the cost of all food and beverages served less the cost of food and beverages served to employees. Depending on the size and type of hotel, food cost generally ranges from 30 to 40 percent of food sales; beverage cost ranges between 20 and 25 percent of beverage sales. The cost of telephone calls includes the total amount billed by the telephone company for local and long-distance calls and equipment rental.

Payroll expenses include salaries, wages, payroll taxes, and employee meals. This expense category together with "related expenses"—which include uniforms, laundry, china, glassware, linen, travel agent commissions, and so forth—

---

*Developed and recommended by the Hotel Association of New York City in 1926, the Uniform System has been revised over the years. It has been adopted in all its revisions by the American Hotel and Motel Association of the United States and Canada. It is the standard by which hotel financial data is reported.

Figure 4-4
Share of Hotel Operational Expenses That Are Typically Fixed and Typically Variable, by Category of Expense

Expense Category	Fixed Expenses	Variable Expenses
Rooms		
Payroll and Related	50–60%	40–50%
Other	25–30	70–75
Food and Beverage		
Payroll and Related	40–50	50–60
Other	50–60	40–50
Administrative and General		
Payroll and Related	90–100	0–10
Other	55–65	35–45
Marketing		
Payroll and Related	90–100	0–10
Other[1]	90–100	0–10
Energy	55–75	25–45
Property Operation and Maintenance		
Payroll and Related	90–100	0–10
Other	55–75	25–45

[1] Includes franchise fees, which usually vary with sales.
Source: PKF Consulting.

generally ranges from 29 to 39 percent of total hotel expenses. The analysts should prepare a detailed five-year staffing schedule for each department, covering positions, the number of persons who will occupy each position, payroll, and related expenses (expressed as a percent of payroll). Payroll expenses should be determined as precisely as possible for key payroll categories: rooms, food and beverage services, minor operating departments, administrative and general, and property maintenance. Employment agencies specializing in the hospitality industry are good sources for wage surveys.

The payroll analysis can be validated by cross-checking the results—expressed variously as a percentage of department revenue, a percentage of total revenue, and per occupied and available room—with payroll expenses at similar facilities. The analysts should project related expenses in these same formats: as a percentage of department revenue and a percentage of total revenue; per occupied room; and per available room.

Development Cost Estimate. For purposes of the consolidated operating and development costs statement, the estimate of development cost can be an order-of-magnitude estimate based on general industry standards and adapted to take local conditions into account. (Various members of the development team, the architect, or the cost estimator can provide a more refined cost estimate later.) A developer should expect to allocate total development expenses as follows:

- Land, 20 to 30 percent;
- Construction, 50 to 55 percent;
- Furnishings, 10 to 15 percent; and
- Miscellaneous, 15 to 20 percent.

Care must be taken to incorporate into the estimate some costs that are often overlooked, including costs associated with the provision of infrastructure to the site; the development of parking garages; site preparation; the construction of elements like roads, retaining walls, and sea walls; and the provision of high-grade furnishings.

Financing Considerations. Chapter 6 describes the financing process in detail. In the context of the feasibility analysis, the key financing consideration is to realize that regardless of who the lenders are—financial institutions, developers, hotel operating companies, brokers, government agencies, or syndicators and passive investors—their basic concern is the project's feasibility.

Day-to-day sales make up the performance of a hotel. Lenders cannot insist on preleasing or presales to lower their risks. Thus, they require strong research and projections. Most hotel lenders require a market study with financial projections, and a full statement of the assumptions used in the operating cash flow analysis and development cost estimates. Most lenders use the first stabilized operating year to assess the cash flow available for debt service and management incentive fees. Often the debt service ratios they require for hotels exceed such ratios for other income-producing real estate, chiefly because hotels depend on the operation of a day-to-day business rather than on the kinds of guaranteed cash flows that typically characterize the operations of office and industrial real estate.

The Operating and Development Costs Statement. When all revenues and expenses are projected, analysts should prepare a statement of projected cash flow from operations before debt service and income taxes. The statement should be in constant and current (inflated) dollars and should cover the initial five years of operation. Because price increases affect each revenue and expense category differently and because the importance of price increases varies with the location, the guest mix, the hotel market's price sensitivity, and the quality of the hotel's management, applying specific rates of inflation to each revenue and expense category is both necessary and complicated. Most experienced hotel analysts use microcomputers to formulate, test, and format these complex cash flow statements. Figure 4-5 shows actual (1993) revenue and expense relationships for U.S. hotels by age, size, and occupancy categories; analysts should compare their revenue and expense projections to such actual experience. Figure 4-6 provides a sample five-year cash flow statement for a proposed 250-room hotel.

Unless the ownership or financing structure has been finally negotiated with firm commitments in hand from all

Figure 4-5

Revenue and Expense Ratios for U.S. Hotels by Age, Size, Occupancy, and Locational Characteristics, 1993 (Percent of Total Revenue)

	Age of Property			Size of Property				Occupancy					Region				
	Over 15 Years	5–15 Years	Less than 15 Years	Under 150 Rooms	150–229 Rooms	300–600 Rooms	Over 600 Rooms	Under 50%	50–59%	60–69%	70–79%	80% and Over	Mountain and Pacific	North Central	New England and Mid-Atlantic	South Atlantic	South Central
Revenue																	
Rooms	63.1%	62.9%	67.6%	83.9%	66.4%	59.1%	57.5%	60.2%	64.9%	63.3%	65.7%	61.9%	59.8%	62.7%	64.5%	66.1%	68.9%
Food, Including Other Income	21.0	21.6	18.7	8.0	20.4	25.9	21.4	20.7	22.4	22.9	21.2	16.2	21.4	22.5	22.0	20.1	19.3
Beverage	5.9	5.7	4.9	2.8	5.9	6.4	5.8	5.2	5.8	6.3	5.4	5.1	5.9	7.1	5.9	5.3	4.2
Telephone	2.4	2.6	2.3	2.3	2.6	2.6	2.4	2.4	2.4	2.6	2.6	2.0	2.3	2.3	3.1	2.5	2.5
Other Operated Departments	5.4	6.0	5.7	2.3	3.4	4.6	10.9	9.3	3.2	3.3	3.5	13.8	9.2	4.2	2.7	4.5	3.9
Rentals and Other Income	2.2	1.2	0.8	0.7	1.3	1.4	2.0	2.2	1.3	1.6	1.6	1.0	1.4	1.2	1.8	1.5	1.2
Total	100.0	100.0	100.0	100.0	100.0	100.0	100.0	100.0	100.0	100.0	100.0	100.0	100.0	100.0	100.0	100.0	100.0
Departmental Expenses																	
Rooms	18.1%	17.3%	16.9%	19.9%	17.7%	16.8%	17.1%	19.5%	18.2%	17.6%	17.8%	16.4%	17.2%	16.4%	20.2%	17.3%	16.4%
Food and Beverage	22.6	22.1	19.1	9.1	21.4	26.4	22.2	22.1	24.0	23.8	21.3	17.3	22.5	23.0	23.8	20.1	19.1
Telelphone	1.5	1.6	1.3	1.5	1.6	1.6	1.4	1.9	1.6	1.6	1.5	1.2	1.4	1.4	1.9	1.5	1.5
Other Operated Departments	2.3	3.1	2.2	1.6	2.2	3.3	3.0	5.8	2.0	2.4	2.6	3.0	2.7	2.8	1.9	3.4	2.8
Total	44.5	44.1	39.5	32.1	42.9	48.1	43.7	49.3	45.8	45.4	43.2	37.9	43.8	43.6	47.8	42.6	39.8
Total Operated Departments Income	55.5%	55.9%	60.5%	67.9%	57.1%	51.9%	56.3%	50.7%	54.2%	54.6%	56.8%	62.1%	56.2%	56.4%	52.2%	57.4%	60.2%
Undistributed Operating Expenses																	
Administrative and General	9.0%	9.4%	9.5%	9.3%	9.6%	9.5%	8.9%	11.4%	10.4%	9.2%	8.8%	9.2%	9.5%	8.9%	9.3%	9.2%	9.3%
Franchise Fees	0.7	1.0	0.7	1.5	1.6	0.8	0.1	1.0	1.1	0.9	0.9	0.8	0.6	1.3	0.9	1.2	0.9
Marketing and Guest Entertainment	6.3	7.2	7.2	6.1	7.0	7.4	6.5	7.7	7.6	7.1	6.9	5.4	6.8	6.8	6.9	7.2	6.8
Property Operations and Maintenance	5.9	5.4	5.2	5.7	5.3	5.5	5.8	6.8	6.5	5.8	5.3	4.9	5.4	5.3	5.6	5.7	6.0
Energy Costs	4.6	4.6	4.6	5.6	5.1	4.5	3.8	7.1	6.3	4.9	4.3	3.4	3.8	4.9	5.5	4.8	4.9
Other Unallocated Operated Departments	0.2	0.1	0.2	0.0	0.1	0.1	0.3	0.0	0.1	0.1	0.1	0.4	0.0	0.1	0.0	0.2	0.4
Total	26.7	27.7	27.4	28.2	28.7	27.8	25.4	34.0	32.0	28.0	26.3	24.1	26.1	27.3	28.2	28.3	28.3
Income before Other Fixed Charges	28.8%	28.2%	33.1%	39.7%	28.4%	24.1%	30.9%	16.7%	22.2%	26.6%	30.5%	38.0%	30.1%	29.1%	24.0%	29.1%	31.9%
Other Fixed Charges																	
Management Fees	2.6%	2.8%	2.6%	3.5%	3.1%	2.7%	1.9%	2.4%	2.7%	2.8%	2.9%	2.6%	2.6%	2.7%	2.5%	2.9%	2.9%
Property Taxes and Other Municipal Charges	3.9	3.4	4.0	3.8	3.5	3.4	4.1	4.2	3.9	4.0	3.5	3.2	2.9	4.7	5.1	3.4	3.4
Insurance on Buildings and Contents	0.6	0.7	0.7	1.2	0.9	0.7	0.3	1.1	1.0	0.7	0.7	0.5	0.7	0.7	0.7	0.7	0.7
Total	7.1	6.9	7.3	8.5	7.5	6.8	6.3	7.7	7.6	7.5	7.1	6.3	6.2	8.1	8.3	7.0	7.0
Income after Other Fixed Charges	21.7%	21.3%	25.8%	31.2%	20.9%	17.3%	24.6%	9.0%	14.6%	19.1%	23.4%	31.7%	23.9%	21.0%	15.7%	22.1%	24.9%

Sources: PKF Consulting.

financing partners for their share of the package, most analysts prepare a consolidated operating and development statement that includes the following elements:

- An operating cash flow statement;
- Estimates of total development cost;
- Financing assumptions;
- Management incentive fees; and
- Loan origination fees.

Management incentive fees tend to be 5 to 20 percent of income before fixed charges. (See Chapter 7 for more on the subject of management incentive fees.) Loan origination fees, in most cases, are 1 to 4 percent of the loan value. The permanent loan typically is presumed to be at prevailing market rates, using an amortization schedule of approximately 30 years but with a term of ten to 15 years, payable monthly, and with a value of 60 to 70 percent of the development cost.

Commonly, the analyst uses the internal rate of return (IRR) to analyze project returns. As of mid-1996, the hurdle rate (the minimum IRR that investors will accept) for freestanding hotels ranged from 13 to 18 percent. For hotels in mixed-use developments, the hurdle rate may be one to two percentage points lower. The analyst then uses sensitivity tests to forecast the IRR under different assumptions about inflation, interest rates, occupancy rates, room rates, and so forth. Changes in any of the assumptions—including financing assumptions, development cost, or ownership structure—can dramatically alter the financial performance of a project. The feasibility study must be updated each time any of its assumptions are changed or any new relevant data on costs or market conditions become known.

Project Implementation

At the conclusion of the feasibility phase, the development team generates the preliminary designs and development schedules that enable documents to be negotiated and executed and development to get underway. The goal of the implementation phase is to complete the project according to established design, market, operational, and cost guidelines. Its elements are the final design, development phasing strategies and timetables, the execution of construction management documents, and the actual building of the hotel.

Initially, at least enough funding cover front-end costs and land assembly is secured and other funding sources are identified and approached. Commitments for land assembly and control are concluded and necessary development agreements are finalized. A franchise agreement or a preliminary management agreement with a hotel operator is negotiated.

The most important step in this phase is securing construction and permanent financing. Financing must cover both direct and indirect costs. Direct costs include land assembly and construction. Indirect costs include legal fees, design fees, interest on loans during construction, the developer's profit, the developer's salaries and overhead, contingency and reserve funds, permit and license fees, consultant fees, and commissions.

The methods used to obtain financing, both debt and equity, will depend on the project team's ability to demonstrate the hotel's viability. It frequently happens that lodging projects fail to generate much lender or investor confidence initially, and so must be developed in stages. However, before actual construction can begin, the final financing terms and relationships must have been negotiated.

Design is another obviously important step. (See Chapter 10.) The design is dictated first by the purpose of the hotel, and then by such design parameters as location, hotel size, and hotel concept. The design of particular elements—public areas, meeting spaces, and so forth—varies according to the type of hotel. For example, the principal gathering place and focal point of a downtown hotel is generally its lobby; for a resort hotel, it may be the beach.

Initial Marketing and Operations

The planning, feasibility analysis, and implementation phases of hotel development tend to focus on external forces—fluctuating market demand, development cycles, capital markets. In the management/operations phase the focus turns more inward—to marketing, staffing, and operating performance. Paying attention early in the development process to management and operational concerns reduces the development risk while it enhances the value and extends the life of the hotel facility. Debt and equity investors will not commit to a hotel project unless it is affiliated with a professional management firm or has access to a national (or global) reservations network.

Typically, the owner/developer hires an independent manager or contracts with a professional management company. Both approaches have advantages and disadvantages, and the decision should be based on the owner's business philosophy and financing considerations. The owner that takes the independent manager route may have to become highly involved in the property's management. A professional management company, on the other hand, provides established systems and procedures for operating the hotel, and owner involvement is not required.

A hotel project will succeed or fail on the strength and expertise of the operating entity that is involved in running the hotel from day to day. Because so much hinges on expert marketing and management, the number of investor/owners that operate their own lodging properties has decreased. Hotel chains and independent operating companies will likely control the hotel management process for some time to come.

Figure 4-6
Projected Operating Results, before Debt Service, for a Proposed 250-Room Hotel

	Representative Year Operating Results (1995 Dollars)			
	Total	Ratio to Total Revenue	Per Available Room	Per Occupied Room Night
Revenue				
Rooms	$4,448,000	56.4%	$17,792	$71.68
Food	1,815,000	23.0	7,260	29.25
Beverage	499,000	6.3	1,996	8.04
Telephone	297,000	3.8	1,188	4.79
Other Operated Departments	356,000	4.5	1,424	5.74
Rentals and Other Income	475,000	6.0	1,900	7.66
Total	7,890,000	100.0	31,560	127.16
Departmental Expenses				
Rooms	1,246,000	28.0	4,984	20.08
Food and Beverage	1,897,000	82.0	7,588	30.57
Telephone	187,000	63.0	748	3.01
Other Operated Departments	228,000	64.0	912	3.67
Total	3,558,000	45.1	14,232	57.34
Departmental Income	4,332,000	54.9	17,328	69.81
Undistributed Operating Expenses				
Administrative and General	700,000	8.9	2,800	11.28
Franchise Fees	0	0.0	0	0.00
Marketing	625,000	7.9	2,500	10.07
Property Maintenance	400,000	5.1	1,600	6.45
Energy and Utilities	255,000	3.2	1,020	4.11
Total	1,980,000	25.1	7,920	31.91
Income before Fixed Charges	2,352,000	29.8	9,408	37.90
Management Fees and Fixed Charges				
Management Fees	237,000	3.0	948	3.82
Rent	0	0.0	0	0.00
Property Taxes	125,000	1.6	500	2.01
Insurance	50,000	0.6	200	0.81
Total	412,000	5.2	1,648	6.64
Income before Reserve	1,940,000	24.6	7,760	31.27
Reserve for Replacement	395,000	5.0	1,580	6.37
Income before Other Charges	1,545,000	19.6	6,180	24.90

Room Occupancy: 65%
Average Room Rate: $75

continued

Figure 4-6 (continued)
Projected Operating Results, before Debt Service, for a Proposed 250-Room Hotel

	Projected Operating Results (Thousands of Dollars)									
	1995	1996	1997	1998	1999	2000	2001	2002	2003	2004
Revenue										
Rooms	$4,448	$4,698	$4,964	$5,302	$5,650	$5,995	$6,212	$6,433	$6,570	$6,844
Food	1,815	1,907	2,034	2,167	2,307	2,421	2,540	2,664	2,758	2,854
Beverage	499	524	559	596	634	666	699	733	758	785
Telephone	297	312	332	354	377	396	415	435	451	466
Other Operated Departments	356	374	399	425	452	475	498	522	541	560
Rentals and Other Income	475	499	532	567	603	633	664	697	721	746
Total	7,890	8,314	8,820	9,411	10,023	10,586	11,028	11,484	11,799	12,255
Departmental Expenses										
Rooms	1,246	1,295	1,353	1,413	1,475	1,534	1,595	1,658	1,716	1,776
Food and Beverage	1,897	1,976	2,070	2,169	2,271	2,365	2,462	2,563	2,652	2,745
Telephone	187	196	209	223	237	249	261	274	284	294
Other Operated Departments	228	239	255	272	289	304	319	334	346	358
Total	3,558	3,706	3,887	4,077	4,272	4,452	4,637	4,829	4,998	5,173
Departmental Income	4,332	4,608	4,933	5,334	5,751	6,134	6,391	6,655	6,801	7,082
Undistributed Operating Expenses										
Administrative and General	700	725	750	776	803	831	860	891	922	954
Franchise Fees	0	0	0	0	0	0	0	0	0	0
Marketing	688	679	670	693	717	742	768	795	823	852
Property Maintenance	400	414	428	443	459	475	492	509	527	545
Energy and Utilities	255	264	273	283	293	303	313	324	336	348
Total	2,043	2,082	2,121	2,195	2,272	2,351	2,433	2,519	2,608	2,699
Income before Fixed Charges	2,289	2,526	2,812	3,139	3,479	3,783	3,958	4,136	4,193	4,383
Management Fees and Fixed Charges										
Management Fees	237	249	265	282	301	318	331	345	354	368
Rent	0	0	0	0	0	0	0	0	0	0
Property Taxes	125	128	130	133	135	138	141	144	146	149
Insurance	50	52	54	55	57	59	61	64	66	68
Total	412	429	449	470	493	515	533	553	566	585
Income before Reserve	1,877	2,097	2,363	2,669	2,986	3,268	3,425	3,583	3,627	3,798
Reserve for Replacement	237	291	353	423	501	529	551	574	590	613
Income before Other Charges	1,640	1,806	2,010	2,246	2,485	2,739	2,874	3,009	3,037	3,185
Room Occupancy	65%	66%	68%	70%	72%	73%	74%	75%	75%	75%
Average Room Rate (Dollars)	75	78	80	83	86	90	92	94	96	100

continued

Figure 4-6 (continued)
Projected Operating Results, before Debt Service, for a Proposed 250-Room Hotel

	Ratio to Total Revenue (Percent)									
	1995	1996	1997	1998	1999	2000	2001	2002	2003	2004
Revenue										
Rooms	56.4%	56.5%	56.3%	56.3%	56.4%	56.6%	56.3%	56.0%	55.7%	55.8%
Food	23.0	22.9	23.1	23.0	23.0	22.9	23.0	23.2	23.4	23.3
Beverage	6.3	6.3	6.3	6.3	6.3	6.3	6.3	6.4	6.4	6.4
Telephone	3.8	3.8	3.8	3.8	3.8	3.7	3.8	3.8	3.8	3.8
Other Operated Departments	4.5	4.5	4.5	4.5	4.5	4.5	4.5	4.5	4.6	4.6
Rentals and Other Income	6.0	6.0	6.0	6.0	6.0	6.0	6.0	6.1	6.1	6.1
Total	100.0	100.0	100.0	100.0	100.0	100.0	100.0	100.0	100.0	100.0
Departmental Expenses[1]										
Rooms	28.0	27.6	27.3	26.7	26.1	25.6	25.7	25.8	26.1	25.9
Food and Beverage	82.0	81.3	79.8	78.5	77.2	76.6	76.0	75.4	75.4	75.4
Telephone	63.0	62.8	63.0	63.0	62.9	62.9	62.9	63.0	63.0	63.1
Other Operated Departments	64.0	63.9	63.9	64.0	63.9	64.0	64.1	64.0	64.0	63.9
Total	45.1	44.6	44.1	43.3	42.6	42.1	42.0	42.0	42.4	42.2
Departmental Income	54.9	55.4	55.9	56.7	57.4	57.9	58.0	58.0	57.6	57.8
Undistributed Operating Expenses										
Administrative and General	8.9	8.7	8.5	8.2	8.0	7.8	7.8	7.8	7.8	7.8
Franchise Fees	0.0	0.0	0.0	0.0	0.0	0.0	0.0	0.0	0.0	0.0
Marketing	8.7	8.2	7.6	7.4	7.2	7.0	7.0	6.9	7.0	7.0
Property Maintenance	5.1	5.0	4.9	4.7	4.6	4.5	4.5	4.4	4.5	4.4
Energy and Utilities	3.2	3.2	3.1	3.0	2.9	2.9	2.8	2.8	2.8	2.8
Total	25.9	25.0	24.0	23.3	22.7	22.2	22.1	21.9	22.1	22.0
Income before Fixed Charges	29.0	30.4	31.9	33.4	34.7	35.7	35.9	36.0	35.5	35.8
Management Fees and Fixed Charges										
Management Fees	3.0	3.0	3.0	3.0	3.0	3.0	3.0	3.0	3.0	3.0
Rent	0.0	0.0	0.0	0.0	0.0	0.0	0.0	0.0	0.0	0.0
Property Taxes	1.6	1.5	1.5	1.4	1.3	1.3	1.3	1.3	1.2	1.2
Insurance	0.6	0.6	0.6	0.6	0.6	0.6	0.6	0.6	0.6	0.6
Total	5.2	5.2	5.1	5.0	4.9	4.9	4.8	4.8	4.8	4.8
Income before Reserve	23.8	25.2	26.8	28.4	29.8	30.9	31.1	31.2	30.7	31.0
Reserve for Replacement	3.0	3.5	4.0	4.5	5.0	5.0	5.0	5.0	5.0	5.0
Income before Other Charges	20.8	21.7	22.8	23.9	24.8	25.9	26.1	26.2	25.7	26.0

continued

[1] Expenses for rooms, food and beverage, telephone, and other departments are expressed as a ratio of their respective departmental revenues.

Figure 4-6 (continued)
Projected Operating Results, before Debt Service, for a Proposed 250-Room Hotel

	Per Available Room (Dollars)									
	1995	*1996*	*1997*	*1998*	*1999*	*2000*	*2001*	*2002*	*2003*	*2004*
Revenue										
Rooms	$17,792	$18,792	$19,856	$21,208	$22,600	$23,900	$24,484	$25,732	$26,280	$27,376
Food	7,260	7,628	8,136	8,668	9,228	9,684	10,160	10,656	11,032	11,416
Beverage	1,996	2,096	2,236	2,384	2,536	2,664	2,796	2,932	3,032	3,140
Telephone	1,188	1,248	1,328	1,416	1,508	1,584	1,660	1,740	1,804	1,864
Other Operated Departments	1,424	1,496	1,596	1,700	1,808	1,900	1,992	2,088	2,164	2,240
Rentals and Other Income	1,900	1,996	2,128	2,268	2,412	2,532	2,656	2,788	2,884	2,984
Total	31,560	33,256	35,280	37,644	40,092	42,344	44,112	45,936	47,196	49,020
Departmental Expenses										
Rooms	4,984	5,180	5,412	5,652	5,900	6,136	6,380	6,632	6,864	7,104
Food and Beverage	7,588	7,904	8,280	8,676	9,084	9,460	9,848	10,252	10,608	10,980
Telephone	748	784	836	892	948	996	1,044	1,096	1,136	1,176
Other Operated Departments	912	956	1,020	1,088	1,156	1,216	1,276	1,356	1,384	1,432
Total	14,232	14,824	15,548	16,308	17,088	17,808	18,548	19,316	19,992	20,692
Departmental Income	17,328	18,432	19,732	21,336	23,004	24,536	25,564	26,620	27,204	28,328
Undistributed Operating Expenses										
Administrative and General	2,800	2,900	3,000	3,104	3,212	3,324	3,440	3,564	3,688	3,816
Franchise Fees	0	0	0	0	0	0	0	0	0	0
Marketing	2,752	2,716	2,680	2,772	2,868	2,968	3,072	3,180	3,292	3,408
Property Maintenance	1,600	1,656	1,712	1,772	1,836	1,900	1,968	2,036	2,108	2,180
Energy and Utilities	1,020	1,056	1,092	1,132	1,172	1,212	1,252	1,296	1,344	1,392
Total	8,172	8,328	8,484	8,780	9,088	9,404	9,732	10,076	10,432	10,796
Income before Fixed Charges	9,156	10,104	11,248	12,556	13,916	15,132	15,832	16,544	16,772	17,532
Management Fees and Fixed Charges										
Management Fees	948	996	1,060	1,128	1,204	1,272	1,324	1,380	1,416	1,472
Rent	0	0	0	0	0	0	0	0	0	0
Property Taxes	500	512	520	532	540	552	564	576	584	596
Insurance	200	208	216	220	228	236	244	256	264	272
Total	1,648	1,716	1,796	1,880	1,972	2,060	2,132	2,212	2,264	2,340
Income before Reserve	7,508	8,388	9,452	10,676	11,944	13,072	13,700	14,332	14,508	15,192
Reserve for Replacement	948	1,164	1,412	1,692	2,004	2,116	2,204	2,296	2,360	2,452
Income before Other Charges	6,560	7,224	8,040	8,984	9,940	10,956	11,496	12,036	12,148	12,740

continued

Figure 4-6 (continued)
Projected Operating Results, before Debt Service, for a Proposed 250-Room Hotel

	Per Occupied Room Night (Dollars)									
	1995	1996	1997	1998	1999	2000	2001	2002	2003	2004
Revenue										
Rooms	$69.64	$71.51	$74.52	$78.52	$82.56	$87.60	$90.77	$94.00	$96.00	100.01
Food	28.41	29.03	30.53	32.09	33.71	35.38	37.11	38.93	40.30	41.70
Beverage	7.81	7.98	8.39	8.83	9.26	9.73	10.21	10.71	11.08	11.47
Telephone	4.65	4.75	4.98	5.24	5.51	5.79	6.06	6.36	6.59	6.81
Other Operated Departments	5.57	5.69	5.99	6.29	6.60	6.94	7.28	7.63	7.91	8.18
Rentals and Other Income	7.44	7.60	7.99	8.40	8.81	9.25	9.70	10.18	10.54	10.90
Total	123.52	126.54	132.41	139.37	146.45	154.68	161.14	167.80	172.41	179.07
Departmental Expenses										
Rooms	19.51	19.71	20.31	20.93	21.55	22.41	23.31	24.23	25.07	25.95
Food and Beverage	29.70	30.08	31.08	32.12	33.18	34.56	35.97	37.45	38.75	40.11
Telephone	2.93	2.98	3.14	3.30	3.46	3.64	3.81	4.00	4.15	4.30
Other Operated Departments	3.57	3.64	3.83	4.03	4.22	4.44	4.66	4.88	5.06	5.23
Total	55.70	56.41	58.35	60.38	62.42	65.05	67.76	70.56	73.03	75.59
Departmental Income	67.82	70.14	74.06	78.99	84.03	89.63	93.38	97.24	99.38	103.48
Undistributed Operating Expenses										
Administrative and General	10.96	11.04	11.26	11.49	11.73	12.14	12.57	13.02	13.47	13.94
Franchise Fees	0.00	0.00	0.00	0.00	0.00	0.00	0.00	0.00	0.00	0.00
Marketing	10.77	10.33	10.06	10.26	10.48	10.84	11.22	11.62	12.03	12.45
Property Maintenance	6.26	6.30	6.43	6.56	6.71	6.94	7.19	7.44	7.70	7.96
Energy and Utilities	3.99	4.02	4.10	4.19	4.28	4.43	4.57	4.73	4.91	5.08
Total	31.98	31.69	31.84	32.51	33.20	34.35	35.55	36.81	38.11	39.44
Income before Fixed Charges	35.84	38.45	42.21	46.49	50.83	55.28	57.83	60.43	61.27	64.04
Management Fees and Fixed Charges										
Management Fees	3.71	3.79	3.98	4.18	4.40	4.65	4.84	5.04	5.17	5.38
Rent	0.00	0.00	0.00	0.00	0.00	0.00	0.00	0.00	0.00	0.00
Property Taxes	1.96	1.95	1.95	1.97	1.97	2.02	2.06	2.10	2.13	2.18
Insurance	0.78	0.79	0.81	0.81	0.83	0.86	0.89	0.94	0.96	0.99
Total	6.45	6.53	6.74	6.96	7.20	7.53	7.79	8.08	8.27	8.55
Income before Reserve	29.39	31.92	35.47	39.53	43.63	47.75	50.05	52.35	53.00	55.50
Reserve for Replacement	3.71	4.43	5.30	6.26	7.32	7.73	8.05	8.39	8.62	8.96
Income before Other Charges	25.68	27.49	30.17	33.26	36.31	40.02	41.99	43.97	44.38	46.54

Source: PKF Consulting.

Chapter 5

Acquisition as a Development Tactic

Bruce Baltin, James R. Butler, Jr., and P. Peter Benudiz

Many hotel projects begin with the acquisition of an existing property. This chapter sets out to assist the developer whose vision begins with buying rather than building "from scratch."

A hotel is a business housed in real estate. Its business is dynamic, and so is its market. There are no major tenant leases. Every room has to be resold every night. Guests in the hotel's dining and meeting rooms come and go on an hourly basis. Given these circumstances, investors that decide to include a hotel in their portfolio must understand why they are doing so, and then make broad assumptions about future market conditions and devise plans to deal with those conditions.

The first question a buyer should ask is: "Why are we buying this property?" The reasons can vary from the pure economics of the deal to the purely emotional. Many acquisitions are driven, at least in part, by dreams of ownership and emotional incentives, including the desire to have a place to visit or a place in which to entertain. Decisions made for other than economic reasons are not inherently wrong. Buying a trophy hotel that produces little or no cash flow yield on the investment is fine if the owner can afford it. However, that trophy hotel should not be financed with the expectation that the property will service the debt.

There are as many strategic reasons for buying a hotel as there are willing buyers. One buyer may see potential in putting a specific type of hotel, like an all-suite hotel or a limited-service hotel, in a particular location, like an industrial park or an airport. Another may find that having a property in a certain city or a certain part of town fits the investor's long-term strategy.

Some owners want active involvement and others prefer to remain passive. Some owners position strategically for the short term, while others take a longer view. Owners base their decisions on yield or return requirements that depend,

The Hotel Sainte Claire in San Jose, California, is listed on the National Register of Historic Places. It has been restored as a first-class, full-service hotel to serve the city's nearby convention center, and its historic ambiance makes it a different hotel product than the nearby Fairmont and Hilton hotels, both of which were constructed as new hotels.

■ Members of the Acquisition Team

Broker
Representing either the buyer or seller, the broker typically helps market the property and bring the seller and buyer together. Often the broker helps negotiate and facilitate a sale. The broker's fee is typically a percentage of the total sales price.

Appraiser
Since the work experience of appraisers can vary widely, it is advisable to select an appraiser who has appraised either similar properties or properties located in the same market.

Accountant
An accountant's review of a hotel's books and records can determine whether funds have been properly applied and whether financial controls and reporting systems are adequate.

Market and Financial Consultant
A market and financial consultant is needed to ascertain how a property might perform and what it would take to achieve desired profit or investment goals. The consultant evaluates prevailing market conditions and prepares projections for both the market and the subject property. The consultant can also review the hotel's revenue and expense reports and help assemble the business plan.

Legal Consultant
An attorney specializing in hotel work has many roles to play on an acquisition team: from helping to formulate the acquisition strategy and coordinate the acquisition team to advising on the terms and structure of transactions. An attorney bird-dogs legal due diligence issues, including pending litigation and regulatory matters, existing contracts, and titles. An attorney must be able to document and close a complex purchase and sale transaction—not merely a plain-vanilla real estate deal. At a minimum, the transaction is likely to involve franchise, labor, real estate, tax, corporate, and trademark issues. In certain cases, litigation, bankruptcy, timeshare, and other specialties may be needed.

Architect
If the acquisition is to involve renovation or upgrading of the property, an architect is needed to design the improvements and review the applicable building codes and regulations. An architect can coordinate the activities of other members of the team who are responsible for the physical property, such as the engineer and the interior designer.

Engineer
A qualified engineer (or engineers) is needed to inspect and make recommendations on the physical components of the property, including mechanical, electrical, plumbing, and structural elements.

---

in turn, on available alternative investments, strategic considerations, and other factors. In short, acquisition criteria are unique to each buyer. Among the factors that an investor seeking to buy a hotel or group of hotels might consider are the following: location; property type; size of property; cost; current and potential cash flow yield; potential appreciation in asset value; risk and stability of earnings; upside potential from repositioning, including renovation or management changes; barriers to entry for new competition; and the new owner's ability to replace the current management or change the franchise affiliation.

There is no right or wrong answer for each asset. But no matter what the underlying motivation may be, a buyer must put in place a clearly defined strategy and decision process before beginning the acquisition process.

The acquisition process begins with an investor identifying an opportunity and formulating a vision for it. The next step is evaluation. The last is acquisition. Caution dictates that many more purchases are started than are completed. A prudent buyer conducts a thorough analysis and due diligence process, which may reveal the need to restructure or terminate a proposed transaction. A prudent buyer keeps an open mind throughout the process.

Given a hotel's dual nature as both a business and real estate, the buyer should be sure to have the advice of professionals who are familiar with the hotel industry. Typically, buyers will assemble a team of about six professionals who will assist in the overall evaluation of a hotel property. The acquisition team may be used sooner rather than later if the buyer needs an initial properties screening team. An acquisition team would include a broker, an appraiser, an accountant, a market and financial consultant, a legal consultant, an architect, and an engineer.

There are practical limitations to the human and financial resources that can be applied to the analysis of potential hotel purchases. Conversely, there is a real benefit to added information, and usually the most informed purchasers make the best deals. In order to optimize the cost/benefit ratio of information, the informed purchaser proceeds through a series of steps as follows:

- Determine acquisition criteria;
- Solicit product;
- Screen initial offerings and decide upon targets;
- Establish a price and a business plan;
- Negotiate the deal to a contract or letter of intent;

- Conduct due diligence; and
- Close the transaction.

The remainder of this chapter discusses these steps and identifies key market and operational issues that affect the acquisition process.

Identifying Potential Acquisition Targets

Having settled on its acquisition criteria, the buyer typically proceeds to "get the word out" that it is interested in acquiring hotels that meet specified criteria. This is accomplished through contacting brokers, asset managers, hotel companies, and industry consultants and, often, through issuing press releases and placing advertisements in trade publications and the general business press.

While continuing to network with industry professionals in hopes of hearing about properties before they are shopped around, the buyer begins to screen preliminary offerings. The screening process is crucial. It allows the buyer to eliminate numerous properties early on, and thus save time and resources for more in-depth investigation of other properties. Too often, the buyer skips the screening step and, as a result, not only misses good opportunities but also wastes resources.

If the buyer lacks an in-house screening team, it can call upon outside due diligence or acquisition consultants with local market knowledge. At this early stage in the process, the buyer can pick their brains to help identify potentially available properties.

Many properties will be eliminated from consideration during the initial screening process, based primarily on descriptions contained in the offering packages submitted, the buyer's or consultant's own knowledge of the properties, and the original acquisition criteria.

Preliminary Evaluation

Before getting to the purchase and sale contract stage, the buyer needs to establish a price and a business plan. In order to do so, it needs to first inspect the property and conduct a preliminary property and market analysis. This analysis and evaluation process will help the buyer determine how to proceed: whether with an appropriately priced buy the hotel represents a turnaround opportunity with great upside potential, or whether the hotel has already reached its maximum earnings level and thus poses a significant downside risk.

For properties that pass the initial screening, the next step is usually a site visit and property inspection, at which point another go/no-go decision will be made. Properties that survive this decision will undergo a preliminary property and market analysis. The next go/no-go decision—develop a bid price and business plan for the hotel, or eliminate it from further consideration—is based on this analysis.

The element that is perhaps the most significant in the buyer's development of a purchase price is the potential earnings. In many purchases, it is the only element. To develop the proposed acquisition price, the buyer must make assumptions about future market conditions and the hotel's performance within its market, and incorporate these assumptions into a discounted cash flow analysis or a projection of stabilized operating income. The buyer's preliminary business plan also will reflect various assumptions about the hotel's physical condition, management, affiliation, and other factors.

■ Figure 5-1

Market Analysis for a 300-Room Hotel

| | Average Daily Rooms | | | | Occupancy Rate | | Average Daily Room Rate | | Performance of Subject Property | |
| | Available | | Occupied | | | | | | | |
	Market	Subject Property	Market	Subject Property	Market	Subject Property	Market	Subject Property	Penetration[1]	Yield[2]
1993	1,500	300	945	165	63%	55%	$81	$74	87.3%	79.8%
1994	1,500	300	1,005	168	67	56	83	74	83.6	74.5
1995	1,500	300	1,065	174	71	58	85	74	81.7	71.1
Projected										
1996	1,500	300	1,097	–	73	–	88	–	–	–
1997	1,650	300	1,163	–	71	–	88	–	–	–
1998	1,700	300	1,186	–	70	–	89	–	–	–
1999	1,700	300	1,210	–	71	–	92	–	–	–

[1] The hotel's share of demand (occupied rooms) divided by its share of supply (available rooms).
[2] The hotel's revPAR (revenue per available room) divided by the market's revPAR.

Market Analysis

Markets change. The causes include growth or decline in the supply of hotel rooms, shifts in market segmentation, and the renovation or repositioning of competitive hotels. A prudent hotel buyer backs up any purchase decision with research on historical market performance and solid forecasts of the supply of competitive hotel rooms and the demand for hotel rooms by market segment (type of traveler). The buyer's research should include an analysis of the ability and willingness of the target market to pay the room rates projected and an analysis of what targeted hotel guests want in terms of facilities, design, amenities, and services.

Figure 5-1 provides an example of market analysis for the proposed purchase of a 300-room hotel. It presents a detailed picture of the historical and projected performance of the competitive market for the subject hotel and of the historical performance of the hotel within the market. It further provides a framework for quantifying the future performance of the property based on possible future actions by the buyer.

Two key measures in this analysis are the subject hotel's penetration and yield. A hotel's penetration is its share of demand (occupied rooms) in relation to its share of supply (available rooms). In 1993, for example, the subject hotel's share of demand was 17.5 percent (165 ÷ 945), and its share of supply was 20 percent (300 ÷ 1500). Thus, its penetration was 87.3 percent (17.5 ÷ 20.0). Comparing the property's and market's occupancy rates is a shortcut method for calculating penetration (55 ÷ 63 = 87.3 percent).

A hotel's yield in this analysis is its revPAR (revenue per available room) divided by the market's revPAR. It reflects the property's relative position in terms of occupancy and room rate. RevPAR is derived by multiplying the average daily room rate by the occupancy percentage. In 1993, the yield for the subject property was 79.8 percent (40.70 ÷ 51.03) based on its $40.70 revPAR ($74.00 x .55). and the market's $51.03 revPAR ($81.00 x .63).

In this example, demand has grown strongly over the past several years, which is typical for a market that is emerging from recession. Demand is projected to grow at more modest levels over the next several years, with the exception of 1997, when a new hotel will be added to the market. (New hotels in a strong market often create demand—supply-induced demand—or accommodate previously unsatisfied demand.) The average room rate has grown modestly, a trend that is projected to continue except while new supply is being absorbed.

Business Plan

While the market in the example appears strong, the subject hotel seems to have problems. Its occupancy rate and room rate have been growing at below-market levels, resulting in declining penetration and yield. The challenge for the buyer is to determine the specific causes of these declines and devise a plan to reverse them.

The buyer's analysis and plan should consider the five basic components of a hotel property: facilities, identification, management, capital structure and financing costs, and marketing strategy.

The evaluation of and plan for the hotel's facilities should focus on the design concept, the configuration (including the mix of guest rooms and suites, restaurants and lounges, banquet and meeting space, recreational facilities, parking, and other facilities), the maintenance needs and durability of the materials, and compliance with current and proposed building and other codes. The buyer's evaluation of the hotel's identification includes the hotel's name and its franchise or brand affiliation, which should be looked at in light of how many room nights it attracts and how the market perceives its price/value ratio. As concerns management, the buyer needs to identify a management company or organization that is well-suited to the needs of the property in terms of quality of service, operating culture, cost control, and marketing strength.

Offering Price

With a plan of action for the property, the buyer can formulate a set of cash flow projections. In order to establish an offering price, the buyer can discount the cash flow projections—including assumptions about capital expenditures and reserves, financing costs, and an exit strategy and disposition price—back to a present value at a discount rate that meets the buyer's return requirements.

In determining the offering price, a prudent buyer will consider also the historical earnings of the hotel and the per room price being achieved for comparable hotel sales in the marketplace. The relationship of the offering price to the discounted cash flow analysis often depends on the strength of the market, the buyer's and seller's relative positions, and other market factors. In a strong seller's market, the offer price must be higher, and vice versa.

Once the initial offer is made, negotiations begin. Either the buyer and seller will come to a meeting of the minds on the purchase price and agree to continue into more refined discussions, or the negotiations will be broken off.

Once an agreement to purchase has been reached, the buyer will often put together an investment memorandum. This useful document is essentially a summary—for internal approval or other purposes—of the analysis that led to the decision to buy. An investment memorandum usually includes a description of the property, a summary of the current and projected market analysis, a projected profit and loss statement, the projected cash flow statements, and the business plan. The business plan includes the key assumptions as to management style, affiliation, marketing, operating costs, capital expenditures by major categories (with schedule), financing, and other elements of any proposed repositioning.

This document can be updated and revised throughout the due diligence process, and used during the operations transition and beyond.

The Purchase and Sale Agreement

Successfully negotiating and preparing a contract for the purchase or sale of real estate require a thorough understanding of the objectives of the buyer or seller, the legal and tax situation, the character of the property, and the interests of third parties, including lenders, brokers, unions, and others that may require contractual provisions for their protection, even though they are not parties to the contract.

Because any transaction costs a substantial sum of money and involves the transfer of valuable assets, the parties and their professional advisers should negotiate the purchase and sale terms with great care and precision.

Key Business Concerns

A buyer should pay particular attention to some crucial business elements of the deal, including the items included in and excluded from the purchase price; adjustments to the purchase price; provisions for the termination (or retention) of the current operator; and contingencies to reduce the buyer's deposit risk.

Included Items. The business nature of hotels means that their assets involve many items other than pure real estate. The negotiation of the items that will be included in the purchase has a substantial impact on the smoothness and cost of transition from old owner to new owner.

As a general rule, hotels involve the following assets, with those marked with an asterisk (*) being the assets that a buyer would normally want included in a hotel purchase.

- *Current Assets.* These include cash, accounts receivable, notes receivable, prepaid expenses, securities, *inventories of food and beverages, *inventories of supplies, *printing and stationery, and *other current assets.
- *Property and Equipment.* This includes land; *buildings and improvements; *furniture, fixtures, and equipment; and *linen, china, glassware, silverware, and uniforms.
- *Other Assets.* These include organization costs, preopening expenses, other deferred charges, *deposits, and *licenses and permits.

A distinction is sometimes made between assets in use and in storage. Nevertheless, a buyer generally seeks a sale price on the basis of a "going concern"—including all the assets with asterisks in the preceding list, plus assignment of leases and contracts, each at the buyer's option, as well as all advance deposits not consumed by the date of closing.

Nonfinancial assets are also a consideration in a hotel acquisition. Accounting books and records, operating statistics, employee records, sales and marketing files, licenses and permits, and numerous other similar items are required to keep a hotel going. A buyer should be certain to have the attorney and operations advisers negotiate purchase terms that will ensure a smooth operating transition from seller to buyer.

The Hotel Roanoke, built by the Norfolk and Western Railway Company in 1883, has been restored to its original grandeur and it has been repositioned as a hotel oriented to an adjacent conference center.

Purchase Price. The final sales price is often affected by related terms in the purchase and sale contract. For example, the purchaser will, perhaps, pay a higher price if the seller will take back purchase money financing. Also, the amount of the earnest money deposit, the length of time over which cash payments can be spread, and the assumability of an existing mortgage can influence the sales price. Other considerations that may affect the final sales price include the track record and financial strength of the purchaser, the speed with which the transaction can be completed, and whether items such as receivables or claims are included in the purchase.

Existing Management. If the purchaser plans to install a new operator, the hotel management contract (if there is one) should be examined by counsel to determine the ability to assign, terminate, or otherwise deal with it. In some instances, the contract can be terminated by paying a cancellation fee. Generally, when a hotel is sold without the requirement that the existing management be retained, the sales price will be higher than it would be if the operator were to remain.

In some acquisitions, the seller is the management company that is operating the property, and the purchaser wants the management company to remain in place. In such cases, the seller may offer cash flow guarantees or take back purchase money financing, which essentially pays out the purchase price over time. Such arrangements generally bring a higher selling price and make it easier for the purchaser to put together the overall financing.

Contingencies. A buyer entering into a purchase and sale contract usually makes a sizable money deposit to demonstrate its commitment to closing the transaction. If the deal is not completed, the buyer may forfeit all or a portion of the deposit. To reduce the risk of losing the deposit, the purchaser usually negotiates a set of contingencies that allow it to back out of the transaction without losing the entire deposit.

Some of the more frequently used contingencies include any inability of the purchaser to obtain specified financing, transfer or obtain a specified franchise affiliation, obtain specified licenses or permits (particularly a liquor license), approve the results of the complete due diligence within a specified period of time, or obtain clear legal title to the hotel's real property.

In a seller's market, the seller usually agrees to encumber a transaction with such contingencies only in exchange for benefits such as a higher price or more favorable terms.

The Initial Contract

One school of thought holds that a letter of intent is the best way to start the process of buying or selling a property. Another holds that a letter of intent wastes time that could be better spent in negotiating a binding definitive agreement with appropriate "outs" or conditions. Although not usually considered as a binding contract, a letter of intent can be binding if the parties indicate that they intend it as such and if sufficient terms are specified. A letter of intent lays out the basic terms of the agreement and serves as an obligation on the part of both the buyer and seller to make an effort in good faith to complete the transaction. After the letter of intent has been accepted by both parties, the buyer must perform due diligence and obtain financing. Negotiations on the final purchase and sale contract should continue throughout the process.

Unless the letter of intent provides otherwise (and the provision is stated to be binding), the seller can negotiate with other interested investors. Meanwhile, the seller has to make a good faith effort to conclude the transaction, which, ethically, somewhat restricts the seller. Nevertheless, letters of intent may serve a legitimate purpose in certain situations. If one of the parties is an institution or investment group, it may, as a matter of policy, require a letter of intent before negotiations can proceed, in order to minimize legal and other expenses or to minimize the risk of undue publicity if the transaction fails to close. If the transaction is to be financed by the public issuance of securities, the underwriter may require a letter of intent as a "comfort document," to justify the time and expense required for the due diligence investigation. In a complex negotiation that will take many months to complete, a letter of intent can help avoid misunderstandings by identifying the purposes of the parties in the negotiation.

Among the items that are likely to be included in a letter of intent are a description of the property that is sufficiently detailed so that both parties understand the nature of the transaction; a description of the price and terms of the transaction and the financing structure; due diligence provisions allowing the purchaser to perform a certain amount of review, documentation, and analysis of the property; a description of contingencies, the specific circumstances that allow one or both of the parties to void the deal; and representations by the seller regarding its legal ability to complete the transaction.

Depending on the language used and legal doctrines that may apply, a letter of intent can be binding, nonbinding, or partly binding and partly nonbinding. The typical letter of intent attempts to detail only the most important deal points. The idea is to be sure the parties fundamentally agree on the big issues before they proceed with due diligence and definitive contract negotiations. When a letter of intent is intended to be nonbinding in its entirety, it is usually just a preliminary step used to confirm a meeting of the minds on key terms.

A binding letter of intent can be dangerous, because one party may be able to compel the other party to perform before agreement has been reached on the details. In many cases, the parties may want binding agreements on certain provisions, while they work on the details of others. Among the provisions they may want to make binding are a forfeitable deposit by the buyer, confidentiality provisions, and a "no shop" or a "stand still" provision that prevents the seller from negotiating with others or selling to another party while due diligence and sale contract negotiations are going on. In such cases, a letter of intent that is intended to be binding only in certain regards and otherwise nonbinding is a good solution.

The language of the letter of intent is very important. For a letter of intent to form a binding contract, it should expressly state that intention and sufficiently specify the material terms of agreement—such as parties, subject matter, price, and terms. If the parties want a letter of intent to be nonbinding, the letter should expressly provide that no legal obligation will be incurred by either party unless evidenced by a formal written contract. In many states, however, it is possible that one party may end up liable for damages on the basis that the obligation to negotiate in good faith was breached. To avoid any such interpretation, the letter of intent should include a specific provision that neither party has a duty to continue negotiating and that either party may withdraw from negotiations for any reason. But a buyer facing the considerable expense of due diligence should understand what rights, if any, it has to force the seller to proceed with the sale.

Under the alternative approach, which is to execute a binding agreement of purchase and sale without benefit of a let-

■ The Purchase and Sale Contract

The basic clauses usually found in a purchase and sale contract are as follows:

Real and Personal Property Being Sold
A description of the real and personal property being transferred.

Business Assets Being Sold
A listing of the various licenses, contracts, franchises, and other miscellaneous and intangible personal property that are being included in the transfer.

Closing
The date, time, and place of closing.

Purchase Price
The purchase price and its composition (relative to equity and debt).

Earnest Money or Deposit
The amount of the deposit and the circumstances under which it would be defaulted or returned.

Due Diligence
The time and conditions under which the purchaser's review of the property and other aspects of the transaction should occur, the rights and obligations of each party during due diligence, and the provision that the purchaser's obligations are subject to satisfactory results from the due diligence investigation.

Terms of Purchase Financing
For transactions in which the seller takes back purchase money, the terms of the mortgage.

Title Commitment and Survey
The specifications for the type and quality of title the purchaser is willing to accept.

Seller's Deliveries
A description of the data and information that the seller must give to the purchaser.

Seller's Representation, Warranties, and Covenants
The various facts and statements made by the seller relative to the transaction that are used to induce the purchaser to buy the property.

Purchaser's Representations and Warranties
The various facts and statements made by the purchaser relative to the transaction that are used to induce the seller to sell the property.

Prorations and Adjustments
The specific prorations of the current revenues and expenses between the purchaser and seller.

Closing Documents and Procedures
A list of the various documents that will be needed to close the transaction and a description of the closing procedure.

Closing Expenses
The allocation of closing expenses between the purchaser and seller.

Eminent Domain and Risk of Loss
The details of what will occur if the property is taken by eminent domain or suffers a casualty loss while it is under contract.

General Clauses
General housekeeping contract clauses.

---

ter of intent, the parties provide that the agreement may be terminated (with or without payment of certain sums) for specified reasons prior to the expiration of the due diligence period. Once under binding contract, a buyer may have greater comfort in spending the money required to complete due diligence, obtain financing, and take the other steps necessary to buy the property. The downside of this approach is the time and money required to negotiate the agreement before due diligence has been performed or financing obtained.

The Purchase and Sale Contract

The final purchase and sale contract establishes the complete terms and conditions of the transaction, covering all the issues in the letter of intent and many other details, including representations and warranties, indemnifications, and closing conditions and terms. (See "The Purchase and Sale Contract" feature box.) The document should be reviewed by an attorney and an accountant familiar with hotel and real estate transactions to ensure its legality.

Employee Issues

Because much of a hotel's success derives from the expertise and cordiality of its employees, the compassionate treatment of employees during the often stressful sale period can go a long way toward protecting the business being purchased. Unfortunately, however, both parties are usually motivated by employment practices liability concerns to make the separation as dramatic as possible.

The Arizona Biltmore, on which Frank Lloyd Wright was a consulting architect, was purchased by Grossman Company Properties in 1992. After a $35 million expansion and renovation, it reopened in 1995.

The buyer usually prefers that all employees be terminated on the day of takeover, at which point the new entity will rehire them on a probationary basis. An analysis should be made of medical and health benefits, pension and retirement plans, vacation and sick day entitlements, and so forth. If appropriate, the buyer may choose to allow all employees to carry their benefits forward as if no sale had taken place, with an accounting between buyer and seller for the accrued liabilities for vacation days, sick days, and retirement thereby assumed by the buyer. Legal counsel can help a buyer avoid unintended successor liability for employment practices of the seller or its predecessors. Legal guidance is particularly important if union contracts are in effect, if union organizing is occurring, or if state or local plant closing laws, like laws found in Hawaii, apply to the hotel.

Due Diligence

A buyer's thorough analysis of the financial condition of the hotel is usually termed a due diligence review. Any letter of intent or purchase and sale agreement should provide that the purchaser's obligations are subject to satisfactory results from the due diligence investigation. Typically, the following reports, contracts, lists, and other documents should be reviewed:

- Annual, audited profit and loss statements, with full supporting schedules, for the last five years;
- Current year-to-date profit and loss statement, with comparison to previous year;
- Monthly profit and loss statements, with full supporting schedules, for the last three years;
- Audited balance sheets for the last five years;
- Occupancy and average room rates for the last three years;
- Capital expenditures for the last five years, with any current projections for expenditures;
- All architectural and engineering plans and specifications;
- All inspection reports, including health, fire, building, and elevator;
- Copies of all studies, including all recent appraisals, market studies, environmental studies, engineering and soil reports, and marketing plans;
- List of all tenants, rent rolls, deposits, and term of leases;
- Inventory of furniture, fixtures, and equipment (FF&E), supplies, consumables, and other goods;
- Real and personal property tax bills for the last three years;
- Schedule of all insurance coverage, including cost and expiration dates;
- Legal property description;
- Service contracts, leases, franchises, licenses, permits, management agreements, union agreements, and any instruments that the purchaser is expected to assume;

- Trademark, trade name, and copyright documents;
- All notes and mortgages currently encumbering the property;
- Details of any governmental action or litigation threatened or pending against the hotel;
- Estoppel letters from any mortgagee;
- List of employees, including name, position, salary or wage scale, and benefits;
- List of future reservations and bookings, including name of party, deposit received, rate guaranteed, dates, and status; and
- List of all purveyors and sources of supplies and services.

The due diligence process involves the performance of a number of discrete tasks. An accountant or firm with experience in the hotel industry should perform a financial audit. A detailed engineering study is needed on all physical components of the property, including the mechanical, electrical, plumbing, and structural elements; the telephone, electronic, and computer systems; and items of decor. A detailed inspection by a qualified environmental engineer is needed to disclose any potential environmental hazards. A skilled local attorney should be used to verify all the property's contracts, licenses, permits, franchises, and other documents, note any potentially adverse provisions, and determine the transferability of the documents to the buyer. An attorney or a title company should conduct a title search.

Finally, it is important to ascertain the current status of the tax assessment. When a hotel property is sold, the local taxing jurisdiction is likely to investigate the terms of the sale and possibly adjust the property's assessed value upward to reflect the sales price. A higher assessed value could reduce the property's future cash flow. A property tax verification performed by a knowledgeable property tax consultant will provide an accurate estimate of future tax liabilities. A property tax consultant can also argue the case for a smaller rise in the assessed value of the hotel.

Closing

When the content, structure, and schedule of the transition are agreed upon, the closing takes place. The closing of a hotel transaction involves the actual transfer of title from the seller to the buyer. Generally, when the buyer assumes management, the closing coincides with the takeover by the new operator. The parties that are normally present at a closing include the seller and the seller's attorney, the buyer and the buyer's attorney, the lender and the lender's attorney, the title company, the real estate broker, and the buyer's and seller's accountants.

An accounting to allocate and prorate the property's existing revenues and expenses takes place. An inventory of all of the assets included in the purchase price is approved. Any items to be transferred that are not included in the purchase price must be inventoried at this time and valued in accordance with the terms of the purchase and sale contract.

After the necessary allocations and prorations are calculated, the mortgages and notes are signed and the requisite money transfers are made. Once this process is concluded, the buyer holds title to the hotel.

Chapter 6
Financing

John M. Keeling

Obtaining financing for a lodging property calls for creativity, tenacity, and flexibility. Today, hotel developers and operators find themselves not only aggressively competing for a constantly changing pool of funds (both equity and debt), but also having to deal with increasingly complex terms and conditions for the use of those funds.

During the relatively stable decades of the 1960s and 1970s, real estate financing remained an orderly, standardized process for matching developers with investors and lenders. Inflation and interest rates fluctuated only slightly. The one wish developers had was for a speedier process. During the late 1970s and early 1980s, real estate financing, stimulated by tax incentives and high inflation rates, increasingly involved financial institutions becoming equity or quasi-equity partners. These institutions sought both income and equity participation. Income participation included sharing in the effective gross revenue, net operating income, cash flow after debt service, or income above a base income. Equity participation included sharing in the proceeds of the sale or refinancing, or sharing in the tax benefits.

When the overbuilding of commercial real estate, including hotels, made itself felt in the late 1980s, financial institutions found themselves reluctant owners of properties for which there was no market, except at drastically reduced prices. As institutions fell into financial difficulty, particularly the S&Ls, many hotel properties were taken over by regulators with the Federal Deposit Insurance Corporation (FDIC), the Federal Savings and Loan Insurance Corporation (FSLIC), and the Resolution Trust Corporation (RTC). Distressed hotels could be purchased at a fraction of their replacement cost. Thus, there was no incentive to build new hotels, and financing for hotel construction was generally not available. With the recovery of the hotel industry in the mid-1990s and much of the distressed inventory sold off, the prices of hotels began to stabilize. In strong markets, lenders cautiously began to consider the financing of new hotels. The revival of hotel construction has focused mostly on the limited-service and all-suite segments of the market.

The financing of lodging properties bears little resemblance to the financing of office, industrial, or residential projects. Lodging properties, which rely on the success of a business, are often viewed as high-risk investments with tremendous upside potential. Lenders, therefore, tend to limit their attention to projects that are well conceived and well located, and that involve experienced developers and operating companies. How much cash flow a lodging property has available for debt service depends on local and national economic conditions, the quality of its management, and unpredictable travel patterns.

Financing Methods

Developers will look in vain for standard methods of financing lodging properties, or for standard financing packages. They do not exist. In fact, financing conditions change almost daily. The ability to analyze, interpret, and predict trends in the equity and debt financing markets is essential for success in developing and operating hotels. A project team's ability to select a proper financing method depends on its experience and on its understanding of the dynamic characteristics of available financing mechanisms. Today, developers and operators commonly turn to specialists in

Like many small hotel development projects, the Sheraton Great Valley Hotel in Chester County, Pennsylvania, was capitalized by a local group with debt financing provided by a miniperm construction loan.

the field of hotel finance for an explication of a project's financing alternatives and a program for obtaining the best financing package.

Available financing methods can be grouped into three categories—short- to intermediate-term debt instruments, long-term debt instruments, and equity structures.

Developers most frequently use short- to intermediate-term loans when a project involves a high risk, when permanent financing does not cover the entire development cost, or when sharing equity is not desirable. The most common short- to intermediate-term debt instruments are the following.

Construction Loans. Generally provided by commercial banks, life insurance companies, and credit companies, construction loans usually have interest rates that float with the prime rate. The loan typically covers the entire development cost and is tied to the ability of the developer to obtain permanent financing.

Combined Construction and Term Loans. These combined loans are packaged to appeal to developers unwilling to share equity with a money partner that is providing debt financing. Lenders generally require guarantees for cost overruns and operating deficits, and the developer usually must provide equity for at least 10 percent of the project. Terms for these loans run between five and seven years, while interest rates float with the prime rate, have a fixing option, or involve a cap percentage. Ordinarily, these loans carry a minimum prepayment penalty to stimulate refinancing. If the hotel operator is a joint venture partner, lenders usually require that incentive management fees be subordinated to the debt service.

Term and Bullet Loans. Limited-term loans and limited-amortization instruments (with the balance due at completion of the term) usually function as interim financing vehicles to cover cost overruns or operating deficits. Interest rates vary within the range of one to four points over prime. The loans generally run from three to five years and take a subordinate position to the primary financing instruments.

There are five major long-term debt instruments as well as some other types of debt financing used generally to fill in the gaps, as described in the following paragraphs.

Convertible Mortgages. The developer receives 100 percent of the project's development cost, control of the property for a period of time (usually ten years), and a loan at or below the market rate. The lender receives a fixed-interest return, participation in 10 to 50 percent of the cash flow after debt service, and the right to convert the mortgage into 50 percent of the equity at an agreed date. Insurance companies, pension funds, and foreign trusts represent the primary sources for convertible mortgages.

Land Sale-Leasebacks and Leasehold Loans. The developer commonly sells the land to the lender at market value and then leases it back at a low rate (10 to 13 percent of the land value, or 3 to 4 percent of gross room sales) for 40 to 50 years. The developer also must pay out a percentage of future cash flow and a share of the property's appreciation. This method provides long-term capital appreciation to the lender (which is usually an insurance company or a pension fund) and a tax-deductible land lease expense to the developer.

Permanent Loans. Most permanent loans involve some lender participation in the future performance of the property. Participation is normally based on gross sales, cash flow after debt service, the appreciation of the property, or some combination of the three. Revenue participation is based specifically on sales or on sales above a certain threshold. Loan principal amounts depend on a debt coverage ratio of 1.10 to 1.35 times the projected cash flow before debt service. These loans run from five to ten years in length, are amortized over 25 to 30 years (with a series of call provisions generally beginning in the tenth year), and carry high prepayment penalties. Insurance companies, pension funds (through separate accounts), and some commercial banks are the principal providers of permanent loans.

Mortgages with a Kicker This financing method provides the developer with a loan at market or below-market rates, but with a long or extra long term. The maximum loan depends on coverage, and the kicker takes the form of a percentage of future cash flows (10 to 50 percent), a share of the residuals, or a combination of the two.

Wraparound Mortgages. Generally provided by sellers or credit companies, these mortgages often entail a lower fixed rate on the original loan being wrapped, thus providing a higher overall yield to the wraparound lender.

Other Long-Term Debt Instruments. Other such instruments include seller financing, exchanges, second mortgages, and standby mortgages. These debt instruments are primarily used when other, more favorable financing methods will not cover all development costs, operating deficits, cost overruns, or land assembly costs.

On the equity side, three major structures are commonly used to finance hotel development, as described in the following paragraphs.

Joint Ventures. A joint venture typically involves a developer, a lender, and, in most cases, an operator. Most lenders prefer that the developer and operator form their own joint venture before entering into a joint venture with the lender. Most JVs bring together "equals"—a developer that is neither larger nor smaller than the operator—and a lender that requires some assurance that the project will succeed under the terms of the joint venture. The division of equity and sharing of revenues and appreciation are based on the cash contributions and the imputed value of each partner's services, and by each partner's investment objectives. When structuring a joint venture, the partners must clarify the payout priorities and the conditions governing the buyout or sale of a partner's interest.

Limited Partnerships. Private offerings of limited partnerships have been a major source of equity financing for small and mid-size lodging facilities. Because each partnership arises from different sets of assumptions, objectives, and products, there are no standard formulas for structuring a limited partnership. Generally, the general partner puts the deal together, receives a 5 to 15 percent development fee for that effort, collects an ongoing development fee that is a percentage of revenues, and takes a percentage of the net cash flow as a partner. The limited partners receive a major portion of the depreciation benefits and tax credits, a preferential return on investment, and a prorated share of the remaining cash flow and sale proceeds.

All-Equity Financing. When interest rates are high and opportunities to obtain debt financing are limited, all-equity financing offers an alternative. A joint venture (developer and lender), a public or private limited partnership, or a single entity (a large insurance company, a developer, or a hotel operator) can provide all-equity financing. With few exceptions, all-equity financing deals are an intermediate step, until more favorable debt financing becomes available or until the property can be sold.

Financing Sources

Which players take the leading roles in hotel finance changes over time. With the dramatic improvement in hotel operating performance in the mid-1990s, lenders gradually began to reenter the hotel lending market. Five major sources—past and present—of hotel financing and their changing roles in this business are profiled in the following paragraphs.

Life Insurance Companies. During the 1970s, life insurance companies provided much of the long-term

Now under construction, the Loews Miami Beach Hotel is scheduled for completion in 1998. The $135 million project was developed under a public/private partnership with $29 million in public financing, a public contribution of $20.6 million for the site, and parking provided in a city-built, 800-space garage.

Some hotel companies, like Red Roof Inns, own and operate their own facilities. Selling a site to an owner/operator may be advantageous for a developer of a project where a lodging facility is needed to support other uses, and such a sale can generate direct and indirect profits.

funds available to the lodging industry. Often they would lend their own funds, but just as often they would use pension fund money they were managing. Because of disintermediation and other severe losses incurred during the 1980s and early 1990s, life companies lost much of their appetite for hotel development. However, by 1995 they were beginning to make funds available for acquisition, renovation, and refinancing.

Savings and Loan Associations. The real estate recession of the 1980s hit the thrift industry hardest. Deregulation of S&Ls in the early 1980s prompted a rush to lend on commercial ventures. Hotels were in the forefront. Lacking expertise, the thrifts funded many low-quality loans, many of which subsequently defaulted. The failure of a large proportion of their loan portfolios drove many savings and loans to insolvency, and led to their takeover by the FSLIC or RTC. By the mid-1990s, new regulations were in place and S&Ls were no longer making hotel loans.

Commercial Banks. Commercial banks shared the stage with S&Ls during the 1980s in terms of furnishing the bulk of the mortgage money. They too have become mostly bit players on the hotel scene. Most banks seem to blame hotels unduly for the bloodletting from the decade's commercial real estate lending excesses, and many still flatly refuse to consider lending on any hotel, new or existing. (Offshore banks, however, and particularly Asian banks, have shown a greater willingness to lend on hotels.) Some commercial banks are cautiously reentering the hotel financing market. In New Orleans, for example, virtually every new hotel project started during the first half of the 1990s was financed, at least in part, by a local bank. While commercial banks have made their share of bad hotel loans and some still eschew them, banks are increasingly providing funds for small, local hotel projects. Ironically, it is small community banks that are lending for construction. Major regional banks and money center banks continue to limit their hotel loans to acquisition and refinancing.

Credit Companies. Sometimes thought of as lenders of last resort, credit companies have been consistent players in the hotel lending market. They charge among the highest rates for loans and often require personal guarantees. Accordingly, they are more willing than most lenders to take on riskier projects. They offer loan-to-value ratios as high as 80 percent.

REMICs. Real estate mortgage investment conduits (REMICs) are conduits established by investment banks, usually through a separate firm. They package commercial real estate loans to be sold on the secondary financial market. Virtually all the major hotel franchise companies have aligned with a conduit company to obtain loans for acquisition and refinancing. In order to attract investors, the loans that make up investment packages must be rated by a rating agency, such as Standard & Poor's. Rating agencies tend to take a very tough stance on hotels, so only the safest hotels are candidates for REMIC financing. The advantages of REMIC financing are that the loans generally are for long terms, nonrecourse, and assumable.

Lending Criteria

Surveys conducted by PKF Consulting since 1986 reveal some major trends in hotel lending criteria. As shown in Figure 6-1, mortgage interest rates rose by one percentage point in 1994 to just under 10 percent. The lower rates offered in 1992 reflect mainly rates negotiated by lenders as part of REO seller-financed sales, rather than loans made by disinterested third parties. While some indicators show a loosening of lender requirements, lenders continue to be reluctant to make hotel loans. Current loan-to-value ratios and debt coverage ratios show only marginal improvement over 1992.

Figure 6-2 shows lending criteria by property type. Not surprisingly, lenders hold limited-service hotels in higher regard than full-service hotels. Limited-service properties have generally outperformed full-service hotels in the 1990s, and what little increase has occurred in the supply of hotel rooms has been principally in the limited-service category. The lending criteria for resort properties—a smaller segment of the industry—are generally the most conservative, but the criteria for all three categories of hotels are in the same range.

■ Figure 6-1

Hotel Lending Criteria, 1986–1994

	1986	1988	1990	1992	1994
Debt Coverage Ratio	1.3	1.3	1.3	1.6	1.4
Interest Rate	10.1%	11.6%	11.5%	8.9%	9.9%
Loan-to-Value Ratio	72.5%	73.6%	69.0%	67.4%	68.0%

Source: PKF Consulting.

Figure 6-2
Mortgage Terms for Hotel Properties, 1995

	High	Low	Average
Loan-to-Value Ratio			
Full-Service Hotels	100.0%	50.0%	68.0%
Limited-Service Hotels	100.0%	50.0%	70.0%
Resort Hotels	80.0%	45.0%	66.0%
All Properties	93.3%	48.3%	68.0%
Interest Rates			
Full-Service Hotels	12.0%	8.0%	9.7%
Limited-Service Hotels	12.0%	8.0%	9.5%
Resort Hotels	13.0%	8.9%	10.6%
All Properties	12.3%	8.3%	9.9%
Amortization (Years)			
Full-Service Hotels	30.0	15.0	21.6
Limited-Service Hotels	30.0	15.0	20.4
Resort Hotels	30.0	15.0	21.4
All Properties	30.0	15.0	21.1
Loan Term (Years)			
Full-Service Hotels	21.5	5.0	8.2
Limited-Service Hotels	21.5	5.0	8.7
Resort Hotels	21.5	5.0	9.1
All Properties	21.5	5.0	8.7
Debt Coverage Ratio			
Full-Service Hotels	1.7	1.2	1.4
Limited-Service Hotels	1.7	1.2	1.4
Resort Hotels	1.8	1.1	1.5
All Properties	1.7	1.2	1.4

Source: PKF Consulting.

Capital for hotel investments is once again available, but its cost is quite high relative to the cost of financing other kinds of real estate. Interest rates on hotel loans remain one to two percentage points above the interest rates for loans on multifamily, retail, office, and manufacturing projects; and the debt coverage requirements for hotels are also higher.

Preparing a Loan Package

All sources of financing for hotels—lenders, parties to limited partnerships and joint ventures, buyers, and sellers—require certain documents and reports, some more and some less detailed depending on the case. Lenders usually require the following documents:

- A transmittal letter to the lender from the project team that clearly states the loan amount requested;
- One-page fact sheet that describes the project, its size, type of ownership and management, operating characteristics, location, and design;
- Rendering of the proposed project, a preliminary site plan, and general design specifications;
- Formal market study prepared by a nationally recognized hotel consulting firm;
- Cash flow statement that projects the cash available for debt service and identifies the first expected stabilized year of operation;
- Any agreements or letters of understanding with a hotel operating company;
- Any franchise agreement;
- Resumes and financial statements on the project's owners and developers;
- Deed, title policy, or lease agreement for the site;
- All documents—such as legal agreements, other leases, constraints, and easements—that affect the site or project;
- Environmental assessment of the site showing that the site is free of soil contaminants, underground storage tanks, or possibly hazardous materials;
- Any environmental impact statements or reports required for development approval; and
- Descriptions and photographs of similar projects developed by the developer and operator.

These documents should be organized and presented in a professionally prepared folder, binder, or booklet. Glossy reports containing mostly superficial information or marketing brochures are materials that lenders do not want.

Evaluating the Financing Package

Developers, investors, and operators set widely different objectives for their investments and thus use different criteria for deciding whether to become involved in a hotel project. The three criteria most commonly used to judge the viability of a hotel project are the internal rate of return (IRR) hurdle rate, debt service coverage, and the size of the loan relative to the value of the project.

The IRR hurdle rate is the minimum acceptable total return on investment. A developer, investor, or operator will each determine its own IRR hurdle rate. As of mid-1996, pretax IRR hurdle rates for equity capital invested range from 12 to 16 percent for freestanding hotels, and from 11 to 20 percent for hotels in mixed-use projects. In determining the IRR, cash flow should be defined as cash available after all operating expenses, property taxes, insurance, reserves for replacement, and incentive management fees are deducted.

For lenders, debt service coverage generally is viewed as the most appropriate indication of a project's ability to secure debt financing. Lenders typically use the project's first stabilized year of cash flow (the third year for most hotel projects and the fifth year for most resort projects) as a basis. Cash flow in this context means cash available after all operating expenses, property taxes, insurance, and reserves for replacement are deducted. Today, acceptable coverage ratios range from 1.1 to 1.8, with most lenders preferring a 1.4 to 1.5 debt coverage. (See Figure 6-1 and Figure 6-2.) In the opinion of most lenders, hotels present more risk than do office or retail projects, which generally have more stable cash flows.

Lenders also look at the size of the loan relative to the project's value. As a rule, lenders cannot make loans that exceed the property's appraised real estate value. Lenders want developers to share in the development risk. Therefore, they look at a developer's equity commitment when they evaluate a loan package.

Some lenders, developers, and investors use other evaluative criteria, as well, as guides to an expected return on investment, including cash-on-cash return, the payback period, net present value, or return on equity.

The primary data that analysts require to evaluate a project's return on investment include an estimate of the overall development cost; an estimate of the productive life of the project, or the hypothetical date of a "forced" sale; and income and cash flow projections.

The hotel development process cannot work without financing. Implicit in this discussion of the sources and methods of hotel financing has been the suggestion that obtaining financing for a proposed hotel takes a project team that is creative, tenacious, and flexible. The fundamentals of financing are fairly constant. However, the ways in which basic financing methods are packaged and used are constantly changing. Securing long-term financing for lodging properties will continue to challenge their developers. The future can be promising, however, for developers that take advantage of the various sources and methods of financing.

Chapter 7
Management Contracts

Karen Johnson

In the history of the hotel business, management contracts are a relatively recent phenomenon. Originally, hotels were managed by the same people who owned them. For the rare hotels that were owned by passive investors, their owners usually were no more involved in operations than investors in any other ongoing business might be.

Management contracts emerged in the 1960s, usually involving an experienced hotel company that operated a property for another entity—usually a government—in an emerging nation. The idea was that the government would assume all the risk in order to get a hotel business off the ground and start the flow of tourism dollars into the country. The operator brought expertise and a world-class brand name, and it would be compensated no matter what the economic outcome of the hotel was.

Before this pump priming approach became popular, national governments and hotel companies had shared the economic risks equally under turnkey leases that were structured with a bottom-line orientation: the operator retained a handsome share of the profits and the owner (a government or quasi-government agency) collected what was left. In business terms, the turnkey lease usually required that the operator/lessee pay the owner/lessor a percentage of sales. If things worked out well, the lease payments would cover the mortgage and compensate the owner for its entrepreneurial risk in constructing the hotel. The operator was in the riskiest position, but it also claimed the lion's share of the upside potential. Through the 1960s and mid-1970s, such leases were the preferred method by which nonhoteliers invested in hotel real estate. Thereafter, the turnkey lease gave way to the management contract.

The First Round of Management Contracts

As explained, the earliest management contracts were designed for hotels that were the emerging country's "loss leader" to gain entry into the tourist industry. The hotels were not expected to make money in the initial years of operation. However, the original rationale for the transfer of the risk from the operator to the owner (government) came to be forgotten. During the 1970s, management contracts took hold in the private sector, with operators more or less running the show. The risk-reward pendulum swung conspicuously in favor of the operator.

In 1970, according to Charles A. Bell, there were fewer than 22 third-party management contracts in the U.S. hotel industry; by 1975, the number had jumped to 182; and, by 1980, there were too many to count.* This rapid growth was spurred by a influx of passive investors. Real estate investors had begun to recognize the hotel as an inflation-resistant investment. Its rents could be adjusted on a daily basis, whereas rents from other forms of real estate were governed by leases that were adjusted for inflation on a far less frequent basis, if at all. Passive hotel investments became attractive to new players who were willing to engage expert management.

Unfortunately for the hotel industry, the transfer of the risk from the operator to the owner was like the opening of

---

*Charles A. Bell, "Agreements with Chain Hotel Companies," *Cornell Quarterly*, February 1993.

Sheraton Society Hill, Philadelphia.

Pandora's box. Hotel owners did not open this box alone. Lenders, recognizing the key role management plays in hotel real estate, began to require that hotel developers obtain an appropriate chain affiliation and a third-party management company before they would approve a loan. Owners began to lose leverage in negotiating management contracts.

Also, many of the hotel developments of the late 1970s and early 1980s were designed to take advantage of tax laws regarding losses on passive real estate investments. If a hotel lost money after depreciation and amortization were taken into account, it did not really matter. The investors would reap their reward in the later years, particularly when the asset was sold at the end of the holding period. Thus, real estate syndicators, which were dependent also upon obtaining a national affiliation and reputable management company for their projects, relinquished more control. The hotel management companies were now firmly in the driver's seat, operating hotels under what can best be described as leases with inverse payments.

That these early management contracts evolved from leases becomes apparent when one considers some of the basic terms of the management contracts of the 1970s and 1980s:

- The contracts survived changes in ownership and foreclosure;
- Since the operator was assured the right of quiet enjoyment, the owner had to request permission to enter and inspect the property; and
- The initial terms were for 20 and 30 years.

For a strong management company (Hilton, Hyatt, Marriott, Sheraton, Inter-Continental, to name but a few), the most common contract in the 1980s entailed a "three-and-twenty" fee structure. The owner paid the management 3 percent of the gross sales, plus 10 to 20 percent of income before fixed charges, such as property tax, building and contents insurance, any ground rent, income taxes, depreciation, amortization, and debt service. In addition, the owner bore the cost of all payroll associated with the property's operation, including the general manager's salary.

The owner also paid for centralized reservations systems and corporate marketing and advertising services, centralized accounting services, centralized employee training, centralized purchasing services, and corporate supervisors' visits to the property. The operator prorated charges for big-ticket central services to the individual owners of the hotels it managed, and included miscellaneous items, such as centralized purchasing, in its overall statements.

In exchange for these fees, the owners received the benefit of the management company's expertise and the brand name of the product. In time, hotel operators that did not own brand names entered the third-party management field. Experienced in operating their own hotels, frequently with a franchise of a brand-name hotel, these independent or unbranded management companies began to sell their services, which were usually to be combined with a separate franchise from a major hotel chain. Typically, the unbranded operators charged lower fees, in that the owner would be paying a separate franchise fee. However, when an independent operator was able to bring a franchise like Marriott to the table, it generally negotiated a contract that mirrored the terms that a chain or branded management company could get.

In the late 1980s, the consequences of separating the risk from the reward became apparent. Tax reforms had made the owners of hotels, which had been developed with the anticipation of barely servicing debt, suddenly anxious to earn a return on their capital during the holding period, not just at the end of the hold. Tax deals and general optimism had pushed supply ahead of demand almost everywhere. Prices (room rates) fell, and hotels, by and large, were unable to service debt. The last hotel management contracts of the 1980s began to subordinate the incentive portion of the fees to debt service, and eventually to an owner's preferred return.

A New Emphasis on Performance

When economic recession struck the United States in 1990, the real estate industry entered its second great depression. Hotel management companies cut some expenses, but worried that deep cuts would compromise their brand names and reputations. Lack of funds for making mortgage payments was shrugged off as an owner's problem. The management companies had troubles of their own, as assumptions of boundless growth in management contracts and fees had failed to materialize and they found themselves overstaffed. Some hotel management companies had become real estate developers, and were encountering the same problems facing other owners. These companies needed the stream of income from the management contracts to keep their corporate offices and debt afloat. Then, virtually overnight, the management companies changed strategies. The change came about for two reasons: competition and legal action.

In the early 1980s, there were fewer than 65 management companies. By 1991, there were more than 500. Lenders, with their swollen portfolios of foreclosed or REO properties, needed short-term management solutions, and the management industry mushroomed as small groups or individuals with hotel operating experience set themselves up as independent management companies and stepped into the void.

At the same time, owners brought a series of lawsuits that sought to revoke old, long-term contracts. Although these management contracts may have looked like leases, the owners argued successfully that they created no legal (leasehold) interest. The relationship between owner and management company, they argued, is not one of landlord and tenant, but of owner and agent.

The 1991 case of *Woolley* v. *Embassy Suites* in California established that the owner could terminate the agent's services at will and thereby regain control of the property. While the decision may appear obvious to someone who has never dealt with hotel management contracts, it came as a shock to the hotel management companies, which were operating under the assumption that they were entitled to retain control through the length of the contract, barring a finding of incompetent management. The "at will" termination allowed by *Woolley* is not without cost or risk, however. If the court were to find that such a termination had been made "without cause" and that the management company had not breached its fiduciary duties to the owner, the owner would be liable for damages for wrongful termination.

The decision on a second and more notable case, *Pacific Landmark Hotel, Ltd.* v. *Marriott,* is still pending as of mid-1996. A California court has already ruled that an investment in a hotel by the management company creates an agency that, when coupled with the company's legal "interest" in the property, is irrevocable. Even if the loan or investment were made under the aegis of a separate incorporated entity, as it was in this case, the agency would hold. *Pacific Landmark Hotel* has caused many owners to rethink their strategies for seeking equity contributions and working capital loans or capital improvement loans from their hotel management companies.

With competitive pressure on the rise and some owners pursuing vigorous legal action, many of the new contracts signed in the early 1990s were far more favorable to the owners. Most newer contracts were being terminated when the assets were sold. Chain management companies were forced to become more competitive, not only to obtain new contracts but also to retain existing ones. Lenders were drawn into the fray. In some cases, they dissolved contracts through foreclosure proceedings. If they were losing money in operations, they sometimes simply shut down the hotels. The threat of foreclosure and the fear of becoming another test case in the court battles between owners and managers persuaded many management companies to reconsider their options and quietly renegotiate their fees or fee structures.

Besides covering shorter terms, these newly negotiated management contracts tied fees more to performance. Base fees might start out as nominal and be stepped up in later years to reflect the likely cash flow pattern. When the competition for fees became extremely intense, one major management company was reported to be offering new contracts that charged no fees in the initial years except for corporate office chargebacks for advertising, marketing, and accounting services. In general, however, contracts still retained

Courtesy Thompson, Ventulett, Stainback & Associates

Hyatt Regency at Bayport Plaza, Tampa, Florida.

base fees, but they were well below the 3 percent applied in the old "three-and-twenty" contracts.

Creative ways to design performance-based fees were found. A second slice (or tranche) of the base fee might be tied to one of a number of different definitions of the net operating income. It might be tied, for example, to an improvement in the NOI, or to the NOI line or the house profit line only if the income or profit reached a specified level. A third tranche of fees might be paid after debt service and a preferred return to the owner.

As lenders worked through and sold off their REO portfolios, their need for third-party management companies dwindled. The majority of the buyers from 1991 to 1994 were owner/operators who had no need of third-party services. By 1993, management companies were downsizing, consolidating, or disappearing.

Conceivably, by 2001 the industry could be back to the same number of management companies as existed in 1981. It is unlikely, however, that it will return to the same kinds of management contracts that were prevalent then. The lesson hotel owners should learn from the 1980s is this: Do not sign any management contract with the encumbrances of a long-term lease unless you, as the landlord, are the one getting paid.

Radisson Plaza at Mark Center, Arlington, Virginia.

Negotiating a Contract

The "ideal" management contract is a fantasy. Contract terms are kept in a state of constant flux by the evolution of the industry and changes induced by litigation and the forces of supply and demand. Also, developer and investor objectives vary. Negotiating a management contract with the most reputable and desirable management companies is a process of give-and-take. Within the matrix of possible alternatives, the developers or investors must decide on which issues they can and cannot compromise. Management contracts favorable to the owner, in length of term and ease of termination, usually come with higher fees.

The importance of retaining an attorney or consultant with current experience in negotiating management contracts cannot be underestimated. Specialist attorneys and consultants know the prevailing terms and understand what is a worthwhile tradeoff. They can save the developer time and help tailor the contract to a specific investment strategy. As a seasoned negotiator is fond of saying, "No matter how good you think your general real estate attorney is, chances are he won't be as knowledgeable as the guy the management company brings to the table." Specialists who negotiate three or four contracts a month know how to look out for their clients' best interests.

How much flexibility an owner wants is one of the key criteria for choosing a management company. If the owner's goal is to build and flip or buy and flip, an independent or unbranded management company is more likely a better choice. The initial cost will probably be more than for a branded operator, because a separate franchise fee must be paid to a second, and unrelated, organization. However, the tradeoff for cost is flexibility; the owner should be able to negotiate a management contract with an independent that allows cancellation in a shorter period of time and at a lower cost. In addition, management fee costs can be lower with an independent management company, since these companies usually generate lower corporate office chargebacks for accounting, marketing, advertising, and other management services.

Contract Termination

It is important for the owner to know precisely what circumstances will enable it to terminate the management contract, and at what cost. Depending on its investment goals, the owner can negotiate specific termination clauses. There follows a discussion of issues and options available for four potential termination circumstances: foreclosure, sale, nonperformance, and at will.

Foreclosure

An unpleasant proposition, foreclosure nevertheless must be dealt with. The owner's odds of financing or refinancing a project improve immeasurably if the contract is designed to terminate upon foreclosure.

Sale

The importance of obtaining a termination-upon-sale clause depends on the owner's investment strategy. A hotel is worth more if it is unencumbered by a management contract, because the pool of potential buyers will be significantly larger when owner/operators can be included, and the greater the pool, the better the chances of obtaining a good price.

Even if the owner intends to hold the asset for the long term, it should plan for the eventuality of an early sale and know beforehand what it will cost to get out of the contract, expressed either in absolute dollars or as a multiple of the previous year's fees.

Typically, the amount of a penalty or buyout of a contract will diminish as the contract ages. A manager must invest considerable time and energy in the opening or repositioning of a hotel, and may not see a significant profit until the second or third year of operation. Managers will expect additional compensation if they are removed before reaping the fruits of this labor, particularly if the contract is structured so that most of their compensation is tied to the bottom line. Historically, buyout terms have been one of the most hotly contested areas in negotiations, particularly for REO properties needing turnaround. The owner must seek to determine at what point in time the manager will have been adequately compensated, and negotiate a clause that lets the owner sell the asset at that point—unencumbered and without the prospect of a significant buyout.

Nonperformance

The owner has the option of negotiating specific performance standards, which will cost the owner in terms of higher fees or a longer term. Management companies will want to be protected from external events, like recessions, overbuilding, interruptions in air service, natural disasters, and so forth. Nevertheless, the owner's debt service must be met regardless of such externalities. The definition of standards for nonperformance can be simple or complex, as demonstrated in the following examples:

- Failure to produce a return on investment to the owner, in any year, that meets a minimum specified percentage or that falls below 17 percent of net operating income after a deduction for a 4 percent reserve and all management fees, real estate taxes, and building and contents insurance. The owner's return on investment is defined as a specified percentage of the project costs, increased by 10 percent of all capital and FF&E (furniture, fixtures, and equipment) expenditures made after the opening of the hotel.
- Failure to meet the stipulated percentages of net house profit (before management fees, property taxes, building and contents insurance, and other fixed charges) in any two years of the contract, as follows: year one—18 percent; year two—24 percent; year three—26 percent; year four and thereafter—28 percent.

Loews Santa Monica Beach Hotel, Santa Monica, California.

- Failure to produce sufficient cash flow to service a specified amount of debt in any three years during the term of the contract.
- Failure to meet a specified net operating income (NOI) or net house profit in any year, except if a third-party source indicates that the hotel's combined occupancy and average daily rate (ADR) penetration is above fair market share.

The first example provides no outs. One could be included to protect the manager from diminished profits caused by an increase in property taxes, utility rates, or some other not easily controlled expense. The second and third examples protect the manager from bad market conditions—for a limited number of years. The fourth example provides the manager with a potential out in every year of the contract. Consider a for-instance in which a manager is achieving above-market penetration, but is spending twice what the competition is spending on marketing to do so. As long as the rooms revenue is at or above the competitive market, the extraordinary cost is not (in the manager's mind) an issue. But the wise owner wants the manager to control expenses, not just generate revenues at any cost, and thus will choose a performance clause that will force management to control all expenses.

Figure 7-1

Sample Statement of Estimated Annual Operating Results for a Hotel

	Year 1	Year 2	Year 3	Year 4
Net House Profit	$723,200	$990,600	$1,179,600	$1,232,300
Property Taxes	122,500	130,000	137,900	163,600
Building and Contents Insurance	44,100	42,400	45,300	46,200
Income before Reserve	556,600	818,200	996,400	1,022,500
Reserve for Replacement	170,000	180,100	186,300	192,800
Net Operating Income	386,600	638,100	810,100	829,700
Debt Service ($5,200,000 principal)	584,100	584,100	584,100	584,100
Cash Flow Available for Depreciation, Amortization, Income Taxes, and the Owner's Return	–197,500	54,000	226,000	245,600
Owner's Preferred Return (8% on $2,800,000 plus $197,500 shortfall in later years)	244,000	239,800	239,800	239,800
Owner's Payout	0	54,000	226,000	239,800
Cash Flow Available for Incentive Fee	0	0	0	5,800

Source: PKF Consulting.

At Will

An at will clause provides for an easy divorce from the management company, for no other reason than that the owner is just not happy with it. This clause is like a prenuptial agreement, except that the longer the relationship continues, the less the settlement will be. A management company that wants to retain or obtain a presence in a strategically important market might be willing to accept at will termination damages of zero after three years. More common, however, would be a stepped-down damage calculation that does not zero out until year five. Branded management companies are generally less willing to grant such at will termination. Regardless of the type of management company, branded or unbranded, the fee schedule associated with contracts having an at will clause is fairly steep.

From a practical standpoint, the developer may find it easier to obtain an unbranded management company for a very short term (one to two years) and make a separate franchise arrangement, than to obtain a no-cost at will termination clause from a national, branded management company.

Fees, Equity Participation, and Chargebacks

The discussion of fees has been left to last, because the base level of fees should not be of foremost concern. A contract that gives the owner maximum control will provide the best value over the long term. The fees charged by a management company will vary according to the following contractual terms and market conditions:

- Contract length;
- Ease of termination and penalties involved;
- The hotel's sales volume;
- Mix between base and incentive fees;
- Whether the company is branded (or whether a separate franchise fee is necessary); and
- Scope and amount of the manager's corporate office chargebacks to the hotel.

In general, the longer the term, the lower the base and incentive fees that a manager requires. A long contract gives the manager time to recoup the extraordinary first-year headquarters' costs of startup or turnaround, and to recover from the headaches.

The less it costs the owner to terminate a contract, the higher the fees will be. One way or another, a good management company will get paid.

The greater the hotel's sales volume, the lower the fee structure. From a manager's standpoint, a 200-room hotel requires just as much oversight as a 400-room hotel. The same reports must be produced and analyzed, and the same number of key executives recruited and screened.

Base fees are typically set as a percent of gross sales. Some operators, typically the independents, are willing to charge flat monthly amounts for base fees, say $6,000 per month. The lower the base fee, the higher will be the portion subject to incentives. At present, base fees can range from 0.5 to 4.0 percent of gross, depending on the factors just discussed. As the method of calculating the incentive fee increases the risk to the management company, the higher the base fees will be.

Incentive fees can be structured any number of ways and are usually calculated as a percentage of one or more income lines. Different hotel companies use different nomenclature for income lines. In setting incentive fees, the income line to be used must be defined very specifically. All the expenses that are and are not included in it must be described. Some managers, for example, consider net house profit as income before the deduction of franchise fees or management fees; others consider it to be net of insurance and property tax deductions.

Four possible bases for calculating incentive fees are worked out in the following paragraphs to show the actual dollar amount of fees that would be paid under each method. The operating results on which the fee calculations are made are shown in Figure 7.1, a sample statement of estimated annual operating results for a hotel.

Method A bases incentive fees on the net house profit (income before property taxes, building and contents insurance, and other fixed charges). If the incentive were set at 10 percent of net house profit the actual fees paid in the first four years would be as follows:

	Base	Fee Paid
Year 1	$723,200 x 10% =	$72,320
Year 2	$990,600 x 10% =	$99,060
Year 3	$1,179,600 x 10% =	$117,960
Year 4	$1,232,600 x 10% =	$123,230
Years 1–4		$412,570

Method B bases incentives on NOI, defined as net house profit less taxes, insurance, and reserve for replacement. To compensate for the smaller base, the incentive is set at a higher rate (in this case 15 percent). The actual fees work out as follows:

	Base	Fee Paid
Year 1	$386,600 x 15% =	$57,990
Year 2	$638,100 x 15% =	$95,715
Year 3	$810,100 x 15% =	$121,515
Year 4	$829,200 x 15% =	$124,455
Years 1–4		$399,675

Using the absolute bottom line as in Method B results in a better sharing of the risk, even though the percentage rate is higher than the one applied in Method A. The use of NOI also ensures that the management company will aggressively appeal property taxes and bid out building and contents insurance.

Method C bases the incentive fee on the excess in NOI over a base amount. The threshold amount over which fees kick in could be related to debt service or to an owner's preferred return in an all-cash deal. The percentage applied is usually fairly steep. This method of calculating management fees is frequently used in takeovers, when it is common to tie the incoming management's incentive to improvements in NOI.

The following example of the application of Method C is for a new hotel. The incentive fee is set at 50 percent of NOI after the property generates the first $500,000 towards debt service. The actual fees work out as follows:

	NOI	Debt Service	Base	Fee Paid
Year 1	$386,600–$500,000 =		$(113,400) x 50% =	No Fee
Year 2	$638,100–$500,000 =		$138,100 x 50% =	$69,050
Year 3	$810,100–$500,000 =		$310,100 x 50% =	$155,050
Year 4	$829,700–$500,000 =		$329,700 x 50% =	$164,850
Years 1–4				$388,950

In this case, the management company's interests are almost perfectly aligned with those of the owners.

The following application of Method C illustrates a takeover scenario. In this example, Year 1 is the first year after takeover and the base for the management fee is the improvement in NOI, which was $386,600 when the hotel was bought. The incentive is calculated at 20 percent of cash flow above $386,600. The incoming management company's fees will be as follows:

	NOI	Year Zero NOI	Base	Fee Paid
Year 1	$638,100–	$386,600 =	$251,500 x 20% =	$50,300
Year 2	$810,100–	$386,600 =	$423,500 x 20% =	$84,700
Year 3	$829,700–	$386,600 =	$443,100 x 20% =	$88,620
Years 1–4				$223,620

Method D also bases the incentive fee on NOI, but subordinates it to debt service and an owner's preferred return. The assumptions for the following example (see Figure 7-1) are that the hotel is valued at $8 million; the loan (at 65 percent of value) has an interest rate of 10.5 percent, calculated on a monthly basis with a 25-year amortization schedule. Annual debt service is $584,100. The owner requires a preferred 8 percent return on its investment. The incentive fee is set at 15 percent, and the actual fees work out as follows:

	Year 1	Year 2	Year 3	Year 4
NOI	$386,600	$638,100	$810,100	$829,700
Debt Service	$584,100	$584,100	$584,100	$584,100
Owner's Return	$244,000	$239,800	$239,800	$239,800
Cash Flow Available for Fee	0	0	0	$5,800
Fee (15% of NOI)	$58,000	$95,700	$121,500	$124,500
Fee Paid	0	0	0	$5,800
Fee Accrued	$58,000	$153,700	$275,200	$393,900

In this example, no portion of the incentive fee is paid out until the fourth year. An incentive fee structure like this would be paired with relatively high base fees. Subordinating the incentive fees does not inherently forgive them if cash flow should be inadequate to pay them out in any year. Depending on provisions in the contract, unpaid incentive fees can accrue at a specified interest rate until the cash flow is adequate to repay them. This could occur when the property is sold. The contract must spell out whether the incentive fees do or do not accrue. Alternatively, the contract could be structured so that the owner's preferred return accrues in those years in which it is not paid out, but the management company's incentive does not. Never paying out unpaid fees would undoubtedly strain the owner-manager relationship, to say the least. If the base fee is not large enough to compensate for the nonpayment of incentive fees, the management compnay's performance would become indifferent. One solution would be to allow management fees to convert to an equity position.

Such a solution leads to the issue of equity participation by management companies. Equity contributions can take many forms, including joint venture partner arrangements, short-term loans, or sweat equity (the conversion of management fees into equity participation in the deal).

As a series of recent court cases has shown, equity participation can be construed to alter the agency relationship inherent in a management contract. An agency "coupled with an interest" is irrevocable. A manager with an interest (that is, a manager that is a partner in the hotel) cannot have its right to possess the hotel terminated at will by the owner. In fact, with the agency relationship altered in this way, termination, even for violations of performance clauses, becomes very difficult. As a minimum, the complete amount owed to the management company must be paid off before any termination clauses can be exercised.

For this reason, many owners are now shying away from any form of equity contribution by the management company, preferring to finance with debt that has fewer strings attached.

Corporate office chargebacks are another issue in the owner-manager relationship. Management companies can charge owners for a variety of services provided by their corporate offices, including national marketing programs, national advertising campaigns, accounting, central purchasing, design services for both new construction and renovations, and employee training programs. In the days of the "three-and-twenty" contracts, corporate office chargebacks easily approximated 2.5 to 3.0 percent of gross sales.

The owner must ask: Are these charges justified? They can be. The owner must ascertain if the charges are for services that are not duplicated at the property level, if the services provided pass the cost-benefit test, and if the charges are indeed legitimate pass-throughs that give the owner benefits derived from the management group's synergy and purchasing power. The hotel owner might well question, for example, an accounting fee of 0.5 percent of gross sales if the hotel's own accounting department processes all payroll, processes all accounts payable and accounts receivable, and produces all but the last page of a 75-page financial report. One bone of contention for many owners is the corporate office's customary practice of deciding on its own how much to spend on national marketing efforts and billing each hotel for its share.

Hotel owners have begun to insist on an accounting of the costs that are passed through, as a way of ensuring that only the actual cost of providing the service is charged to the hotel. Some owners have set a ceiling for corporate office charges, expressed as a percent of total sales. The next decade should see significant changes in the area of corporate office chargebacks.

CHAPTER 8
TRENDS IN HOTEL DEVELOPMENT

Thomas E. Callahan

Shifts in the lodging industry—past and future—can be traced to two broad forces: socioeconomic changes and the evolution of the hotel business. Over the last four decades, the industry has prospered from the emergence of new sources of demand for lodging and it has weathered economic downturns. In the process, the hotel industry has reached maturity and now is forced to confront the realities of a mature market.

Successful hotel developers are sensitive to the market's needs and they find opportunities to provide services and products at good value (with an acceptable profit). The opportunities to be found in a mature market are not the same as those offered in new or maturing markets. In the coming decade, developers will do well to focus on the following realities of a mature market: price competitiveness, branding, franchising, educated consumers, and new technologies.

To understand the key issues that the lodging industry will have to face in order to succeed in the coming decade, some knowledge of historical trends is required. This chapter summarizes these past trends before turning to the future.

Historic Trends

Growth

The quarter century beginning in 1972 has seen (and will continue to see) tremendous changes. It also serves as a valuable guide for future expectations. Figure 8-1 provides thumbnail descriptions of the lodging market since 1972 in four- to six-year time periods, in terms of the major factors that affect it: the economy, supply and demand con-

Amicola Falls Lodge and Conference Center in Dahlonego, Georgia, is a 60-room inn that attracts seekers of rural quiet from nearby Atlanta.

Courtesy Thompson, Ventulett, Stainback & Associates

Figure 8-1
U.S. Lodging Market Periods, 1972–1998

	1972–1975	**1976–1979**	**1980–1983**	**1984–1989**	**1990–1993**	**1994–1998**
Economy	Long period of growth ending with recession	Recovery, followed by a mild recession	Strong recovery, followed by recession in 3rd quarter 1982	Strong expansion	Recession in 1990, followed by growing sense of fragility	Moderate growth; rising interest rates and large federal deficit
Lodging Demand	Weak	Improving at beginning; tapering off at end	Growing at beginning, tempered at end by recession	Very strong	Weakening as volume of travel declines and consumers become rate sensitive	Moderate; keeping pace with the economy; consumers looking for price/value relationship
Lodging Supply	Strong; growth cycle ending	Moderate at beginning; picks up over time	Strong upsurge; beginning of a period of high growth	Extraordinary boom at beginning; slowdown at end; market starts to segment	Stagnant; properties taken back by unwilling owners; many changes in affiliation	Slight increase; stable
Property Values	Stagnant	Resurgent	Strongly appreciating	Appreciating more slowly; variations by region	In decline, ending at a fraction of replacement costs	Stabilized; appreciating in many markets
Volume of Transactions	Brisk at beginning; weak at end	Moderate	Brisk	Very brisk	Weak	Moderate
Capital for Real Estate	Fairly accessible; interest rates rising	Difficult to come by at beginning; fairly accessible at end	Readily accessible; very high interest rates	Too accessible	Extremely difficult to come by; rates drop	Not readily accessible
Investor Interest	Strong at beginning; weak at end	Restrained at beginning; moderate at end	Strong and growing	Still strong with some falloff due to tax reform	Cautious at beginning; nonexistent at end	Reluctant at beginning; selective at end
Tax Climate	Uncertainty about tax reform	Elimination of favorable capital gains treatment (in 1976)	Extraordinary stimulus from 1981 tax reform	End of real estate stimulus in 1986 tax reform	Lack of tax incentives felt	Reintroduction of incentives to stimulate economic recovery

Source: PKF Consulting.

ditions, hotel sales and prices, and capital (availability, investor interest, and the tax climate). The figure is a brief catalog through time of the basic indicators in the development equation.

Overall economic conditions, employment levels, and the amount of discretionary income available to consumers clearly affect the level of demand for lodging facilities—and cause the industry to come up with new products and services in response. In general, lodging demand is very sensitive to economic conditions and some product types are more sensitive than others. For example, during periods of economic uncertainty, companies looking to cut costs tend to home in on business travel as one of the first budget items to be reduced. And households trying to hold down expenses tend to change their vacation plans, usually by traveling closer to home and searching for additional value. Resorts and budget hotels often suffer the most during recessions, while lodging facilities in strategic urban or suburban locations typically fare much better.

From 1984 to 1994, growth in the supply of hotels was strong. In the United States, the number of rooms increased by an average of 2.2 percent a year, total sales by 8.5 percent

■ The Hospitality Industry Cycle

The hospitality cycle comprises five characteristic periods.

Growth
During the growth period, occupancy levels and average room rates increase, usually by more than inflation. Hotels generate strong cash flows. Capital markets jump on the bandwagon with equity capital and loans for new development. Market values for hotel properties increase.

Peak
During the peak period, occupancy levels and room rates continue to be strong. Cash flows remain high. Equity and debt capital continues to be available. Market values continue to rise, but at a slower rate, before stabilizing. Everyone is happy.

Decline
The decline period is led by a downward trend in occupancy. Room rates grow at or below the rate of inflation. Cash flows stabilize or decrease slightly. As investors sense risks rising, they require higher returns and begin to look for other investments. Decreasing cash flows and investors' demands for higher rates of return push market values downward.

Gutter
During the gutter period, occupancy levels, room rates, and cash flows reach rock bottom. As the competition becomes fierce, the market becomes a buyer's market. Perceiving the risks to be extremely high, investors look for even higher returns. Financing is not available, and values bottom out—often at below-replacement costs.

Resuscitation
At this stage, occupancy levels and room rates begin to rebound. Overleveraged players have vanished and bankruptcies have removed some rooms from the market, at least for a time. The survivors start making profits again. Equity investors come out of hiding and begin to lower their return requirements. Lenders cautiously lend money. Market values start slowly to improve.

And, the cycle begins all over again.

---

a year, employment by 3.5 percent a year, and the number of guests served by 1.7 percent a year. By 1994, there were 3.3 million rooms generating sales of $61.7 billion, employing 1.5 million people, and serving approximately 575 million guests.

Like most industries, the hospitality industry experiences its share of cyclical swings, and an understanding of where the industry as a whole is in its cycle can shed light on what is likely to happen next. The hospitality cycle is influenced by any number of supply and demand factors. On the demand side are the economy (local, regional, and national) and travel patterns, to name only a couple. On the supply side are, among other factors, the availability of capital and interest rates. The feature box on this page describes the role of some of these factors in each period of the cycle.

Industry Structure

To analysts seeking to sketch the outlines of the lodging industry of the future, trends in the structure of the industry—in how hotels are owned and managed—are of even greater interest than performance trends. Each decade since World War II has put its own stamp on hotel industry ownership and management arrangements, as shown in Figure 8-2.

The Era of Brand Names. In the beginning, brand names told the consumer what to expect. With only a few companies owning and operating all hotels in the United States, their names—which were often family names like Hilton and Marriott—became almost synonymous with the word "hotel." The hotel owners also managed their properties, and a brand of hotel nearly always looked the same and provided the same level of service no matter where it was located. Hiltons were Hiltons and Hyatts were Hyatts. Guests knew what kind of hotel experience they would have.

■ Figure 8-2
The Maturing U.S. Lodging Industry

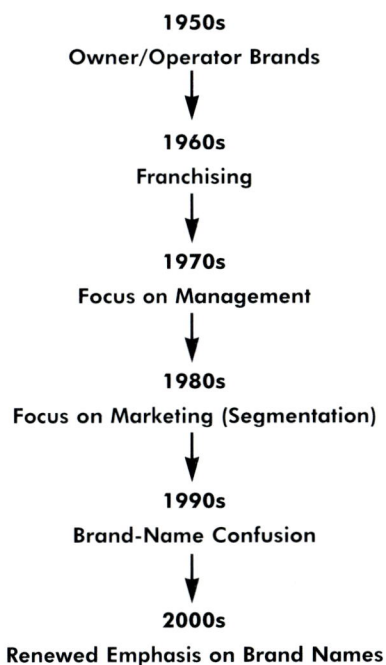

1950s
Owner/Operator Brands
↓
1960s
Franchising
↓
1970s
Focus on Management
↓
1980s
Focus on Marketing (Segmentation)
↓
1990s
Brand-Name Confusion
↓
2000s
Renewed Emphasis on Brand Names

Through the 1960s, the majority of big hotel companies were privately owned. As they added properties and became more profitable, they took advantage of their name values and became public corporations. As public companies, they faced even greater pressure to increase revenue and profits.

The allure of hotels and their profits began attracting wealthy individuals and institutional investors, which began to purchase properties. These new players found themselves in need of qualified management at the same time that the traditional hotel companies were looking for new sources of revenue. The hotel companies offered their services as second-party managers. In such cases, the hotel company's brand name went on the hotels it managed but did not necessarily own. Although these second-party managers did not enjoy the rights and benefits of ownership, they retained control over the quality of the facilities and the guest services and thus preserved the quality of their company name and maintained the uniformity of their system.

The Spread of Franchising. In the 1960s and 1970s, hotel companies placed great emphasis on the growth and operations of their systems. As interstate highway miles and airports were developed, the need for distributed product grew. To meet the demand for new hotels, major companies began to let go of management. Entrepreneurs like Holiday Inn founder Kemmons Wilson traveled the country selling franchises to doctors, construction companies, and other financially qualified buyers. Detailed how-to books came with each franchise. Distributed by the central corporate office, these exhaustive construction and operating manuals were supposed to guide novice hoteliers through the intricacies of building and running a hotel. Corporate headquarters also dispatched a cadre of inspectors whose role was to guarantee the hotel company's product and service standards throughout its variously-owned or -operated system of hotels.

As franchising spread, a new ownership category emerged: franchise owners that had no interest in operating their properties. At first, the hotel companies offered their management services. But, as the number of disinterested owners grew, talented industry executives with management experience at the property level formed independent management companies. They specialized in the management of hotels for disinterested owners and competed with the management divisions of the old hotel companies. Single independent management companies operated hotels under many different franchises.

Segmentation and the Reign of Confusion. Several bouts of double-digit inflation during the 1970s forced the hotel industry to hone its management skills. An industry-wide effort to control expenses and improve profits through management succeeded, and a 25 to 30 percent operational profit margin became the standard.

By the start of the 1980s, hotels were operating efficiently and the major hotels were represented in all major markets. Once again, hotel companies needed to be creative in finding ways to grow their revenues. Their emphasis began to shift away from operations and toward marketing. Sales efforts were beefed up at the property level and the major hotel companies began to invent niche products aimed at specific types of demand.

Like makes of automobiles, common hotel names began to take on more than one meaning. A Hilton could be an inn or a hotel. Hampton Inns and Embassy Suites joined the Holiday Inns family; Comfort Inns and Quality Royale were added to the Quality Inns family. From the perspective of the hotel companies, niche products—owned, franchised, or managed—offered a way to grow. For the traveling public, they offered variety and, because of price wars, better prices. But the meaning of once-specific brand names became fuzzy. Customers to whom brand names meant little would make their choices on the basis of price.

As a result of the far-reaching segmentation of brands and the complex interweaving of ownership and management, the hotel industry has reached a stage that can be described best as confusion. Consumers, investors, and even people in the industry find it difficult to define any hotel company's character or "personality." Naming a hotel a Sheraton, a Hilton, or a Marriott, does not reveal what company owns or operates it. What can an independent management company that manages multiple brands represent to a hotel customer who sees the brand name, not the manager's, on the sign out front and on the bill?

Perhaps history is repeating itself. The hotel industry seems to be about to revive the concept of brand identity and the owner/operator form of doing business. Major hotel management companies are starting to invest in properties that they manage and take on the risks and rewards of ownership. Wanting to ensure their positions in the hotels they manage, these companies are also extending equity contributions during management contract negotiations with owners/developers. The move back toward owner operations should improve quality control and consistency of standards within hotel brands.

Hoteliers may be taking their cue from other industries where events have proved that expansion for its own sake offers only short-term benefits. Corporations of all sorts are

Holiday Express, Springfield, Virginia, a minimum-service lodging.

Residence Inn by Marriott, Arlington, Virginia.

doing a booming business in selling off subsidiaries that are not related to their primary businesses. "We do chicken right!" is more than a restaurant chain's slogan; it is a management concept with merit.

Hotel Development in The Future

Industry experts think that the growth trends registered by the U.S. hotel sector between 1984 and 1994 will continue to strengthen. Their forecasts predict that growth rates for hotel rooms and sales over the next ten years or more will be at least as high as the growth rate of the overall economy.

Within this framework of growth, developers and operators will have to remain attentive to a changing work environment and changing family structures as they design, market, and operate lodging facilities into the 21st century. Among the trends and changes in the society at large and within the lodging industry that will affect the long-term development and profit potential of hotels are the baby boom's becoming 50, the continuing diversification of U.S. households, consumers' growing value consciousness, time pressures on consumers, changes in the distribution process (marketing and advertising, reservations, and travel agency commissions), the popularity of destination gaming and entertainment attractions, and the incorporation of information and communications technologies into everyday aspects of family life and business operations.

Boomers and Retirees

The baby boom generation, made up of people born between 1946 and 1965, is starting to turn 50 years old. Because it is so large, the baby boom generation makes itself felt in economic and societal matters. When the baby boom was young, the society was youth-oriented. Now that boomers are reaching middle age, they are tilting the whole society in a more mature direction. From now on into the 21st century as the members of the baby boom generation reach their age of greatest discretionary income and leisure time, this economically powerful generation will become the most sought-after consumer market.

In 1994, according to the U.S. Travel Data Center, the vacation destinations preferred by boomers involved recreation or adventure. High on their list of potential vacation activities were golf, fishing, skiing, theme parks, and resorts. As the group matures, its tastes will change. Weekend trips to nearby destinations are popular among boomers.

The retiree segment of the population (people aged 55 or older) is growing in size and financial power, two attributes that make retirees of particular interest to the lodging industry. By 2010, this group will number 75 million and make up one-quarter of the total population. Current retirees tend to have lower consumer debt than younger segments of the population.

According to the U.S. Travel Data Center, retirees travel further per trip than other travelers, are twice as likely to travel in a group program, and prefer sightseeing and entertainment to active recreation. The purpose of their travel is overwhelmingly for pleasure, and for the majority it is to visit friends and relatives. Forty percent of the retiree travel market relies on friends and relatives for accommodation.

Hotels outside the United States frequently include amenities not found in U.S. facilities, like this croquet green at the Canberra Hyatt in Australia's capital.

A lush indoor/outdoor lobby, like this one at the Hyatt Regency Aruba (Netherlands Antilles), is a common feature in tropical locations.

Changing Household Structures

Ward and June Cleaver and the kids on the road for a two-week vacation is no longer the vacation market's bread and butter. The vacationing family today is just as or more likely to be a married couple with no dependents, a two-income household with a good deal of discretionary income but not a lot of time, or a single person.

The number of single-person households has risen rapidly as well. In 1992, there were 23.6 million of them, making up 24 percent of total households. About 49 million Americans aged 25 and older have never married or are divorced or widowed. The continued increase in the number of single-person households will affect the travel industry.

Two-income households pose a particular challenge to the travel industry to invent facilities and services that cater to them. The members of these households are more likely than people in other types of households to travel more frequently and on shorter trips—for both business and pleasure.

Perceptions of Value

Satisfying the demands of value-conscious consumers for expanded services and higher-quality product—often at discount prices—poses a growing challenge for the lodging industry. Studies indicate that boomers and retirees, the major markets, will hold onto their discretionary dollars if they are not satisfied with the quality of what those dollars can buy.

Time-Pressed Consumers

According to the Economic Policy Institute, Americans work 158 hours (or about one month) more per year than they did 20 years ago. Longer workdays, less paid time off, and more two-worker families allow people less time or less flexibility for vacation trips. The solution for many has been shorter but more frequent trips. Weekend travel increased more than 46 percent between 1987 and 1994. Time-pressed consumers are likely to favor prepackaged vacations, accessible destinations, and holidays crammed with activity.

The Distribution Process

After hoteliers succeeded in lowering operational expenses as far as most observers felt to be possible, they began to focus on distribution (marketing, sales, reservations, and commissions) costs. Review of the entire distribution process with an eye on improved efficiency is a next step for the industry. Technology promises to be the key to cost-effective distribution.

One element of the system that is likely to change radically is the travel agent. Technology will provide consumers with more direct and convenient access to the suppliers of lodging and other travel services, encroaching on the travel agent's traditional role. Online services will turn personal computers into desktop travel systems through which customers can buy airline tickets, rent cars, and book hotels. Certainly there will always be a role for experts to help consumers through the maze of choices, but to play this role the travel agent will have to become better informed and better equipped. The information and hardware required cost money, so the future is likely to bring alliances among agents as well as greater vertical integration throughout the travel industry.

Gaming and Entertainment Centers

Entertainment as a component of hotels is an emerging trend that is spreading. Megahotels with casino and other entertainment attractions have caught the imagination of consumers and taught the lodging industry how to showcase products. The combination of entertainment and lodging has created some strong destination markets and will become an important segment for the hotel industry. In Las Vegas, tourism has grown by 15 percent since 1992, which is more than three times the rate of growth for total U.S. travel. With its famous country-and-western theaters, Branson, Missouri, once a quiet rural backwater, has become the second most popular summer destination in the United States. The number of available hotel rooms in Branson has increased more than tenfold in ten years.

Financial results have stimulated interest in the expansion of casino gambling and other forms of gaming. Gross revenues from U.S. gaming have been growing at a compound annual rate of 11.4 percent (from $11.8 billion in 1983 to $34.7 billion in 1993). In 1993, nearly $400 billion was wagered, up by 17 percent from the previous year. In 1989, only two states allowed gaming; in 1994, 23 states did. And interest in legalized gaming is growing in light of its increasing acceptability as a form of entertainment, its potential contributions to local and state tax revenue, and its positive impact on tourism and economic development.

The long-term outlook, however, is cloudy. Although many analysts in the early 1990s projected that as many as 20 additional states would pass some form of gaming legislation by 2000, enthusiasm stalled in 1995. The legalization of gaming involves a political process that can take unexpected turns. The future of gaming will not depend on its revenue potential alone. Legislative restrictions more than market demographics will be a paramount consideration in how many gaming facilities are developed and what their operational characteristics might be.

Tent cabins at Maho Bay on St. John in the U.S. Virgin Islands stretch the envelope of choice for vacation travelers. Maho Bay is considered a prototype of environmentally-sensitive resort development.

Gaming has become a major attraction in many locations. Shown here is the proposed Mohegan Sun Casino in Uncasville, Connecticut.

75

A multimedia meetings facility at the Hotel Roanoke and Conference Center in Roanoke, Virginia.

Information and Communications Technologies

As sophisticated information and communications technology becomes more a part of the everyday life of travelers—both business and leisure travelers—they will expect to have it available when they check into a hotel. To a large degree, the ability of hotels to anticipate and provide for the needs of their guests in this area will spell the hotels' success or failure. Even leisure travelers expect the most up-to-date phone system with call waiting and voice mail. Before long, they will expect in-room entertainment to consist of considerably more than the current offering of cable TV with up to 50 channels. Interactive multimedia centers and access to the Internet will be as important as in-room checkout and a wide selection of current movies.

Business travelers will expect even more communications services. To remain competitive, hotels will have to provide business guests with (at least) the following in-room technological amenities:

- Modular phone jacks;
- Modem ports;
- Wiring for fax transmission;
- Wiring for quick communication access to the Internet and World Wide Web;
- Call waiting and custom messages;
- Automated message systems;
- Setups for picture phones;
- Multimedia centers;
- Large desks; and
- Internet access.

Communications services for meetings are a promising new hotel service. When videoconferencing was first being developed, it was thought that the technology would eliminate the need for most meetings and training sessions outside the office conference room. Just the opposite seems to have happened. According to recent experience, instead of heralding the demise of meetings, communications technology—including videoconferencing—may even increase the need for meetings. In the near future, competitive hotels will be providing the following equipment and services in their meeting rooms or for meetings in the hotel:

- A videoconference wall screen;
- Multiple modem ports;
- Computer jacks;
- Satellite dishes;
- Desktop publishing and other PC services;
- Overhead projector with computerized video capability; and
- Internet connections.

Automated meeting facilitation techniques make it possible for groups of up to 500 people to meet in one large room and gather into small groups without the use of breakout rooms. Sufficient electrical outlets and computer jacks in correct positions will be important for meetings that are supported by high-tech machinery. Upgraded audiovisual equipment will also be necessary.

As needs change, hotels change functions. Yesterday's hotel came to function as its community's banquet hall and ballroom. Tomorrow's hotel is destined to become a center for business groups needing face-to-face contact in high-tech surroundings.

CHAPTER 9

HOTEL DEVELOPMENT AROUND THE WORLD

Corey Limbach and Patrick Quek

The number of tourists arriving in foreign countries grew from 69 million in 1960 to more than 528 million in 1994, according to the World Tourism Organization. This corresponds to a compound annual growth rate of 6 percent. The World Travel and Tourism Council reports that the tourism and travel sector makes up the world's largest industry, with a gross output estimated at $3.4 trillion (U.S. dollars) in 1994.

While Europe remains the number one tourist market in terms of both arrivals and total receipts, the East Asia/Pacific region has been the fastest growing market in recent years. From 1986 to 1993, the annual growth rate (compounded annually) of tourist arrivals in the East Asia/Pacific region was 11.2 percent (compared with 5.6 percent worldwide) and receipts grew 17.8 percent per year (compared with 9.2 percent worldwide).

Not surprisingly, travel and tourism has become a consolidated and global industry, global in terms of both the development of facilities and the nationalities of tourists. The key factors in the globalization of tourism include the following:

- Increasing availability and affordability of air service;
- Growing exposure of far-flung destinations in mass media;
- Expansion of hotel development groups' pursuits well beyond their traditional geographic boundaries; and
- Consolidation of the travel business and tour operator segment of the industry (which controls a large number of air seats and blocks of hotel rooms), and the growing popularity of travel/tour services across the spectrum of the travel market.

The opening up of tourism and lodging investment opportunities worldwide gives investors a choice of markets in different stages of the development cycle. When certain markets present weak opportunities for new development, they may be buyers' markets for existing properties. The United States and Canada fit this category in 1995 (see Figure 9-2). At the same time, other markets may offer tremendous opportunities for new development but be sellers' mar-

Pan Pacific Hotel, Vancouver, British Columbia.

Figure 9-1
International Tourist Arrivals and Receipts by Region, 1986 and 1993

	1986[1]				1993[2]			
	Arrivals		Receipts[3]		Arrivals		Receipts[3]	
	Number (Thousands)	Percent Share	Amount (Billions of U.S. Dollars)	Percent Share	Number (Thousands)	Percent Share	Amount (Billions of U.S. Dollars)	Percent Share
World	340,891	100%	$140	100%	500,000	100%	$259	100%
Africa	9,458	3	3	2	17,900	4	6	2
Americas	70,972	21	38	27	106,500	21	88	34
East Asia/Pacific	32,539	10	17	12	68,500	14	53	20
Europe	217,218	64	76	54	296,500	59	106	41
Middle East	7,973	2	5	4	7,200	1	5	2
South Asia	2,731	1	2	1	3,400	0	2	1

[1] Revised figures.
[2] Provisional revised estimates.
[3] Receipts exclude international transport.
Source: World Tourism Organization.

kets for existing product. Latin America in 1995 was a case in point (see Figure 9-2).

Global markets give investors opportunities to take positions at any time in the stage(s) of the development cycle they want to target, to form strategies to maximize their potential while balancing their risks.

Figure 9-2
Hotel Investment Climates, 1995

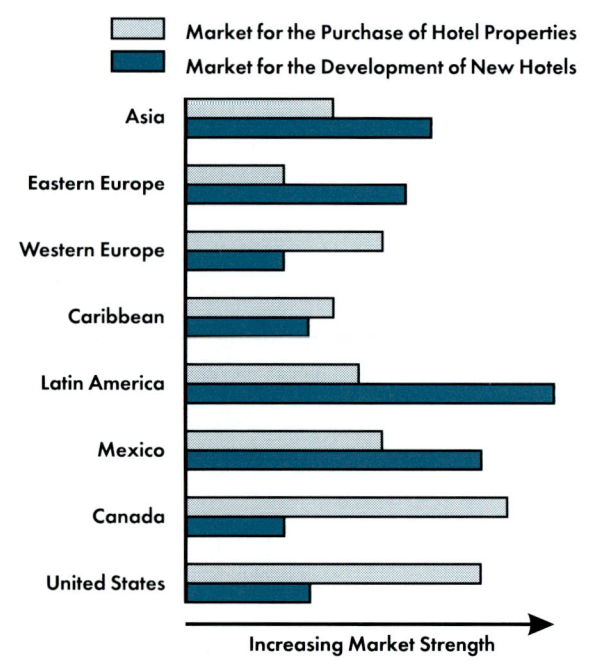

Source: PKF Consulting.

The remainder of this chapter covers trends in lodging markets outside the United States and Canada, by major market region: Europe, Middle East and Africa, the Caribbean, Latin America, and Asia.

Europe

The upswing in the majority of European economies during 1993 and into 1994 resulted in a slight improvement in hotel performances. As of 1995, the British hotel market was entering a period of growth, with London performing particularly well. Although occupancies were showing tentative signs of recovery in Germany, average room rates and overall room yields continued to decline. As the Scandinavian countries moved from recession into recovery, their hotel markets showed some improvement. With the devaluation of their currencies making Spain and Portugal more attractive and affordable destinations, their hotel markets have entered a recovery phase.

Issues facing the hotel industry in Europe over the next few years include increased price competitiveness, hotel branding, and the development of franchising.

The last recession highlighted the need to trim costs, and hoteliers have sought ways to reduce the payroll burden. These have included more flexible work rules, the reduction of management tiers, and the introduction of multitask roles. In some countries, however, legislation limits what can be done on the labor front. The recession also taught customers to negotiate the best deal. This will inhibit growth in room rates. It is likely that there will be a marked decline in business secured at rack rates in many countries.

The makeup of the hotel market in Europe is changing with the adoption of American style branding. In France and

Hyatt La Manga Club, in Cartagena on the southeast coast of Spain.

the United Kingdom, branding is well established and has been a feature of recent growth in hotel chains. Although the diversity of European hotel stock limits branding opportunities, it is likely to become more significant.

The development of franchising is a major opportunity. Chains represent just over 20 percent of the stock in Europe. (In the United States, chains control closer to 60 percent.) Hotel companies such as Accor, Choice, and Holiday Inn Worldwide already franchise in western Europe. While France's Accor is one of the leaders in this area, just 5 percent of its hotel stock is franchised.

Middle East and Africa

Political instability limits the growth of the hotel market. Current peace talks between Jordan and Israel provide some hope for stability in the Middle East region, although the political isolation of Iraq remains a concern. Hotel markets in Egypt remain in the doldrums, following terrorist attacks on tourists by religious fundamentalists.

Several countries in the Middle East are seeking to diversify their oil-dominated economies, and the development of tourism represents an opportunity. Oman and Syria are among the countries that are encouraging the development of a wider range of tourist facilities and infrastructure projects and engaging in proactive marketing.

In Lebanon, the end of the civil war has allowed Beirut's reconstruction to begin. Large amounts of capital have been attracted, and international hotel groups are showing considerable interest. Beirut is likely to be one of the boom centers for hotel development over the next few years. The United Arab Emirates are witnessing a period of strong growth, and a number of new hotels have opened in Dubai. The recovery in Bahrain is being led by mid-market hotels.

The hotel market in South Africa is likely to see considerable growth in the aftermath of the country's opening up, politically and economically, to the rest of the world. The recovery in Kenya continues to be patchy.

The Caribbean

The Caribbean region has experienced significant growth in hotel inventory. The number of rooms almost doubled from 1980 to 1993. A large percentage of this growth has taken place in a relatively small number of destinations, like Cuba, Aruba, the Dominican Republic, and Jamaica.

Hotel Categories

The Caribbean hotel market is made up of four main types of projects: traditional, freestanding resort hotels; all-inclusive resorts; mixed-use, master-planned destination resorts; and boutique hotels.

Traditional Resort Hotels. Frenchmen's Reef Hotel in St. Thomas exemplifies a freestanding resort hotel. These usually are at beachfront locations and feature food and beverage outlets, some meeting space, and resort amenities such as swimming pools and water sports equipment and instruction.

In most circumstances in the Caribbean, these kinds of projects cannot be developed profitably. Land costs are too high. Long-term financing is difficult to obtain. Expensive labor (resulting from union considerations and training needs) and the high costs associated with the need to import most supplies make many projects unattractive from the perspective of return on equity.

Locations with an existing base of tourism infrastructure, such as Puerto Rico and Aruba, are the exception. Hotels in these places are able to achieve year-round occupancies and strong room rates. In such locations, the development of chain-affiliated properties has been occurring, with many

Hyatt Regency Aruba, a resort hotel and casino in the Netherlands Antilles.

U.S. hotel management groups increasing their presence in the Caribbean.

All-Inclusive Resorts. A typical all-inclusive resort offers a vacation package that includes lodging, meals, drinks, recreational activities, airport transfers, gratuities (tipping usually is not allowed), and other items at one prepaid price. The Club Mediterranean (known as Club Med) originated the concept at its first resort in Majorca, Spain, in 1950. Club Med's vacation package included accommodations, all meals, wine with meals, gratuities, and use of all the facilities.

The character of vacation packages has become more sophisticated in recent years. For example, SuperClubs, based in Jamaica, introduced a more upscale format in Jamaica in the mid-1970s. Negril Beach Village (later renamed Hedonism II) proved to be a sensation, outperforming all market trends and running at near capacity shortly after opening. Couples, in Ocho Rios, another Jamaican resort by SuperClubs, ushered in a new generation of all-inclusive vacation resorts. Couples and Hedonism II have enjoyed outstanding occupancy and some resistance to the downturns that have affected other segments of the island's tourism industry, such as the traditional resort hotels in Montego Bay.

Development of all-inclusive Caribbean resorts is likely to increase. They achieve substantially higher than average levels of year-round occupancy. Perceived by tourists to offer a high value, all-inclusive resorts generate a relatively consistent travel pattern and thus suffer less than the traditional resorts from seasonality.

Certain emerging demographic trends intensify the demand for all-inclusive resorts. People who are 36 to 54 show a high propensity to travel and have high disposable incomes. Many are members of two-worker families and therefore desire vacations that relieve stress and require little decision making, yet offer a variety of activities. Another plus is that there are no hidden costs in all-inclusive packages. Eliminating the constant money worries of tourists in a foreign country enhances their satisfaction.

Mixed-Use, Master-Planned Resorts. Tailored after the megaresorts found in Hawaii, mixed-use, master-planned resorts feature a variety of land uses. The hotel normally is the project's centerpiece. Components typically found at such developments include primary homes and second homes, golf courses, marinas, tennis centers, and spas. These resorts offer a sufficient variety of facilities and amenities for guests to enjoy their vacations without having to leave the resort.

The El Conquistador Resort and Country Club exemplifies a master-planned destination resort. Opened in November of 1993 in Fajardo, Puerto Rico, the resort contains 751 hotel rooms and an additional 167 keys provided by condominium units in a rental pool. In addition to a vast complement of meeting facilities, the resort offers numerous food and beverage outlets, a casino, an 18-hole championship golf course, a tennis center, a 55-slip marina, and several other amenities and recreational facilities. A 15,000-square-foot health and fitness facility is planned.

By virtue of the range of its offerings and the sheer size of its room inventory, such a resort can attract a variety of market demand segments at any one time. The availability of several sources of income, especially real estate sales, provides the development with cash flows that may be especially needed during the initial years of operation before the hotel component has stabilized.

On the other hand, development costs are extremely high, and operational expenses and ongoing capital maintenance requirements can also be high. Obtaining the necessary funding for such resorts and clearing enough cash for debt servicing can thus be difficult.

Boutique Hotels. Targeted at the upper end of the frequent, independent travel market, boutique hotels usually are smaller than 100 rooms, and many have fewer than 50 rooms. They generally feature personalized service with a high employee/guest ratio, private and somewhat isolated locations, few recreational facilities within a sophisticated and relaxing environment, limited but elegant food and beverage facilities, and high-quality finishes throughout.

Boutique hotels usually rely on repeat traffic. Several have been developed in the Caribbean over the last few years, most of them on small islands lacking extensive tourism infrastructure, such as Anguilla and St. Barts.

Boutique hotels are generally either owner operated or managed by a luxury chain, such as Rosewood Hotels.

Several factors limit opportunities for the development of boutique hotels in the Caribbean, especially the following: high per room construction costs, heavy equity requirements, limited demand, and a lack of sites providing both a secluded environment and supporting tourism infrastructure.

Hotel Development Potential

The following products and locations represent hotel development opportunities in the Caribbean:

- Chain-affiliated resort hotels in mature tourist destinations with an established air transportation network (such as Puerto Rico, which is and should continue to be the hub of the Caribbean);
- All-inclusive resorts in destinations with an inventory of traditional resort hotels, some of which may offer conversion opportunities;
- Hotels within mixed-use resorts (not necessarily master-planned destination resorts), where the hotel is designed as the focal point of the resort, while residential sales provide the cash flow that makes development feasible;
- Boutique hotels in selected destinations that will attract targeted guests or where such hotels might complement the existing hotel inventory;
- Environmentally-sensitive resorts featuring a no-frills package targeted to adventure tourists and divers;
- Limited-service hotels in destinations with a commercial base (such as Puerto Rico or the Dominican Republic); and

- Cuba, which, though currently off-limits to U.S. hotel developers, offers development opportunities for the gamut of Caribbean hotel products.

Latin America

The lodging market in Latin America, a large and complex region, can be divided very broadly into three segments: commercial, resort, and tourist. The commercial market is composed of hotels in primary cities (like Mexico City, Sao Paulo, Buenos Aires, or Santiago) and in secondary and tertiary cities. The resort market focuses on beach-oriented destinations and specifically on master-planned megaresorts such as Cancun and Ixtapa in Mexico, both sponsored by a public agency: FONATUR (National Fund for Tourism). The tourist market includes hotels in areas of historic, archeological, or natural interest, as well as hotels, including mountain resorts, that cater to (primarily domestic) leisure travelers seeking sports and outdoor activities.

As economic and political stabilization continue to take place in Central and South America, the hospitality and tourism development industry in most countries is early in the growth or revitalization stages of the development cycle.

Mexico, on the other hand, experienced tremendous growth beginning in the mid-1980s through the early 1990s. As a developing country, Mexico is susceptible to wide swings of the economic and fiscal pendulum. However, the country's large size, economic diversity, and ties to the United States and Canada should result in overall growth tempered with periods of recession and other negative trends.

Four Seasons Hotel, Mexico City.

Modernization of the Lodging Industry

In general, a number of economic, market, and hotel business changes are being felt throughout the region's lodging sector. These include the following:

- Increased demand from business travelers—international, domestic, and group—with cities of all sizes feeling the effects;
- Increases in the inventory of mid-market guest rooms in secondary and tertiary markets;
- More frequent air travel and more arrivals by automobile;
- A growing sophistication on the part of owners, developers, and managers with regard to capitalization, development, and operating systems;
- More strategic alliances between hotel operators and investors;
- Overall higher levels of investment, as capital becomes more affordable and available; and
- Operating cost uncertainties as economies become dollarized and individual markets become more competitive.

Related major trends in Latin America's lodging industry include modernization, segmentation, hotel branding, and the emergence of group business demand. New products, better locations (closer to demand generators), and modern management systems are beginning to replace current hotel product, which is mostly independently owned and operated, very old (dating back as far as the 1920s and 1930s), poorly located, and outdated in design and layout.

Product segmentation for mid-market hotels is a current trend. Holiday Inn Express, Days Inn, Comfort Inns, and Posadas de Mexico's Fiesta Inn are all active in the market. As suburban areas and secondary cities begin to develop, the need for financially viable product segmentation will increase.

International hotel chains have become interested in many segments of the Latin American market.

Finally, group business travel is emerging as a separate hotel market, thanks to the more frequent staging of (larger) trade shows, exhibitions, and conventions and the development of modern convention centers and hotels with expanded meeting facilities to meet this demand.

Hotel Development Potential

As Latin American countries become members of the free trade agreement now encompassing North America, an eventuality that many trade experts foresee, the region will become economically stronger. Even without this, current patterns of growth will create opportunities for hotel development in many areas, including the following:

- *Resorts.* With the added enhancement of government incentives, the northeastern coast of Brazil is ripe for the development of various types of resorts targeted at domestic and foreign markets. Infrastructure costs and the appeal of this part of the country to foreigners are key development issues.
- *Limited-Service Hotels.* Secondary and tertiary cities in Latin American countries like Brazil, Argentina, Chile, Peru, and Mexico generally lack consistent,

well-managed hotels. Limited-service hotels could fill this niche. Given the high cost of land associated with well-located sites even in secondary and tertiary markets, finding equity partners that control land parcels is a necessity.

- *Full-Service, Chain-Affiliated Hotels.* In key capitals, such as Sao Paulo or Santiago, this market, which is quickly becoming saturated elsewhere, offers some potential. New cities will become candidates for such hotels as their economies strengthen.
- *Mixed-Use Resorts.* In a few locations, as more disposable income comes under the control of more Latin American households, a market for second homes in resort environments may emerge.
- *Ecotourist Destination Hotels.* Latin America's many ecologically-rich areas are potential destinations for the traveling public that is drawn to such places. Various locations in Brazil's Amazon Basin, Argentina's Patagonian region, Chile (near Antarctica), and Peru could be considered for hotel projects.
- *Mid-Market Hotels.* Mexico's strongest-growing northern area should continue to provide good opportunities for the development of limited-service, mid-market hotels to serve an expanding market.

Asia

As illustrated in Figure 9-1, international travel in the East Asia/Pacific region is growing faster than anywhere in the world. This growth is fueled largely by the increase in travel between countries within the region (intraregional travel). When the United States and Europe sank into recession in the early 1990s, Asian destinations began to focus their marketing efforts on their own backyard, to good effect.

Although relatively few people in many countries in Asia travel, travel growth rates are tremendous. In the first half of 1993, departures from Thailand grew by over 25 percent compared with the same period in 1992, and Hong Kong and Singapore both registered increases of more than 16 percent. A high proportion of this travel is intraregional and will continue to be so as the attractiveness of regional destinations grows.

The largely untapped Chinese market is one of the strong spots for growth. Restrictions on overseas travel by citizens of China have been eased, and tour operators have seized the opportunity to provide intraregional travel packages. Should conditions lead to greater travel opportunities for China's population, the hotel industry could reap a massive windfall.

Manhattan Hotel, Makukai (Tokyo region), Japan.

Fueling this increase in Asian travel is the economic success that continues in the region. China, the third largest economy in the world, is expected to continue to achieve growth rates of 7 to 8 percent through the turn of the century. Overall, Asia prospered in the early 1990s. Compared with world averages, its average gross domestic product (GDP) grew faster by 2 to 3 percentage points and, compared with the industrialized world, its personal consumption spending increased at a much faster rate. Increasing affluence has been accompanied by more leisure time, which, more and more, is being spent on travel.

Intraregional travelers prefer to visit the larger cities, and their favored activity continues to be shopping. In the eyes of vacationers from outside the region, on the other hand, Asia is the world's newest playground. The search for new resorts is unceasing and resort destinations are being planned at a fast and furious pace in places like Thailand, Indonesia, and Malaysia. There are tremendous opportunities for eco-tourism or adventure-tourism development in Asia. Experiences like cave kayaking in Phuket, Thailand, rafting in Sulawesi, Indonesia, or jungle trekking in Malaysia are drawing adventurers to the region.

In Asian cities, the focus of development over the past decade was luxury hotels. Regional chains like Regent, Shangri-La, and Mandarin Oriental represented the height of luxury in their facilities and service. While many of the top luxury properties show no signs of losing favor, development opportunities for additional upscale properties is limited in most major markets.

Asia's intraregional travel market, like many domestic markets, is interested in value. Therefore, interest in developing mid-scale product is currently strong. Shangri-La hotels has introduced a new brand, Trader's Inns, which it believes can expand rapidly in coming years. A Trader's Inn has opened in Singapore, and plans have been announced for additional properties throughout China. This move by a major Asian chain could signal the beginning of American style market segmentation. Asian mid-scale chains will compete with international chains like Holiday Inn, Choice Hotels, and Days Inn, which have expansion in Asia on their agendas.

In Hong Kong, some peculiarities of property values are prompting the replacement of hotels by other commercial land uses. The Hong Kong Hilton has been razed, and as many as a half-dozen other hotels may meet the same fate. The reason: the superheated property market has driven up retail and other commercial rents beyond the revenue hotels can achieve, and to the point where the costs of acquiring and demolishing a hotel are justified. (One factor bidding up land values was the relocation of the airport, which led to the relaxation of height restrictions in several prime real estate neighborhoods.)

In 1995, hotel occupancy in Hong Kong rose into the 80 percent range. The loss of major hotels is predicted to bring on an acute shortage before new properties can be added. A new wave of hotel construction should follow the completion of the Chep Lap Kok airport and transportation project, which is opening up new sites on reclaimed land.

Grand Hyatt, Hong Kong.

Governmental promotion of tourism as a means of economic development is a major factor in resort development in Asia. To further resort development, governments offer tax breaks, investment credits, or favorable land leases. They provide infrastructure, including airports, roads, and utilities. Public/private development partnerships through tourism development corporations are common. And Asian governments typically market tourism heavily, with healthy ordinary travel promotion budgets that are supplemented by special events planning, such as Visit Malaysia Year or Visit ASEAN (Association of Southeast Asian Nations) Year.

Bintan Beach International Resort is a fairly typical example of development opportunities generated by government. Bintan is a joint venture between the governments of Singapore and Indonesia and a consortium of major companies from both countries. The governments provided the agreements that allowed for the development of an 89-square-mile beachfront parcel on Bintan Island, approximately 28 miles from Singapore. The consortium formed a development company that has prepared a master plan and will provide infrastructure, including a ferry and terminal service, roads and utilities, and public recreation amenities. The individual parcels that are being developed along with the resort facilities will enjoy the benefits of environmentally-sensitive planning.

While China has been occupying the attention of so many international investors, another sleeping giant has awoken in Asia. India, its massive market long held in check by government controls, is opening its doors to the world and finding that the world wants in. This holds true for the travel market, making India a country of high interest for hotel developers and operators alike.

Following years of unmet expectations of travel growth, travel to India finally has risen substantially, driven largely by commerce. New foreign investment has led to a surge in business travel, with major cities like New Delhi, the capital, and Bombay, the leading financial center, benefiting most directly. In other hubs of industry, such as Hyderabad and Bangalore, new hotels tend to be more budget-oriented.

In India, seasonality has traditionally played havoc with the hotel market. Vacation visits are concentrated in the cooler months from October through February, and off-season tour business usually pays heavily discounted rates. Thus, annual hotel occupancies and overall average room rates are depressed. The strong emergence of business travel has helped offset tourist seasonality. This travel is less seasonal and less reactive to certain events such as riots in Ayodhya or terrorist bombings in Bombay.

Erratic arrival patterns in India over the past several years make projecting a steady increase in future arrivals difficult. However, the fluctuations have been caused by events that are unpredictable and give little basis for forecasting a downturn in demand. The travel market seems to be poised for a period of sustained, strong growth.

Therefore, interest in hotel development will continue to be strong. In the major cities, interest will be focused primarily on first-class hotels, since high land prices rule out small hotels or mid-price hotels. Secondary cities offer tremendous potential for mid-level accommodations, and the domestic market provides a strong base for budget accommodations. In the northern state of Haryana, which has no natural tourist attractions, more than 30 vacation centers have been developed, aimed at the local holiday traveler, primarily from Delhi. These areas have tapped into this market very successfully.

Chains such as Choice, Holiday Inn, Accor, and Radisson have moved into India, and will soon be players in the domestic and foreign traveler markets. With each state tourism department angling for its own piece of the expanding travel pie, opportunities for the development of new hotel properties over the next several years will be ample.

Chapter 10

Architecture and Design

Howard J. Wolff, Ronald J. Holecek, and Ronald O. Van Pelt

Very few types of buildings involve the array of business and design specialists that the creation of a hotel requires. A hotel project needs specialized design expertise. The project team moves through a process by which design concepts are transformed into a solid reality, responsive to the many site and market variables involved. This chapter describes this process and indicates some of the myriad market and operational considerations that must be incorporated into a hotel's design.

Defining the Project

The single most important item for the architect about to undertake a hotel project is the client's program (or brief, as it is often called outside the United States). Properly configured, this document sets out the objectives for the project in clear, measurable terms, including such fundamental parameters as the level of the hotel (two-star, three-star, four-star, five-star), its orientation (business travelers, conventions and groups, vacationers), and the amenities and services that are to be provided.

The program lists the size requirements for each area of the hotel. It describes the operator's philosophy and criteria, together with definitions of the levels of service it wishes to provide for the various operations—food service, laundry and valet service, housekeeping, staff facilities, and many other operations. (See Appendix 3 for a sample brief for a 350-room luxury hotel.)

For most U.S. and international hotel operating companies, many of the relevant design standards are contained in their own manuals of corporate standards. These extensive manuals are constantly revised and updated by the technical services and development departments to keep up with changes in operating procedures and development requirements and changes necessitated by government regulations.

As the foundation for the project, the program document must be revisited during the various design phases. It should serve as a guidepost and checklist, as well as a tool for documenting and managing the project. As the project evolves and specific design, market, and cost information becomes available, it is common for some of the early parameters and criteria to change. It is important to update and revise the program to reflect such changes.

In defining the project, a tug-of-war can arise between the operator's criteria (its wish list) and the developer's budget or scope. Negotiations and discussions centering on the operational necessity versus the budget impact (additional costs involved and potential income generation) of disputed items normally resolve the differences, and the architect may be asked to help explore various alternatives for particular program items.

To work, the project definition must clearly communicate the owner's and operator's requirements, identify any particular constraints or restrictions imposed on the project by other parties, and establish a careful balance among all the complex parameters and factors that together make a hotel. The importance of this fundamental step cannot be overstated: poorly developed or incomplete programs invariably lead to major problems and projects that come in over budget and behind schedule.

Memorable, consistent, and repeated signage aids brand-name recognition, which is critical in obtaining and keeping market share. Standards of price, quality, and amenities are part and parcel of brand-name recognition.

The Team

On the Client Side

A hotel project requires a leader, perhaps even a driver. Usually, this is the developer. A principal of a development company might have the vision, energy, and drive to undertake a hotel project. In other cases, the leader could be a principal of an operating company that is developing a project in a prime location on its own or with a local development group. The developer/operator is the client of the project team and any specialty consultants. As such, the developer needs to be represented by a number of key players who will have to commit a significant portion of their time for three to four years to develop the project. The client's lead representative should be an experienced, development-oriented person. The operator's representative is typically a vice president of development or a senior member of the technical services department.

In most cases, a number of specialty consultants work directly for the client. Usually, these include a legal consultant—normally a lawyer or a real estate development specialist—who assists with the preparation of agreements between the developer and regulatory agencies, becomes involved in other legal issues, and advises the developer on any agreements with the operating company.

On projects that encounter stringent environmental controls or complex planning restrictions, a planning consultant may become involved. This specialist assists with the initial negotiations, helps develop mitigation measures, and prepares the reports and documents needed for planning and environmental approval.

If critical environmental issues are involved, an environmental consultant may be brought in. A consultancy can be chosen for its expertise in particular areas, such as archeology, wildlife, or wetlands. The developer may choose to bring in consultants to provide various preconstruction and construction management services, instead of taking the traditional path, which consists of preparing a complete set of documents, putting the project out to bid, and selecting a contractor. Major construction companies offer a variety of preconstruction and construction services, from the selection and management of consultants to a full turnkey operation. Whatever the approach to construction management—fast track, design/build, or management contracting—it will involve construction specialists on the development team. The structure of the construction procurement process also will help determine who does what on the consultant team. In some cases, the developer's design consultants may be assigned to the contractor, which uses them to produce the technical documentation.

Many of the changes that have been taking place in the how and who of project and construction management are intended to limit the developer's risk and exposure in the

Fitting into the low-profile, small-scale fabric of old Charleston, South Carolina, was important in the design of Charleston Place.

costly and, at times, highly contentious construction phase. These changes often aim for a one-stop, one-responsible-party approach to design and construction.

On the Consultant Side

It is imperative to put together a cohesive team in which each member clearly understands and adheres to his or her responsibilities from the beginning. When projects develop problems, it is often because certain key players are not performing their roles effectively or have overstepped the bounds of their responsibilities.

The team is usually set up, managed, and directed by the client, often with a project manager or a lead consultant in charge. Typically, the lead consultant is the architect, in which case his or her role as architect is expanded to include project management services such as scheduling, managing, and directing the work of the other consultants. Normally, the architect is responsible for the site planning, architectural design, production of technical drawings, and the coordination of the prime consultants on a project. To execute this work effectively, an architectural firm appoints a principal-in-charge. Some firms appoint both a design principal and an administrative principal to oversee the project jointly.

The principal-in-charge is supported by a senior designer, who is responsible for the architectural design of the project, and a senior project manager, who manages the process, the consultants, and the interface with the owner. The project manager—together with the client—establishes a schedule, budget, and other guidelines necessary to run the project. These key team members also interact with planning agencies and building officials to secure the necessary approvals and permits. On a firm's foreign projects, the project manager and the principal are the primary contacts with the local architect and consultants.

The senior architectural managers are supported by additional design and technical staff, including the all-important

Atlantis, Paradise Island, a resort in Nassau, illustrates the complexity of design of a large-scale resort.

project coordinators. These are usually senior technical architects responsible for both the execution of the architectural work and the day-to-day coordination and interface with the other consultants involved in the production of the drawings and specifications.

The architect assists the client with the interviewing and selection process for the consultant team. All the consultants must understand the complexities and nuances of hotel layout, operations, servicing, and design. (See Figure 10-1 for a chart of the design team.)

The interior design firm selected for a hotel project is usually a specialist in hospitality design. Its responsibilities extend from initial space planning to the detailed development of the interior design package, including floor, wall,

Room design can range from formal to rustic and from upscale to utilitarian, depending on the market served.

■Figure 10-1
The Hotel Design Team

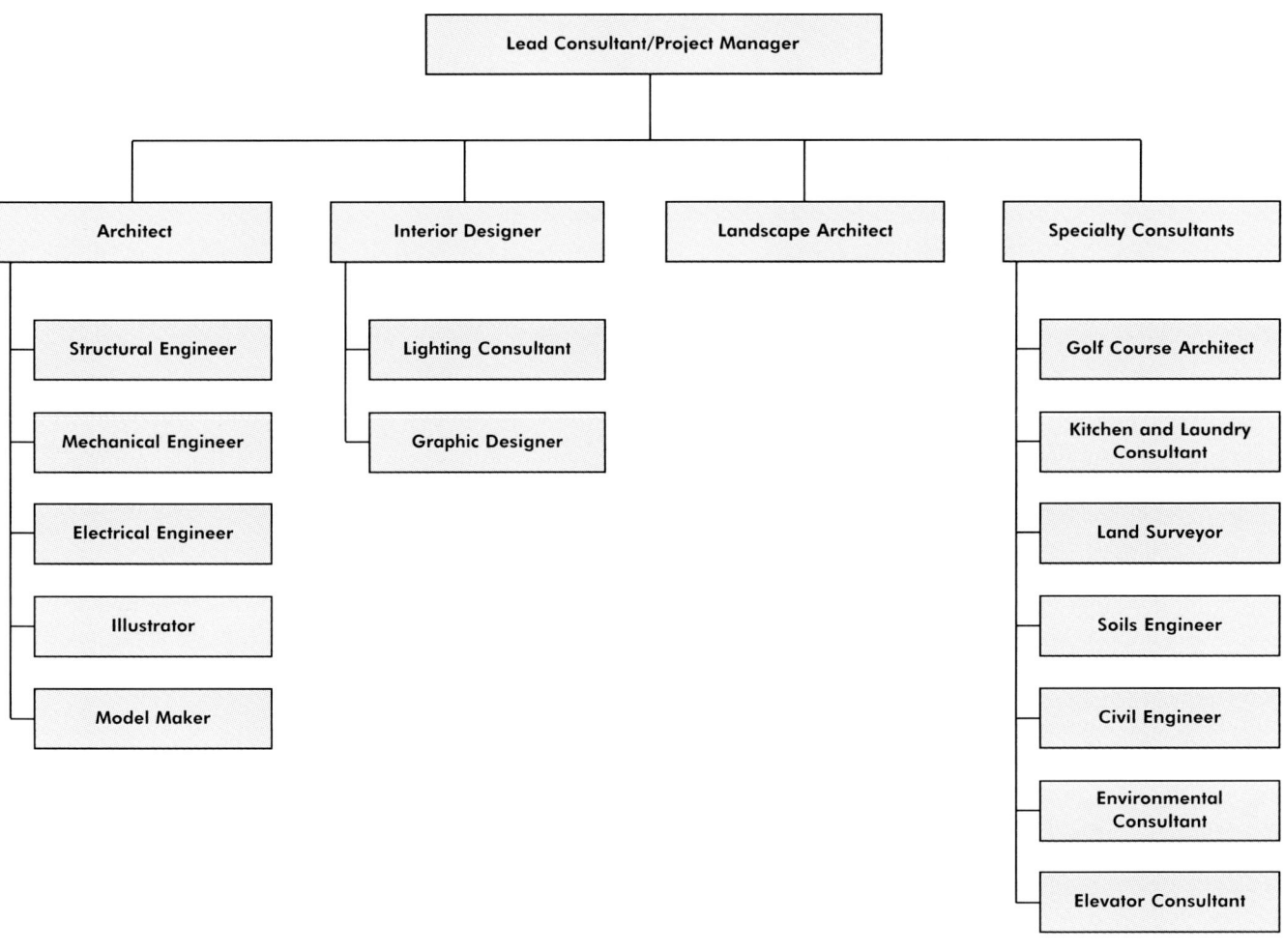

and ceiling finishes; fixed decor; furnishings; and decorations. The interior designer selects the furniture and fixtures (including the colors and materials) and prepares a specifications book from which the interior design elements can be priced and purchased. It may also be involved in purchasing the furniture and fixtures and overseeing their installation.

The landscape architect plays an especially prominent role in the design of resort hotels and other projects that have large outside areas, and is involved also in the design of hardscape paving and furnishings and plantings for a variety of small but important outdoor spaces in urban hotels. The landscape architect produces detailed drawings and specifications covering hardscape (walls, paving, benches, light fixtures), softscape (plants, shrubs, ground cover), decorative fountains and fittings, pools, spas and other outdoor recreation facilities, and irrigation. It is critical for the architect to work with engineers who are skilled in grading, drainage, irrigation, electrical supply, and lighting on the design of these elements.

Various kinds of engineers are involved in the design, technical documentation, detailing, and specifications. The primary engineering disciplines required are structural, mechanical, electrical, and plumbing. Typically, these last three disciplines are provided by a single multidisciplinary engineering firm that handles HVAC (heating, ventilation, and air conditioning), electrical power, lighting, telecommunications, emergency life-safety systems, plumbing, water supply, sewerage, and drainage.

Structural engineers make the calculations necessary for designing and sizing the foundations, columns, structural walls, floor framing, and roof framing. They are involved throughout the design and construction process, coordinating their work with that of the other engineers.

The mechanical, electric, and plumbing (MEP) engineers size, design, and coordinate the layout of various key building elements. They must have a thorough understanding of the hotel's operational requirements and be cognizant of utility options in terms of sources, costs, and availability. In some cases, engineers must design hotels to be self-sufficient:

producing their own power, providing their own water through desalinization or a well, and treating and handling their own sewage and refuse.

The soils engineer, sometimes in conjunction with an engineering geologist, is responsible for ascertaining the bearing capacities and properties of the soil and making recommendations to the structural engineer for the design of the building's foundations and superstructure. In areas prone to seismic activity or having other complex soil conditions, input from a soils specialist is essential.

The civil engineer is responsible for grading and drainage and the design and layout of roadways, parking lots, and other public structures, which may include bridges, extensive drainage systems, and paths. A quantity surveyor or cost consultant uses up-to-date data to make project cost estimates. On many projects outside the United States, the cost consultant prepares contract documents for the bid or tender process. A cost consultant can be helpful, regardless of the construction procurement method.

Kitchen and laundry consultants, who may be employed by separate firms or a single firm, work with the operator to create kitchen and laundry layouts that meet the operator's particular food and laundry philosophy and objectives. Food and laundry operations are quite complex in large hotels with multiple food and beverage outlets, large banquet facilities, and outdoor entertainment areas. Food service can be further complicated when it is offered in remote areas such as pool bars and grills, tennis clubs, and other facilities away from the main building. Kitchen and laundry consultants help design food delivery, preparation, and storage areas and establish procedures for handling food service trash and garbage. They must coordinate their efforts with the MEP consultants who design the power, drainage, and mechanical systems.

A land surveyor may be needed to survey the site and provide an accurate topographic description of its features. The surveyor can also assist the construction contractor in setting out the building. The elevator consultant helps determine the type, number, and technical specifications of passenger and service elevators. He or she provides technical information to the structural and MEP engineers and prepares the documents for elevator procurement.

Most projects include a lighting consultant, who works either independently or directly for the interior designer to design the lighting and specify fixtures. On projects with a large spa or health club, a leisure and fitness consultant is usually involved. This specialist provides detailed information on the operational aspects of these facilities and prepares specifications for any specialized FF&E (furniture, fixtures, and equipment) needed.

For golf course resorts, a golf course architect and sometimes a golf course operations consultant are included on the team. The client can choose the golf course architect from an international golf celebrity's firm that provides design consulting services or from a smaller, independent company that specializes in golf course design. Other major recreational amenities will also involve specialized consultants.

The interface between the Riverwalk and the hotel was a key consideration in the design of the Hyatt Regency, San Antonio.

While rarely visible to the general public, back-of-house areas like this kitchen at the Radisson Plaza at Mark Center in Arlington, Virginia, must be designed well for efficiency.

The Hyatt Regency Hill Country, San Antonio, offers a range of amenities from golf for adults to floats for kids to ride down the Ramblin' River.

A graphic designer is often called upon. Some of the major chains have in stock a significant body of signage and graphics work that can be readily adapted for new hotels. However, the naming and branding of food and beverage outlets, meeting facilities, and a host of other identity and communications graphics will require design work.

The design team often employs a professional artist or illustrator to assist in preparing materials for client presentations, public relations, and premarketing efforts. The services of a model maker may also be required for approvals, presentations, or marketing purposes.

A careful structuring of the team, the clear establishment of a scope of services for each of the consultants, the definition of their roles and responsibilities, and the clear articulation of the organizational structure and reporting process are essential. In today's highly complex design and construction projects, one of the most critical factors is timely decision making. The client must have the ability to communicate clearly and decisively. Accurate information and the ability to act on it within a reasonable time frame are fundamental to the success of a project.

First the Site

Site Selection

By the time architects or planners become involved in hotel projects, the client usually has selected the site. Sometimes, however, developers call upon architects or planners to assist in site selection. These professionals can assess the physical attributes of a site and foresee how various conditions—planning restrictions, environmental considerations, topography, and other factors—will influence the design of a hotel. Accessibility (travel modes, distance from airports), surrounding land uses, and other locational criteria must be analyzed. Findings can be expressed in a diagram showing the opportunities and constraints of each site.

Master Planning

Since the hotel boom of the 1960s, there has been an upward trend in the size of properties that developers acquire for hotel and resort developments. These properties need long-term master plans setting out appropriate land uses, development criteria, and phasing. Good master plans integrate the various components of the development and establish workable relationships between them. They have a certain degree of flexibility designed into them, allowing the developer to make modifications in a prescribed fashion in response to changes in market demand or economic conditions.

Among the key planning issues that should be considered in developing a piece of property for a hotel or resort are the following:

- *Land Uses.* Allowed uses should be graphically represented on a land use plan.

Master plan for Hilton Hawaiian Village, Honolulu.

At Pentagon City, a mixed-use development in northern Virginia, a discrete but understated entrance brings people into the Ritz Carlton hotel from an adjacent, upscale shopping mall.

- *Densities.* Specifying the amount of actual built-up area that is allowed on a piece of property, density guidelines can be used to restrict the height and bulk of buildings and define spaces between buildings and between different land uses.
- *View Corridors and Open Space.* A key factor in a resort is the spaces between developed parcels. Open-space buffers are necessary; a golf course can serve as such. View corridors opening on prominent features or vistas are essential. The planning for view corridors should take into consideration existing views from developed land and seek to minimize the impacts that the project will have on valued views. Open-space and view restrictions help maintain the character and quality of a resort and ensure that future development phases retain their value.
- *Environmental Sensitivity.* Environmental sensitivity extends beyond sensitivity to the site's natural features and ecology and the development's impact on local and regional natural systems, to include any areas of historic or archeological interest, as well as the development's impact on indigenous cultures and nearby historic precincts. It is not unusual for governmental agencies to require extensive environmental impact reports. These reports must address myriad issues, including impacts on the local culture and economy as well as on the natural environment.

Site Design

In designing a hotel, most architects and planners begin with site design. The graphic analysis of the client's program applied on the actual site seeks to determine the best location of the building(s) relative to various physical and

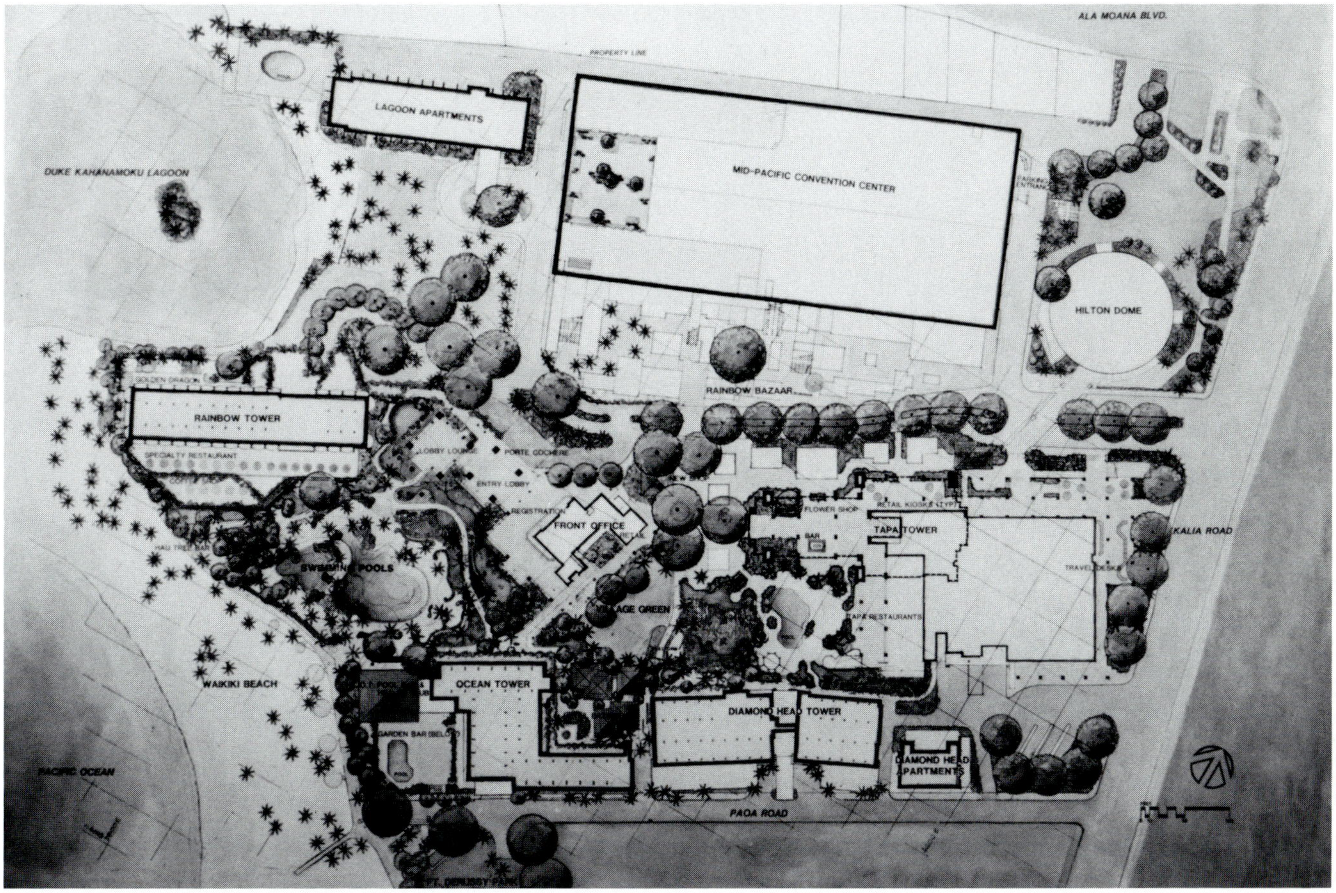

The site plan for Hilton Hawaiian Village shows the hotel in more detail than does the master plan.

A prominent architectural profile on a city's skyline is an important design feature for hotels. Here the distinct top of the San Francisco Marriott stands out against its San Francisco Bay backdrop.

Jane Lidz Photography

other constraints. The location of vehicular and pedestrian circulation is important for giving guests a sense of arrival. The location of service entries and separate service drives (if required) and the screening of service areas are other site design factors.

Depending on the size of the site and the value of the property, the parking element can exert considerable influence on the design approach to the project. On a large site, landscaped parking lots can be located near the hotel. In urban or suburban areas, where land may be limited or highly valued, parking structures—raised or subterranean—may be the best solution. In mixed-use developments, which often include stores, offices, residences, and a hotel, parking structures are sized according to the overlap of parking use between the various components.

Designing the Hotel

The architectural design process has six primary phases that serve as a framework for scheduling and coordinating the architectural and engineering work. The process comprises the following phases: conceptual design, schematic design, design development, construction document preparation, bidding or negotiating for construction, and construction administration. The interior design process also progresses through six phases: planning, concept, design development (architectural information), contract documents (working drawings and specifications), bidding and negotiation, and implementation.

With two design processes proceeding simultaneously, careful planning and coordination of the work efforts of all design disciplines is required. Because of pressures of time and cost, the design phases frequently overlap, making the effective coordination of the design team's work efforts even more critical.

The following sections provide details on the phases of the architectural design process.

Conceptual Design

During the conceptual design phase, the design team visits the site to collect data on its features, view planes, and surrounding areas. It begins the design of the building according to approved parameters, which include the project program and budget. Concept plans (single-line drawings) are prepared, addressing the functional relationships of the project components and taking into consideration the site features and governmental planning and building requirements. Written descriptions of the building(s), interiors, and landscaping are prepared. Gross building areas by program are tabulated and compared with the original program. The drawings completed during this phase include the following:

	Scale	
Conceptual Design Drawings	International	U.S.
1. Illustrative site and roof plan	1:500	1:480
2. Lobby floor plan	1:400	1:384
3. Back-of-house floor plan	1:400	1:384
4. Typical guest wing floor plan	1:400	1:384
5. Typical guest room plan	1:100	1:96
6. Exterior elevation to describe character	1:200	1:192
7. Building section to describe massing and scale	1:200	1:192
8. Character sketches	–	–

Schematic Design

Once the client approves the concept, the design team prepares schematic design drawings to illustrate the scale and relationships of the components. In this phase, a definitive program is established, building areas are tabulated, the items that will be included in the specifications are outlined, and a written description of the aesthetic character of the project is prepared for the use of a cost consultant in establishing probable construction costs. During this phase, the landscape architect, the engineers, the interior designer, and the kitchen/laundry and elevator consultants begin work on the design of the building systems, grounds, and interiors. The drawings prepared by the architect during this phase include the following:

Schematic Design Drawings	Scale International	U.S.
1. Site and roof plan in sufficient detail to indicate overall scope and intent	1:500	1:480
2. Public area and back-of-house floor plans	1:200	1:192
3. Typical guest wing floor plans	1:200	1:192
4. Typical guest room and suite floor plans	1:50	1:48
5. Exterior elevations	1:200	1:192
6. Major building and site sections	1:200	1:192
7. Sketch sections of exterior walls in key areas	1:100	1:96

Design Development

Based on approved schematic design documents, the design team prepares design development documents to further fix and describe the project's form, size, and basic materials. All the design consultants prepare drawings and documents that describe their own portion of the work. The documents are scaled to indicate the overall building configuration in relation to the site and nearby buildings. Preliminary estimates of construction costs are completed. Design development documents prepared by the architect include the following:

Design Development Drawings	Scale International	U.S.
1. Site plan	1:500	1:480
2. Floor plans for all floors	1:200	1:192
3. Exterior elevations	1:200	1:192
4. Longitudinal and transverse building sections	1:200	1:192
5. Large-scale sketch sections of typical exterior walls illustrating design intent and materials	1:50	1:48
6. Typical guest room plans (in coordination with the interior designer)	1:50	1:48
7. Suite plans (in coordination with the interior designer)	1:50	1:48
8. Reflected ceiling plans of non-public areas	1:100	1:96
9. Roof plans	1:100	1:96
10. Drawings of design feature details	1:20	1:24
11. Color/materials selection boards	–	–

Construction Phases

Based on approved design documents, the design team prepares detailed construction drawings, specifications, and calculations. The team then assists the owner in obtaining bids or negotiated proposals and in awarding and preparing contracts for construction. Finally, the architect and other members of the design team provide administration of the construction contracts. They visit the site during appropriate stages of construction, and observe the construction work for design intent and quality of installation. The design team reviews shop drawings and materials samples, and advises the owner. The amount of effort required from the design team during this phase can vary greatly, depending on the complexity of the project and the capabilities of the client's development staff.

Hotels from a Design Perspective

The great paradox in hotel design is that while most hotels are generally the same programmatically, no two are alike. Although an oversimplification, it can be said that 90 percent of the hotels in the three-star range and above contain almost all the same physical spaces, housing similar functions that have the same specific physical relationship to each other. Within this sameness, variables such as site constraints, the number of rooms, operator's requirements, and quality differences can help define a hotel and give it its own character. For example, most five-star hotel chains

A two-lane lap pool is a feature of the health club at the Georgetown Four Seasons Hotel in Washington, D.C.

93

The Hyatt Regency Kauai nestles in the foreground of a magnificent landscape.

offer club areas located on their own floor or in their own wing or even building.

Types of Hotels

Although the urban hotel and the resort hotel are nearly identical programmatically, they present two interestingly different design challenges. The typical urban property usually has a limited site area that requires a design focus on concerns such as traffic, access, setbacks, and density. The architecture of the hotel, supported by exterior hardscape and interior design, is the hotel's dominant visual statement. The architectural challenge often is to create an icon in the cityscape (within a context of mass, scale, and form).

In contrast, the design challenge posed by the typical resort property is to reinforce a sense of place within a cultural context. The architecture of a resort hotel frequently is the background for the landscaping. The landscape, architecture, and interior design are balanced elements. They blend together to create the desired environment and ambiance.

The casino hotel, while frequently located in an urban environment, has come to rival the resort property in terms of being a design challenge. As with resort hotels, the design goal for the newest casino hotels is to create a sense of place, albeit in a themed context. The recent introduction of entertainment components into casino hotels has added another layer to the design process, and has necessitated adding other kinds of expertise to the design team.

For the hotel architect, the special design challenge of the urban mixed-use property is to accommodate the hotel's requirements for back-of-house functions and for guest security. The design of structural systems, including vertical transportation systems, that can effectively serve multiple land uses is a major concern in vertical mixed-use projects.

The basic programmatic components of luxury properties are similar to what is provided in other types of hotels. The distinguishing design difference is a high level of finish in luxury hotels.

Dedicated conference centers impose special requirements for the food and beverage areas. As would be expected, the meeting areas and meeting support systems in these facilities often are designed for dedicated use, in contrast to the more flexible arrangements that other hotels prefer.

The spa is another specialized hospitality property. Design parameters for spas vary significantly, depending on the spa's focus, which can range from pampering to exercise, from weight loss to medical evaluation and treatment.

Hotel Components

Hotels are generally conceived as having three major components: guest rooms, public areas (front-of-house), and administrative and support areas (back-of-house). Each component presents its own design issues.

A conference center at the Four Seasons Hotel, Tokyo.

This 62-room "retreat" connected to the Radisson Plaza at Mark Center has its own meeting rooms and great room.

A hotel's personality is revealed in its dining facilities—whether a high-end, white-tablecloth restaurant or a family-oriented facility.

Each component has its own long list of elements. For example, guest rooms come in many varieties—kings, double/doubles, junior suites, executive suites, presidential suites, villas, and so forth. Also included in the guest rooms component are guest corridors, stairs and elevators, and areas supplying guest room services (such as housekeeping rooms, butlers' pantries, and vending rooms).

Guest Rooms. Almost every hotel design project starts out with a fresh look at the guest room. The standard guest room module becomes the basic building block for the project, whether it is a low-density resort hotel or a high-rise tower. Groupings of guest rooms form the guest room floors.

The designers may have considerable flexibility in locating and interrelating guest rooms and in placing guest room wings on the site. In projects at the lower end of the quality spectrum or in projects with tight budgets, design flexibility tends to be limited and guest room wings are kept compact. In five-star resort hotels, architects are freer to conceive guest room wing layouts that might, for example, create courtyards, respond to dramatic views, or reduce the physical scale or mass of the building.

Public Areas. The layout of the public areas is usually the most challenging element of a hotel's design. Public areas must interrelate with back-of-house areas and also be readily accessible from the main lobby and other public entry points. In high-rise hotels, the presence of service ducts and structural columns that come down from the guest rooms through the base (or podium) of the building makes achieving a satisfactory interrelationship between the public areas, support spaces, and primary public circulation areas even more complicated. Many public areas—restaurants, meeting spaces, and ballrooms—typically require a higher floor-to-ceiling height than the average guest room floor. Fitting these large areas, both vertically and horizontally, with other hotel components can be difficult.

The complicated interrelationships between the back-of-house support spaces and the various public areas—such as food and beverage outlets, meeting spaces, pools, and health club—require careful study. The key design objectives are to prevent the crossover of public and service circulation, to provide guest circulation that is direct and easy to understand, and to enable the hotel to meet its standard of quality in service.

Administrative and Support Areas. Back-of-house design is also complex. Safety and security, the smooth flow of supplies and materials into and through the hotel, and the quick and easy circulation of staff through the hotel are important design parameters. The proper location of the mechanical plant is important. It should be close to the kitchen and laundry—and the engineering and maintenance offices should be close to it.

Special Features and Amenities

Hotels—whether two-star economy or five-star deluxe—offer a growing assortment of special features and amenities, from live entertainment to state-of-the-art video conferencing facilities and from spas and fitness centers to business support services. These guest services have at least one thing in common: they need to be incorporated into the design.

Guest room layouts and fittings, for example, are changing in response to technology advances across a wide range of applications: energy-conserving lighting, water-saving bathroom fixtures, HVAC systems that provide more comfort (and are more efficient), personal entertainment centers, and wiring and connections for personal computers and fax machines.

Fitness centers have become standard fare in many hotels and resorts, but their design is evolving with the introduction of new state-of-the-art equipment and the increasing popularity of such innovations as specialized treatment rooms and healthcare products retailing within the fitness centers.

A number of hotels program activities and provide care for guests' children. The design of hotel childcare facilities and amenities for older children is an area in which there is room for improvement. Hotel facilities for children take many

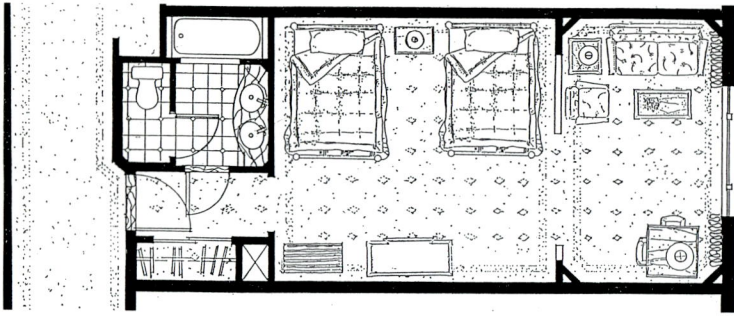
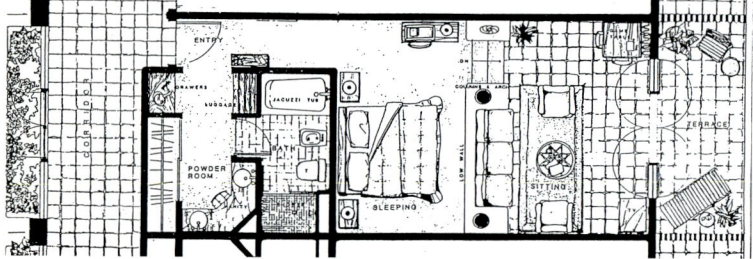

Guest room layout is a critical element of a hotel's positioning.

forms, including playgrounds, children's pools, and youth activity centers. Children in their teens traveling with their parents can generate revenue for a hotel. This customer group needs youth-oriented amenities that provide entertainment and opportunities for interaction independent from parents. Activity centers for teens, with video game machines, pool tables and Ping-Pong tables, and big-screen music video amphitheaters, are being incorporated into new hotels. Almost every hotel has some retail space, which can range from a small sundries shop in the lobby to a full-blown shopping galleria. The scale and scope of a hotel's retail offering depend greatly on its size and type, its location, and the potential spending patterns of its guests. Shopping is a major leisure pastime. Strategically located retail facilities provide entertainment for hotel guests, and the hotel can use them as a locale for events as well as restaurants and

The atrium at the Grand Floridian, Walt Disney World, Orlando, Florida.

bars. Retail space can contribute significantly to the revenue generation of a project. Name-brand outlets are commonplace in the galleries of high-end hotels, adding to the hotel's cachet and, if properly located, capturing considerable impulse spending.

For most hotels, the provision of security poses a dilemma. On the one hand, guests consider security for their persons and their valuables to be of utmost importance. On the other hand, the presence of overt security measures and guards tends to make guests—and visitors—feel unwelcome and as if they were staying in a prison. Security-conscious design and the careful planning of security systems—by experts with knowledge of the innovations in technology—can create secure hotel environments in which guests and the general public can feel welcome. For business hotels that cater to government officials and diplomats, extra security features may be required.

The Renovation Process

The architect's work is not limited to new hotel construction. A significant percentage of engagements are performed for developers who require the upgrading and renovation of their existing properties. The process is virtually the same. Hotel renovations involve design professionals, and the de-

A guest room at the Ritz Carlton Huntington in Pasadena, California.

The Ritz Carlton Huntington was partially torn down and rebuilt in order to meet seismic design standards.

sign process for major renovations is akin to the design process for a new hotel.

Hotels are constantly being upgraded, sometimes merely cosmetically but frequently quite dramatically. Major and rapid shifts in concepts of leisure, the nature of recreation, and ways of doing business are shortening the competitive life span of many hotels, and thus accelerating the pace of renovation. Upgrading is becoming an ongoing activity, as shown in Figure 10-2, and the time elapsing between major reconstruction programs has been halved.

There are essentially three classes of hotel renovation activity based on the degree of physical change involved—the three Rs—as follows:

- *Refurbishment.* In many hotels, cosmetic changes—such as new carpets or fresh paint—are made fairly frequently, if not continuously, as styles change or as materials and finishes show wear and tear and equipment becomes outdated.
- *Renovations and Additions.* Now and then, as dictated by operational needs or changes in the market, some components may be upgraded and amenities—like a conference center, a fitness facility, or a wedding chapel—may be added.
- *Rehabilitation.* At some point, which is sooner rather than later for hotels that have not been well maintained, a major rehabilitation must be performed to remedy functional and physical obsolescence. The comprehensive rehabilitation of a whole property often involves repositioning it as well.

Reasons for Renovating

At times, hotel owners have no alternative but to renovate—a natural disaster has caused extensive damage, equipment has failed, or the roof leaks. But being forced to renovate is only one reason to do so. Often there are positive and

■ Figure 10-2

The Changing Frequency of Hotel Renovations

	Occurring Every...	
	In the Past	In the Future
Cosmetic Refurbishment	3–5 years	Ongoing
Minor Renovations and Additions	10–20 years	3–5 years
Major Rehabilitation	25–30 years	10–20 years

compelling economic reasons for embarking on a hotel renovation program.

To keep a hotel competitive and profitable, its owners may need to extend its useful life. An older property may be physically or functionally obsolete, particularly if maintenance and regular upgrades have been deferred for many years. A property may simply look out-of-date. It may be advisable to reposition the property within the marketplace.

Hotels often undergo physical modifications in response to guest feedback, industry trends, and technological changes. The need to comply with changes in codes and regulations, like the Americans with Disabilities Act (ADA), can trigger a renovation program.

Improving operational and functional efficiency is another common reason for renovation. Properties that have grown helter-skelter over a number of years can gain a great deal from physical remakes aimed at improving the efficiency of various operations.

The drawing power of nostalgia can provide a good economic reason for rehabilitating a historic hotel, particularly one with the all-important qualities of character and location. A hotel that offers the amenities of today and the ambiance of yesteryear can be highly marketable.

Planning and Implementing Renovations

In many ways, renovating a hotel is like building a hotel, although renovation involves some added considerations of operational continuity and the compatibility of new and old elements—in terms of design, construction, and operations.

The first phase of the renovation process is preplanning, which involves establishing goals and determining if the renovation is economically viable; and then developing a

The Conrad International Hong Kong is part of Pacific Place, a multitower mixed-use development. The hotel shares a tower with a 243-unit apartment and service-suite complex.

The Pine Room at the Hotel Roanoke in Roanoke, Virginia, was restored to its original clubby elegance.

program, schedule, and phasing strategy. Time spent in this phase will help circumvent problems later on.

Budgeting for renovation requires planning for potentially costly discoveries during construction. Even after the property has been thoroughly investigated, higher than normal contingency funds are still necessary. A key part of the renovation budget is the decision on whether the hotel will be closed or remain open during construction. Closing the hotel entails loss of revenue. Keeping it open raises the cost of construction.

If the property remains open during renovation, it might be advisable to fast-track the construction process with extended work hours, in order to finish it in a shorter period of time. The potential impact of construction on the guests needs to be assessed. In key guest areas, the noise, dust, and inconvenience of construction work needs to be mitigated. Discount rates can be offered and other steps taken as part of the guest relations program to make guests feel that they have a stake in the project, and thus make them want to return to see the results.

If the renovation can occur during a seasonally slow period, closing the hotel—and fast-tracking the construction—could be more cost-effective. When the hotel is closed, the retention of employees is an issue.

Whether or not the property stays open, public relations is an important element in renovations. Guests and the public should be kept informed. Staging a grand reopening is usually de rigueur.

A complex renovation needs a specialized project team. All its key members, including the owner, operator, designer, and contractor, should have had experience with major renovations. Perhaps even more than for a new construction project, teamwork and a win-win attitude are prerequisites for a successful renovation project. The team must be involved in the preplanning stage to help establish budgets, schedules, phasing strategies, and contingencies.

In renovations, an existing design style often needs to be taken into account. Construction phasing studies should be undertaken early in the process in order to establish the practicality of the design concept. The project team must anticipate field revisions and be flexible about design and construction solutions. Most renovation projects need as-built drawings to establish a baseline, in addition to new design drawings. Demolition drawings must identify the elements being affected by the renovation, and the older the building, the more difficult the task.

The International Arena

The travel and tourism industry is a global giant that will grow dramatically, well into the 21st century. U.S. architects and designers working on hotels in foreign countries encounter many conditions that are different than those to which they are accustomed, including the following:

- Local sensitivities—religious, cultural or historic;
- Nuances in the way that business is conducted;
- Regional differences in construction technology;
- Development processes that involve different roles for consultants; and
- Local political conditions and planning and regulatory practices.

In the spa at the Four Seasons Hotel, Tokyo, different bathing and swimming cultures meet.

Cultural, business, and regulatory practices affect how hotels are developed and designed in various countries.

World-class hospitality projects adhere to recognized international standards of service. Yet many successful hotels in every corner of the world incorporate and evoke local culture, history, and technology. The days of standard chain hotels that are interchangeable worldwide are over. The hallmark of a successful hotel company is not so much a standard, recognizable design, as it is a particular approach to service and guest satisfaction and a particular signature in terms of graphics and amenities. The planning and design of hotels and leisure projects are likely to reflect local customs—food, music, art, dance, and crafts. To work in the international arena, hotel architects must understand more than the hotel project itself. The success of such world-class projects depends, to a large extent, on the ability of their designers and developers to establish a meaningful rapport with their local counterparts that transcends national boundaries.

Chapter 11
The Construction Process

Walter A. Rutes

As a complex mixed-use building type, hotels present significant challenges in both design and construction. Key issues in hotel construction today include the form of the construction contract, construction management and completion schedules, new technologies, and postoccupancy evaluation.

Construction Contract Options

The form of the construction contract has much to do with the construction quality, delivery time, and cost of the final product. Three forms of construction contracts are used widely in hotel development today: design-award-build, fast track, and design/build. The comparative advantages and disadvantages of these three forms for the major parties are described in Figure 11-1.

Design-Award-Build

The design-award-build contract is the traditional building method. Despite the time it takes to first design and specify the building, design-award-build is still the best overall contracting option. This building method puts the emphasis on instituting tight construction management procedures to avoid budget and schedule overruns. It begins with the design effort, which must develop clear, complete, and concise construction documents. A competitive bidding process resulting in a guaranteed maximum price (GMP) contract can consistently provide a high-quality project on time and within budget.

Fast Track

In a fast-track construction contract, the design effort is still underway when construction begins, and it continues throughout the building process. Generally, for reasons of economics or availability, major decisions on structure, materials, mechanical systems, and vertical circulation elements are made early and imposed on the preliminary design as givens. Thus, items with long lead times can be ordered before the design is completed. The major benefit is speed. However, if items ordered ahead are canceled or changed, the result can be large monetary penalties. To help coordinate the many subcontractors, design professionals, and regulatory bodies that a complex building program entails, many fast-track projects use the services of a construction manager (CM). The CM is responsible for managing the contracts with the various parties engaged in the effort.

An experienced CM can shorten the construction period considerably—particularly if the project uses components with which the CM is familiar from previous projects—without jeopardizing the quality of the finished hotel. The CM can be a valuable addition to the project team when fast track is the construction method. In general, however, unless time is especially tight, fast track is not the best contract option for high-end hotel projects.

Design/Build

Design/build has evolved from efforts to reduce the delivery time of projects. It assigns the design and construction responsibilities to a single entity. This approach best serves projects in which the design needs and solutions are known, and the owner is comfortable with the contractor relationship. By using this option, the owner can often do without the services of an independent architect and, as well, without the services of a CM. The contractor is responsible for providing design services and for managing the construc-

■Figure 11-1

Comparative Advantages and Disadvantages of Construction Contract Options

		Design-Award-Build	Fast Track	Design/Build
For the Client	Advantages	■ Professional advice on contract and construction quality issues ■ Good industry understanding of how method operates ■ Budgets most accurately resemble actual costs ■ Easier guaranteed maximum price negotiations ■ Clear penalties for cost overruns	■ Shorter project delivery time ■ Lower project costs ■ Professional advice on contract and construction quality issues ■ Clearly defined sharing of cost overages and underages	■ Shorter project delivery time ■ Lower project costs ■ Single responsible party ■ Inventive design/construction solutions ■ Reduced project management stress ■ Reduced number of claims ■ Single fee to pay
	Disadvantages	■ Longer start-to-finish time ■ Multiple fees to pay	■ Project management stress ■ Decision-making responsibilities blurred	■ No independent professional design advice
For the Contractor	Advantages	■ Definitive plans and specifications on which to base bids ■ Role clearly understood by all parties	■ Difficulty in establishing guaranteed maximum price ■ Early completion bonuses ■ Easier to recommend substitutions	■ More control over project ■ Minimum risk and uncertainty ■ Improved design ■ Opportunity to increase profits
	Disadvantages	■ Less flexibility for substitutions of materials, equipment, and systems ■ Adversarial relationships with design professionals	■ Coordination failures result in delay ■ Penalties ■ Gaps in insurance coverage	■ Responsibility for design ■ Responsibility for design errors and omissions
For the Designer	Advantages	■ Greatest control over design and construction quality ■ Role clearly understood by all parties	■ More involvement in the field ■ Quick decisions by all parties	■ More control over project quality ■ Opportunity to increase profits ■ Field experience ■ Greater credibility with clients ■ Reduced number of claims from contractor
	Disadvantages	■ Adversarial relationships with contractors	■ Decision-making responsibilities blurred ■ Priorities blurred ■ Timeliness more important than quality ■ Coordination stress	■ Responsibility for errors and omissions of the contractor

The Omni Rosen Hotel in Orlando, Florida, with the eighth of 24 floors under construction.

tion process. Design/build does not function as well when the development objective is an innovative hotel product.

No matter whether design/build or the fast-track option is chosen, all hotel construction contracts are moving toward negotiated guaranteed maximum prices based on completed plans and specifications. The design/build formula can consistently provide a high-quality hotel on time and within budget, if the developer obeys the following guidelines:

- Deliver complete contract documents before the bidding and construction phase.
- Keep fast tracking to a minimum. Restrict its use to ordering certain equipment, like transformers and boilers, with long lead times, and then only if the order can be canceled without significant penalty. Fast tracking is risky, since complete drawings are lacking at the time of contract.
- Base competitive bidding on equivalent quality.
- Make it a policy that no change orders will be accepted unless they were initiated by the owner.

Construction Management

Cost management—upon which the timely, prudent allocation of resources and the successful realization of the project depend—begins with a well-organized control system. Because of the complexity and financial risk of hotel development, decision makers need constantly updated and clearly understandable information on a project's status. Effective control systems monitor not only costs but also schedules and performance levels. A good control system continually measures expenditures against budgets, and thus identifies variances and alerts decision makers to opportunities for corrective action.

The first step in establishing an effective control system is to plan the work fully, well in advance of construction. Each aspect of the work plan must be reduced to a level of tasks and subtasks that will allow adequate monitoring and control. Project managers must carefully identify the scope and priority of various tasks—from land acquisition through postoccupancy evaluation. The work plan should highlight any special needs for labor, materials, and equipment that will be encountered at any time during the entire run of the project, from planning through occupancy. Regulatory reviews and inspections are often overlooked. They require time and resources and thus should be anticipated and given a place in the work plan.

The work schedule is an outgrowth of the work plan. Prepared and administered by the project manager, the work schedule delineates the time lines for all tasks and delivery dates for all parties involved. The project manager must approve any variances in the work schedule and is responsible for detecting any changes in the work program that will result in cost overages or savings. After the basic design decisions have been made, the major influence on construc-

Building projects like the Wyndham Cleveland Hotel at Playhouse Square in Cleveland, Ohio, on a tight urban site complicates construction management.

tion budgets is unforeseen change orders. They must be dealt with or negotiated at once.

The project manager also sets forth key measurement points (milestones or benchmarks). Contract delivery dates, for example, can be key measurement points. The measurement points are critical performance indicators for the owner and the contractor. The contractor can also use them in scheduling, budgeting, and resource allocation.

With the work plan, schedule, and measurement points in place, project budgets can be finalized. Care must be taken to make the budget reasonable, attainable, and based upon the contractually negotiated costs that are identified in the statement of work. Constructing a hotel is a dynamic multidimensional event, not a statistical study. For the budget to serve its purpose as a baseline for the cost control system, cost control and cost analysis must be interlocked.

Reserves and contingency funds are a key element in the control system. If the project is large and complex, basing the reserves and contingencies on such broad rules of thumb as "5 percent of budget" or "10 percent of materials cost" can be both risky and naive. These lines in the budget should reflect the risks and complexities of the project and should receive the same level of thought and consideration as every other line item.

Control is impossible without a system of measurement that gives project managers, owners, and investors the information that they need to track and evaluate the project's consumption of resources—money, time, materials, and labor. The most useful measurement for evaluating resource consumption is variance, or the deviation, either positive or negative, in costs, technical performance, or schedule from the budget, work plan, or work schedule. Reporting both underages and overages allows the parties to properly negotiate change orders and assess penalties. Measuring the completed work and comparing it to the work plan allows the parties to reschedule tasks and the employment of resources —either forward or back—and to coordinate related or dependent tasks. In complex hotel projects, a measurement system based on performance specifications rather than prescriptive specifications provides a true cost-benefit basis for evaluating substitutions and analyzing change orders. Such a system is critical in assuring the financial success of the project.

The critical path method (CPM) is an increasingly popular tool in hotel project management. A CPM diagram clearly shows each step of the process, the amount of time each step requires, and its dependency upon the completion of other tasks. As the project moves forward, the allocation of performance bonuses or penalties at the completion of the project can be forecast by analyzing the early or late start or the early or late finish of each task. CPM quickly resolves many disputes over which party is responsible for project delays and what, if any, penalties should be assessed, without protracted arguments. Successful use of CPM requires regular (at least monthly and preferably weekly) monitoring, evaluation, and maintenance of the CPM diagram.

For hotel projects, completion dates are generally more critical than they are for other types of buildings. Hotels under construction prebook rooms to guests and groups. A delayed opening entails not only a loss of revenue, but also a more serious tarnishing of the hotel's reputation among travel agents, corporate groups, and affected guests. In addition, staff payroll, training, and other fixed preopening expenses must be carried through the period between the scheduled and actual opening. To help ensure that opening dates are met, many contruction contracts include liquidated damage and bonus clauses.

Hotel projects involve complex completion schedules. This is because some key areas must be turned over for early occupancy to permit the installation of furnishings and equipment and the training of employees. Hotel construction contracts generally contain early certificate-of-occupancy schedules for specific areas, as follows: the kitchen and laundry, communications and computer rooms, training room, and loading dock to be turned over three months before opening; and the guest room floors and one elevator, front desk, and office, to be turned over six weeks before opening.

New Construction Technologies

As the 21st century approaches, old building materials are making way for new ones, new kinds of structures and "smarter" buildings are being designed, and certain labor-saving and timesaving construction practices are being more widely adopted despite resistance from interest groups. The adoption of new technologies to building design and construction practices is being spurred on by continual pressures to bring projects in on time and within budget.

Stronger and lighter composite materials come onto the market daily. In the next decade, many costly metal and stone elements in hotels will be replaced by high-impact, durable plastics and polymer composites. Improvements in fire, smoke, and toxic retardants in floor, wall, and ceiling materials, as well as furniture coverings, will make tomorrow's hotels safer.

As concerns building structures and systems, new technologies will bring many changes. Fabric-covered tensile structures and positive pressure (inflatable) structures, for example, will be used to provide larger, flexible rooms—permanent or temporary—for a wide range of events from dining to championship boxing. Advances in technology will continue to smarten building systems, making hotels more efficient to operate and more user-friendly.

Finally, technology is changing the actual process of construction. An increasing number of components that make up the hotel are coming to the job site preassembled, and are installed with quick-connect couplings and mounting systems.

Postoccupancy Evaluation

The design and construction of a hotel are actually just the beginning of the construction process. Knowing how well the building responds to the guests' needs and staffing functions is critical for its continued success. This requires a postoccupancy evaluation (POE), a rigorous and systematic evaluation process that takes place after the hotel has been occupied for some period of time. Two kinds of evaluation are especially useful: the investigative POE and the diagnostic POE. The investigative POE measures the variance between expected and actual levels of performance. It forms the basis for corrective actions. The diagnostic POE analyzes the fit (or lack of fit) between various design concepts and intentions and actual performance and use. Such analysis is extremely useful in designing renovations or adaptive uses.

POE provides many benefits. Among its short-term benefits are the following: POE identifies problems with the hotel facility, and suggests solutions. It identifies guests' likes and dislikes, thus giving the operator a basis for proactive management of the hotel. POE can help the operator see where improvements can be made in space utilization and maintenance. It allows systems performance to be monitored until the initial kinks are worked out.

For the medium term, continuing systematic evaluation offers the following benefits. It can be used to analyze the capability of the hotel to respond to market changes, growth, and adaptations. It provides verification of the savings realized from initial design and construction decisions made on the basis of life-cycle costs or value-engineering. It can be used to allocate accountability for building performance. The long-term benefits of continued POE include improvements in overall building performance, improvements in the measurement of building performance, and valuable input for the developer's or operator's design database and design standards. POE provides information that can be used in the design of similar hotels in the future.

The scramble to complete interior finishes and install fixtures under a hotel opening deadline can be a scheduling nightmare. Shown here is the Kuwait Sheraton Hotel reconstruction, Kuwait City, Kuwait.

Topped out, the Orlando Clarion Plaza, Orlando, Florida.

Hotel Megatrends

In the last part of the 1990s, two seemingly conflicting megatrends—environmental preservation and high technology—can be unified into a single positive force. The challenge will be to confront the issue of saving the environment by showing no-growth forces that exquisite hotels and resorts that both preserve and enhance the natural and cultural environment can be built.

Among the design concepts ready to be extended and perfected are the following: small, understated, and decorative but not gaudy hotels; low-profile, all-villa hotels; hotels catering to ecotourism and ethnotourism; wellness spas; and hotels that help conserve and preserve natural and historic urban areas.

Hotel designers will be further challenged by demographic and psychographic trends, such as the maturing of the population; travelers' greater appreciation for art and nature; the end of the Cold War and the opening of new regions to travel; and a return to economically sensible lifestyles, where nostalgic charms exist side by side with the most advanced technology.

The growing science of "marketechture" asks important questions. Why build costly glass hotels that waste energy, when most guests prefer ivy-covered stucco? Why build suburban skyscrapers, when most guests prefer staying close to the ground? Why build extravagant, monumental commercial hotels, when the majority of business travelers prefer a more resortlike ambiance?

The contemporary traveler's growing mood of healthy curiosity is a megatrend that may be the sleeper of the decade. This curiosity embraces learning and the pursuit of ecological adventures, the arts, and entertainment. Could the continued phenomenon of segmentation and the public's apparently insatiable desire for different travel experiences and "unhotels" be simply signs of cultural pluralism finally coming of age, as we "boom" and bloom into the next century?

CHAPTER 12
DEVELOPMENT PROFILES

Projects Profiled

Luxury Resort
Arizona Biltmore Hotel and Resort, Phoenix, Arizona
Restoration and expansion of a hotel and condominium resort, and its repositioning under independent management..

Downtown
Chateau Sonesta, New Orleans, Louisiana
Adaptive use of the 1849 D.H. Holmes Department Store and its 1919 warehouse as a hotel and apartment building on the edge of the city's French Quarter, by means of a public/private development process.

International Market
Conrad International Hong Kong
A deluxe but conservative hotel catering to overseas business travelers and, to a lesser extent, upscale leisure travelers, and located within a mixed-use complex that includes three hotels.

Resort/Convention
Walt Disney World Dolphin and Swan Hotels, Orlando, Florida
Two convention hotels within Walt Disney World with shared recreational amenities and special design themes.

Downtown, All-Suite
Doubletree Guest Suites/New York City, New York, New York
The performance of an all-suite hotel in a highly competitive market, through a renovation process and brand-name changes.

Mid-Market, Commercial
Hilton Garden Inns, Prototype Design
A prototype of a hotel chain's second generation mid-price hotel targeted to business travelers.

Economy
Holiday Inn Express/Strathclyde Country Park, Strathclyde, Scotland
A hotel chain's own development and management of a franchise brand hotel in a new market, in order to introduce the hotel concept to potential investors.

Downtown, Conference
Hotel Roanoke and Conference Center, Roanoke, Virginia
The renovation of a historic railroad hotel and the development of a conference center, under the auspices of a public/private team that included the city, a university, and a civic association.

Themed Resort
Hyatt Regency Hill Country Resort, San Antonio, Texas
A luxury resort on a 200-acre, wooded ranch, using a regional theme.

Convention
Loews Miami Beach Hotel, Miami Beach, Florida
Public/private construction of a 17-story tower and renovation of a 100-room historic art deco style hotel, to provide an 800-room hotel to support the city's convention center.

Suburban, Economy
Red Roof Inn/Alamo Downs, San Antonio, Texas
An owner-operated hotel in a suburban business corridor.

Nonmetropolitan
Sheraton Great Valley Hotel, Chester County, Pennsylvania
A full-service hotel outside a metropolitan area, catering to business travelers and tourists.

The Arizona Biltmore Hotel and Resort

Phoenix, Arizona

With the renovation and repositioning of the Arizona Biltmore Hotel and Resort in Phoenix, a historically significant hotel was transformed from obsolescence to a real estate opportunity.

Originally built in 1929, the 500-room resort is widely recognized for its architectural design and detail. Frank Lloyd Wright played a valuable role in the resort's original design, serving as the consulting architect. Over the years, however, the property lost much of its luster, becoming physically dated and lacking in the level of services and amenities required in an increasingly competitive luxury hotel and resort market.

The resort was acquired for $61.5 million in June 1992 by the principals of the Grossman Company Properties (GCP). To reposition the underperforming property, GCP devised a strategy that combined value-added rehabilitation and refurbishment, new construction, and strengthened management and marketing. The $32.6 million hotel project included refurbishment of the guest rooms, lobby, and kitchen, as well as the construction of a new pool complex and a conference and banquet facility. In addition, 78 resort condominium units in 18 multifamily villas, expected to cost $16.9 million are planned, with more than half built and all sold.

Throughout the project, GCP was faced with the formidable challenge of preserving the property's architectural integrity, while simultaneously keeping the construction budget competitive.

Frank Lloyd Wright inspired the design of the Arizona Biltmore's main building, which opened in 1929.

Development Process

In an effort to adhere to the resort's original design, the developer hired architect Vernon Swaback, formerly an apprentice of Frank Lloyd Wright, to supervise the project. Early in the development process, the design team researched the hotel's prominent history and original design concepts by studying archival photographs. As the resort is made up of several architecturally significant buildings, each designed and developed during different time periods, the design and construction team had to learn, and adapt to, a variety of different construction methodologies.

To decrease the exposure to risk typically associated with the hidden conditions of buildings in need of rehabilitation, the development team avoided wall and demolition work wherever possible. Dated fixtures and furnishings, most of which had been installed during a previous renovation, were stripped away. For the hotel's guest rooms and common areas, the aim was to achieve a casual elegance with more of a residential feel than had existed in recent years. Fixtures designed in the Arts and Crafts idiom were installed,

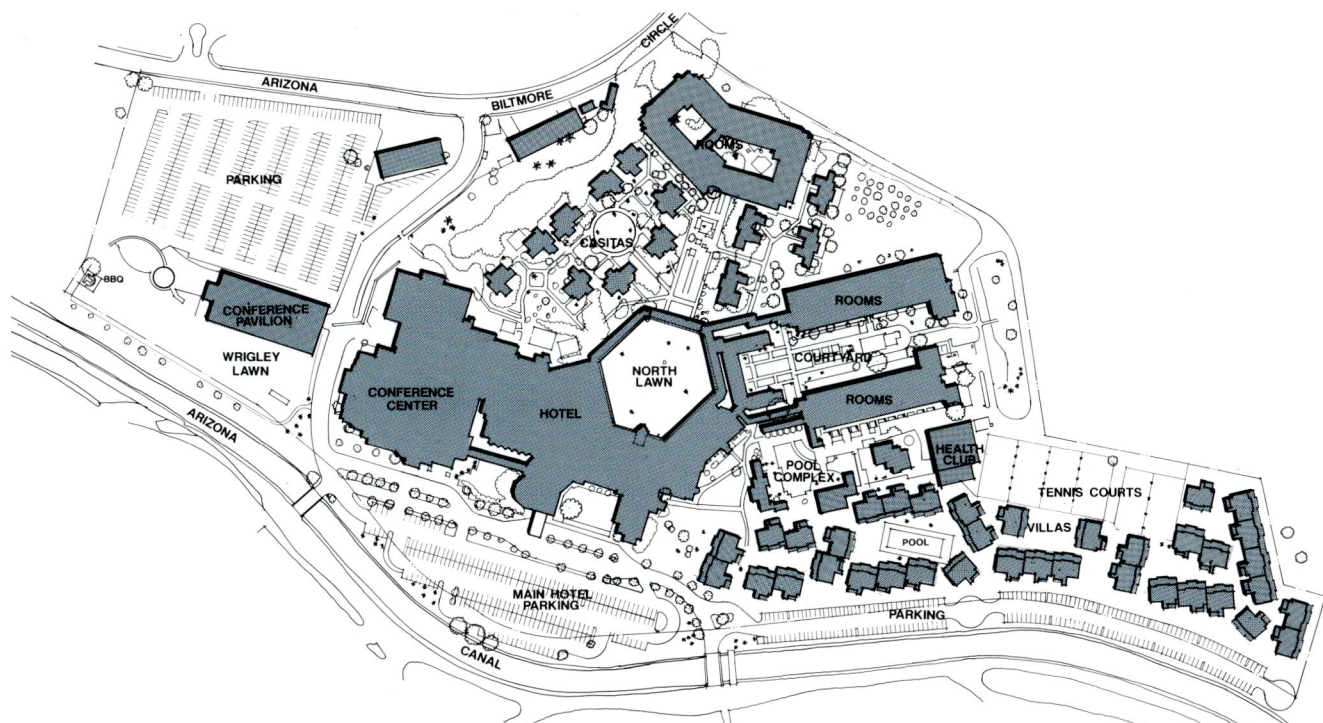

Site plan.

creating a more integrated, elegant, and historically correct interior design. To meet market expectations for upscale resort accommodations, all guest bathrooms were detailed with marble.

The Biltmore's central kitchen facility was so outdated that health officials required GCP to renovate it to comply with local codes. Expanding and renovating the kitchen cost approximately $1 million more than the pro forma had projected, largely due to hidden conditions that came to light as work proceeded.

Phasing of the 30-month construction process allowed the hotel to continue to operate efficiently. No more than half the guest rooms were removed from the rental pool at any one time, allowing the hotel to maintain reasonable occupancy rates and cash flow throughout.

Villa sales started in November 1994, halfway through the hotel renovation process. With an average sales price of $204 per square foot, all 78 villas were sold by December 1995, 12 months sooner than had been expected. The developer was able to generate profitable yields from these sales and thus finance the expansion of the hotel with a minimal capital investment and no future debt service obligations.

Design and Construction

The resort occupies only 29.9 acres. However, strategic building placement and view corridors, combined with extensive landscaping, make the property appear far larger and more spacious. Into this confined, but extremely well-laid-out site, GCP built several essential improvements, including: a pool complex, a large conference/ballroom facility, and 78 two-bedroom condominium units. In improving and adding, the developer managed to retain the resort's Frank Lloyd Wright character and sense of openness and elegance.

To compete with the growing number of upscale hotel resorts within the Phoenix market, GCP added a luxurious pool complex, which includes six pools and two spas, an elegant bar and café, guest cabanas, and a waterslide. The 92-foot-long waterslide, designed to attract and accommodate young guests, was built within an architecturally prominent structure.

Banquet and conference facilities were added in response to a predevelopment feasibility analysis indicating that an expansion of the Biltmore's conference facilities was essen-

New condominium villas.

The Arizona Biltmore Hotel and Resort Project Data

Land Use Information
Site Area: 29.9 acres
Condominium Units Planned/Built: 78/40[1]
Hotel Rooms Planned: 600

Land Use Plan

	Acres	Percent of Site
Villas	4.9	16%
Hotel	25.0	84

Guest Room and Condominium Unit Information

Guest Rooms
Average Daily Room Rate: $190
Average Annual Occupancy Rate: 68%

Condominium Units
Average Daily Rent: $1,850
Typical Sales Price: $372,000
Range of Current Sales Prices: $289,000 to $435,000[2]

Villa Development Cost Information

Site Improvement Costs	$675,283
Excavation/Grading	110,315
Sewer/Water/Drainage	173,801
Paving/Curbs/Sidewalks	229,715
Landscaping/Irrigation	38,874
Fees/General Conditions	122,578
Construction Costs	$6,927,867
Superstructure	4,065,205
HVAC	196,629
Electrical	220,828
Plumbing/Sprinklers	13,673
Finishes	2,103,272
Graphics/Specialties	20,000
Fees/General Conditions	308,260
Soft Costs	$591,324
Architecture/Engineering	93,722
Project Management	74,583
Marketing	250,000
Legal/Accounting	54,331
Construction Interest and Fees	118,688
Total Development Costs (as of March 1996)	$8,194,474
Total Projected Development Costs at Buildout	$16,899,684

Hotel Renovation and Expansion Cost Information

Construction Costs	$28,171,159
Rooms Renovation and Upgrade	8,936,006
New Pools, Tennis, and Spa Facility	3,023,195
Public Area and Site Upgrades	1,981,296
New Pavilion and Renovated Conference Facility	4,021,554
Engineering, HVAC, Roofs, Fire Safety	3,435,484
Systems Upgrades and Electronic Locks	760,307
Laundry Expansion and Upgrade	322,868
Food and Beverage Renovation and Expansion	5,690,449
Soft Costs	$4,443,138
Total Renovation and Expansion Costs	$32,614,297

Project Team

Developer
Grossman Company Properties

Architect
Vernon Swaback Associates

Notes
1. 78 units sold.
2. Plus furniture package at $45,000.

One of 23 poolside cabanas featuring teakwood furnishings, a bathroom, and a shower.

tial to the financial success of the resort. The new 16,000-square-foot conference pavilion can accommodate up to 1,500 guests. The innovative design emphasizes high-tech features, including a rear screen projection system and a state-of-the-art lighting system, as well as high-quality fixtures and furniture—plush carpeting, ceiling finishes, and chandeliers. A marketing CD-ROM allows prospective clients to visualize the pavilion's space and its many possible applications. The facility was built for approximately $60 per square foot.

A central component of the resort's repositioning was the development of 78 second-home condominium units. Constructed on 4.9 acres surrounding the historic 1929 Catalina Pool, the villa complex comprises 18 individual structures, each housing four to six units. Also designed by Swaback, the two-story, stick-built villas have scored stucco exteriors to resemble the historic concrete block buildings. The decorative brickwork (a.k.a. Wrightian Block)

The pool complex.

The renovated main lobby, the design of which was inspired by historic photographs.

found on buildings throughout the resort has been incorporated into the villas by means of cost-efficient reproductions (trademarked by the developer as the Biltmore Block) using a lightweight, but extremely dense, molded polyurethane foam painted to resemble the original ornate concrete blocks.

Built for approximately $118 per square foot, the villas cost more than had been originally projected. After the model units were designed, built to residential specifications, and sold, local officials required that the remainder of the units be built in compliance with commercial specifications, which required added fire protection features including a two-hour firewall separation between units and extensive sprinkling systems.

Operation and Management

Condominium Management. Biltmore condominium owners can place their units in the resort's rental pool when they are not using them. With this in mind, the 1,626-square-foot, two-bedroom, two-bathroom units were designed with two separate outside entrances and a locking door that divides each unit into a one-bedroom suite and an upscale hotel room. Approximately 80 percent of the owners participate in the rental program, increasing the resort's room inventory by approximately 20 percent.

The management of the participating villa rentals is relatively straightforward. The total room revenue generated by the villas is divided among the villa owners and the developer: once the villa owners achieve a predetermined level of return, the developer receives approximately 65 percent of the total rent revenues. This percentage compensation gives the hotel an incentive to maximize villa rental occupancy.

Hotel Management. Shortly after assuming ownership of the hotel, GCP dismissed the national hotel management corporation that had been operating the property for approximately 17 years. The typical standardization and institutional practices of a national management entity were contrary both to GCP's repositioning and management philosophies and to the image of the Arizona Biltmore. Independent management and operation have proven to be a successful initiative for the Biltmore owners. In 1990, two years before acquisition, the property generated a $4.1 million loss before debt service and capital expenditures. In 1995, the hotel produced a positive cash flow exceeding $11 million, also before debt service and capital expenditures.

In Perspective

- Meeting resort guest expectations while construction is underway can be challenging. It requires considerable management finesse. Nevertheless, the construction period can provide valuable training for resort employees, forcing them to devise appropriate and cost-effective solutions to problems that arise.
- The developer was able to use condominium development to increase the resort's profitability, room inventory, and future cash flow. However, this approach has a possible drawback: condominium owners may perceive that they have an interest in the resort's management and operational decisions, thereby requiring strong property management and residential services efforts.
- By embracing the resort's unique historic and architectural assets, the developer successfully repositioned the property in a sensitive, yet market-driven and cost-effective manner.
- By choosing to operate and manage the upscale resort independently, GCP was able to enhance and capitalize on its distinctive attributes and historic reputation and avoid any conflicting identity that an institutional hotel management entity might bring into the picture.

The Chateau Sonesta Hotel

New Orleans, Louisiana

The Chateau Sonesta Hotel is a study in perseverance. An assortment of public and private financing was used to convert two historic assets in downtown New Orleans—the 1849 D.H. Holmes Department Store and its 1919 warehouse—into, respectively, a modern, 243-room hotel facility and an 88-unit apartment building. This conversion required not only a public/private partnership and a complex financing package, but also a great deal of specialized design and construction expertise. Development planning began in 1989. The hotel opened in April 1995 and the apartment building was completed in January 1996.

The developer, Historic Restoration Inc. (HRI) headed by Ed Boettner and Pres Kabacoff, has set a mission for itself to contribute to the renewal of cities large and small through the preservation and adaptive use of historic buildings and through new construction in historic neighborhoods, in partnership with other players from the public, private, and nonprofit sectors. HRI's first projects involved the conversion

The hotel's Canal Street facade is a replica of the building's original facade.

A swimming pool occupies one of the courtyards that were created in the building's redesign.

of obsolete warehouse buildings in the old Warehouse District of New Orleans to residential uses.

The Site and Development Process

The hotel site covers approximately two-thirds of the block bounded by Canal, Bourbon, Iberville, and Dauphine streets on the edge of the French Quarter, and faces onto all of these streets. The site for the apartment building is an adjacent block across Iberville Street. A bridge connected the two structures. The two blocks are steps away from the central business district across Canal Street.

Built in 1849 by Daniel Henry Holmes, the D.H. Holmes Department Store was one of the first commercial establishments to serve the public from Canal Street, a wide boulevard that separated the old and new sections of the city. The original store was expanded several times over the years. An annex was added in 1905, the five-story warehouse was constructed in 1919 and a parking garage was constructed in 1969, also across Iberville Street.

In 1988, Dillard Department Stores bought the D.H. Holmes company and closed the store on Canal. Dillard donated the property to the city in 1989.

Concerned about the future of the site, the city of New Orleans quickly brought in HRI to redevelop the property. After several false starts, and only after splitting the project into two components—a hotel in the main building and a luxury apartment building in the warehouse—HRI managed to arrange and secure financing. The deal that was struck involved a lease arrangement between HRI and the Canal Street Development Corporation (CSDC), an entity created by the city of New Orleans in 1989 to oversee the redevelopment of Canal Street.

Financing

Financing for the project took three years and involved a mix of private and public sector sources. In the early 1990s, when the original financing plan with a New York bank fell through and national financial institutions appeared generally hesitant to finance a hotel in Louisiana, the developer turned to local sources. Financing was finally arranged through a bank consortium led by the First National Bank of Commerce in New Orleans.

The bank consortium provided a $12.6 million first mortgage on the hotel, with Premier Bank of Baton Rouge lending another $5.4 million for construction of the apartments. The U.S. Department of Housing and Urban Development provided a $5.6 million second mortgage through the city. Boh Brothers Construction Company, the parent of the construction company, Broadmoor Construction, that built the project, provided a $3 million bridge loan. Chevron Land and Development Company contributed $6.5 million in equity at the end of the construction period, which was

The restored Iberville Street facade.

used to repay the bridge loan. In return, Chevron received federal tax credits for restoration of a landmark building. The developer deferred up to $2 million in development fees and contributed an additional $1.2 million in equity.

To finalize the deal, Sonesta International, the hotel management company, provided a five-year guarantee of the hotel's debt service on the first mortgage by means of a lease.

The total financing arranged—$36.3 million—exceeded the actual cost of the project, which was reduced from the original estimate of $36 million by the application of innovative construction methods the developer had learned on its first apartment projects. The project cost was approximately $29.5 million, $23 million of which was for the hotel.

As the owner of the hotel building, CSDC receives a lease payment of approximately $260,000 to $270,000 per year or 6 percent of the hotel's gross revenue, whichever is higher. It also receives 15 percent of the hotel's net profit and 40 percent of its commercial rents.

Planning and Design

The only way to make the extensive four-story department store building work as a hotel was to create internal courtyards and atriums. Thus, the hotel design features two open courtyards and an enclosed atrium—all centrally located in the core areas of the rectangular building. The interior rooms open onto these spaces.

Once the courtyard solution was incorporated into the building design, the primary problem involved laying out the rooms around the existing columns. The solution to this problem involved giving many of the rooms unusual floor plans. Some included small sitting nooks. Most rooms are larger than typical hotel rooms, and, taking advantage of one of the primary assets of the building, all have 12-foot ceilings. Many of the rooms have original wooden windows and wainscoting.

Construction workers ran into many unexpected problems that caused delays, such as steel supports hidden behind brick or masonry. The bridge across Iberville Street connecting the store and warehouse buildings was visually obstructive and was therefore removed.

The most significant historic feature of the department store building—its 1913 neoclassic Canal Street facade of ivory-colored, glazed terra-cotta tile—had been covered by a new facade in 1964, a process that destroyed the tile. Removing the 1964 facade, which included modern arches and token cast-iron balconies, was a major undertaking in itself. Then, based on the original drawings, which were intact, workers were able to recreate the 1913 facade, using fiberglass rather than terra cotta.

The primary lobby entrance was placed on the corner of Iberville and Dauphine, with a car drop-off area cutting through the corner of the building at this location. A second entrance was located on Canal Street (where the department store's main entrance had been but where the hotel's frontage was limited).

Marketing and Management

The New Orleans hotel market has performed quite well for the past several years. Demand has increased in response to

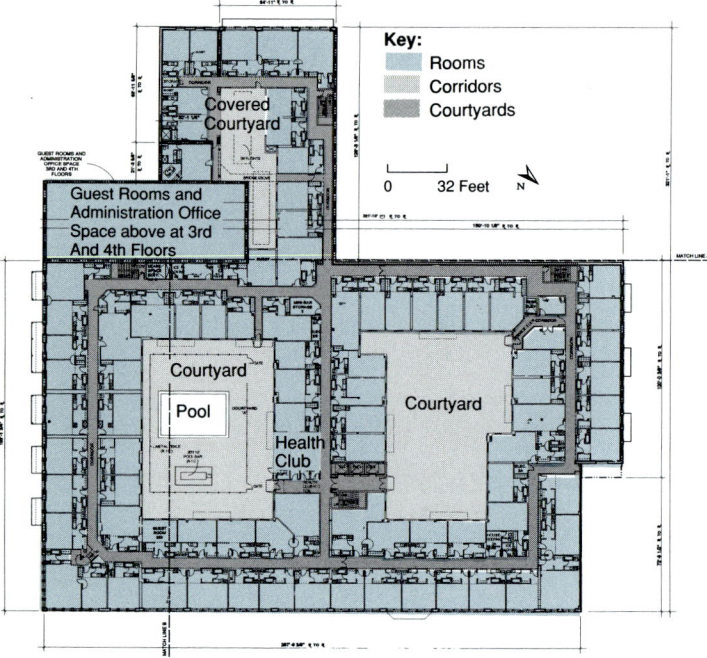

Second-floor plan.

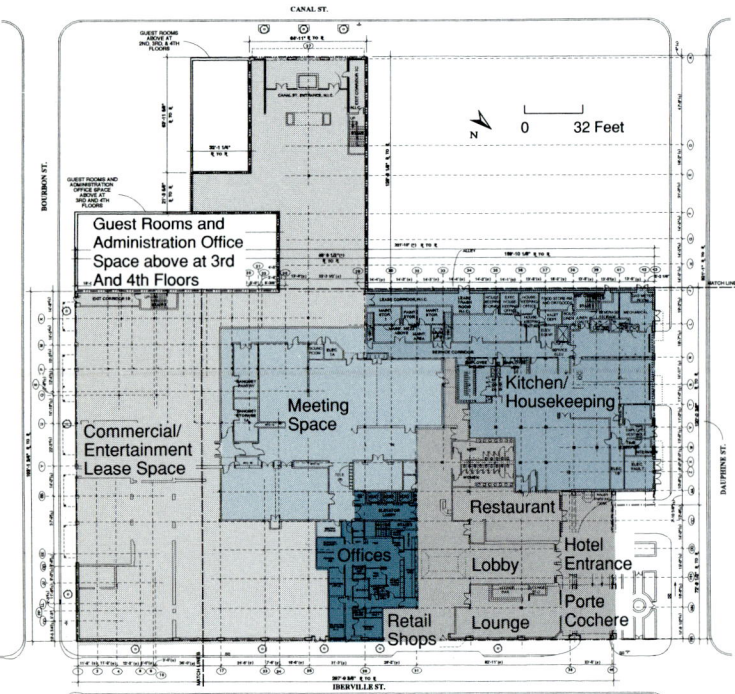

First-floor plan.

a strong community effort to promote tourism and no new construction has taken place. The Chateau Sonesta Hotel, the first major hotel to open in several years, has been able to take advantage of the growing demand. Hotel amenities include an outdoor pool, an exercise room, a gift shop, and a tour desk.

An original plan to master lease the restaurant and club space to one firm—which would then sublease the space—fell through, and the developer has decided to handle the leasing internally. The space, which is in a prime location at the end of the Bourbon Street strip of clubs and entertainment venues, is not expected to be difficult to lease. As of August 1996, negotiations were underway for both the restaurant and club.

In Perspective

- The developer's attempts to arrange financing from out-of-state sources was a frustrating experience. In the end, it was local banking institutions, investors, corporations, and government that made the project work. Appealing to the civic pride and interest of local players is crucial for the success of this kind of development.
- Converting a historic department store building into a hotel presents formidable design problems, but creating solutions to these problems can be rewarding. For example, internal courtyards and unusual room layouts—practical solutions that make the project functional—also give the hotel an unusual and memorable character that can be quite appealing to hotel guests.

An entrance on Iberville Street.

■ Chateau Sonesta Hotel Project Data

Land Use Information

Site Area: 2.3 acres
Hotel Site: 1.6 acres
Apartment Site: 0.7 acres

Building Use Information

Gross Building Area (Hotel): 250,000 square feet

Guest Rooms (Hotel): 243
On Second Floor: 82
On Third Floor: 85
On Fourth Floor: 76

Meeting Space (Hotel): 5,937 square feet
Apartment Units: 88
Parking Spaces: 323

Guest Room Information

Average Daily Room Rate: $125
Range of Daily Room Rates: $90 to $190
Average Annual Occupancy Rate: 70%

Hotel Development Cost Information

Site Costs	$514,626
Site Acquisition	508,876
Site Improvement (Landscaping)	5,750
Construction Costs	$15,366,366
Finishes	3,700,000
Other	11,666,366
Soft Costs	$7,121,341
Architecture/Engineering	496,500
Marketing	635,000
Legal/Accounting	1,135,298
Taxes/Insurance	76,532
Construction Interest and Fees	2,122,090
Other	2,655,921
Total Development Costs	$23,002,333

Total Development Cost per Room: $94,660

Project Team

Owner
Canal Street Development Corporation

Developer
Historic Restoration Inc.

Hotel Manager
Sonesta International

CONRAD INTERNATIONAL HONG KONG
HONG KONG

The five-star Conrad International Hong Kong is one of three hotels within Pacific Place, a four-tower, mixed-use complex in the central area of Hong Kong, on a barracks site vacated by the army in the early 1980s. Pacific Place was developed by Swire Properties Limited, and it consists of three five-star hotels with a total of 1,682 rooms, more than 1.6 million square feet of office space, 380 apartment units including service suites, 800,000 square feet of retail space, and 500 parking spaces on two levels.

Two towers were developed in Phase I, one dedicated to office space and the other containing a JW Marriott Hotel (lower portion) and the Atrium Apartments (upper portion). These towers sit atop a podium that houses shopping, entertainment, and parking facilities. The same podium serves as the base for two more towers constructed in Phase II. Both these towers contain stacked uses. In one, the Conrad International Hong Kong occupies levels 40 through 61, sharing the building with the Parkside Apartments on the lower levels. In the other tower, the Island Shangri-La Hotel occupies the upper levels, with office space underneath.

Both towers built in Phase II dedicate lower-level floors for hotel uses—lobby, reception, restaurants, and banquet facilities. The Conrad International Hong Kong has only guest rooms on the upper levels, while the Island Shangri-La uses the upper levels for guest rooms and a restaurant and bar.

The four-level shopping center underpins the entire complex and provides an upscale retail and entertainment environment that supports the hotel, office, and residential uses. The complex offers ample parking and rail and bus transit and taxi access for the more than 130,000 daily visitors to Pacific Place.

Hotel Design

Groundbreaking for Conrad International's tower took place in February 1987, and construction was completed by June 1990. The hotel officially opened on September 1, 1990. Unlike the two rectangular towers built in Phase I, the two towers built in Phase II are elliptical and have a distinctive exterior design—an architecture that clearly identifies Pacific Place on the central business district skyline. These two towers differ greatly in respect to interior use of space, which has allowed the hotel operators to design environments that meet their specific preferences.

The guest rooms at Conrad International Hong Kong offer excellent views of both Hong Kong Harbour and Victoria Peak. The views in either direction are enhanced by

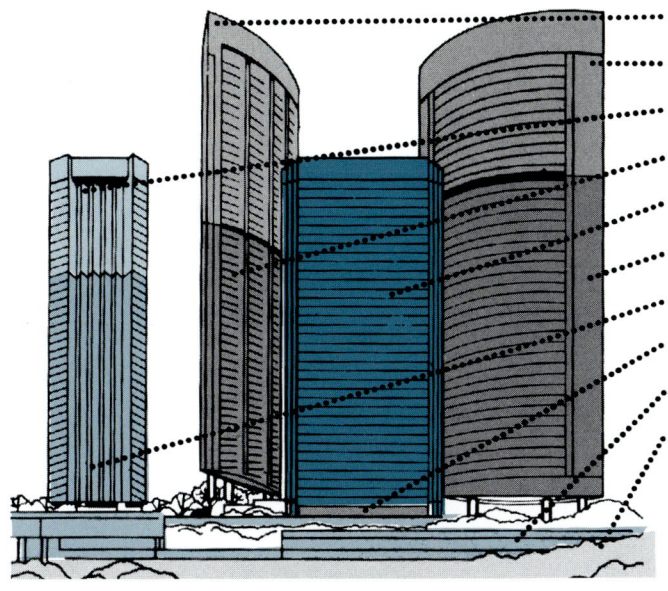

- Conrad International Hong Kong (513 rooms)
- Island Shangri-La (565 rooms)
- The Atrium (136 service suites)
- Parkside (243 apartments and service suites)
- One Pacific Place (860,000-square-foot office tower)
- Two Pacific Place (680,000-square-foot office tower)
- JW Marriott Hotel (604 rooms)
- Conference Center (750-delegate meeting facility)
- Shopping Center (800,000 square feet)
- Parking Garage (500 spaces)

the elliptical design. The building's shape made the design of the public areas and back-of-house areas challenging, a challenge that was met by using the spaces on the narrow ends of the ellipse for relatively small public areas and the space located in the wider portions of the building for restaurants, bars, and function rooms.

A hillside location allowed the architects of Pacific Place the opportunity to explore and design a myriad of convenient entrances to the complex at different levels. Above-

■ Conrad International Hong Kong Project Data

Land Use Information
Site Area (Pacific Place): 12.7 acres
Hotel Rooms: 513

Building Use Information

	Square Feet
Gross Floor Area	553,300
Lobby and Reception Areas	8,800
Guest Rooms	362,200
Business Center	300
Restaurants/Lounges	20,000
Convention/Meeting/Banquet Facilities	20,000
Health Center	3,800
Administrative Offices	8,300
Back-of-House Areas	51,100
Circulation	25,300
Mechanical Rooms/Elevators	53,500

Guest Room Information
Average Room Size[1]: 433 square feet
Average Daily Room Rate[2]: $240

Development Cost Information

Land and Site Improvement Costs	$38,975,800
Land	38,804,900
Excavation/Infrastructure	170,900
Construction Costs	$38,959,000
Furniture, Fixtures, and Equipment	14,787,300
Soft Costs	$23,898,500
Taxes/Insurance	409,800
Other	23,488,700
Total Development Costs	$165,620,600

Average Development Cost per Room: $322,847

Annual Operating Expenses

Fees	$5,710,100
Property Taxes	0
Income Taxes[3]	0
Annual Audit	32,800
Insurance	263,850
Marketing	3,755,300
Maintenance	2,455,000
Utilities	2,333,000
Legal	8,600
Management/Administration	2,812,600
Reserves (FF&E)	1,854,600
Total Annual Operating Expenses	$19,225,850

Project Team

Developer
Swire Properties Limited

Hotel Manager
Conrad International

Notes
1. Net area per module.
2. August 1996.
3. Net capital loss carryover.

ground and below-ground entrances to the hotels, shopping center, offices, apartments, and transport facilities make all corners of the complex accessible without the need to venture outside. At the same time, all three hotels are freestanding structures, each with its own porte-cochere and driveways.

Financing and Marketing

The mall, office, and apartment components of Pacific Place were financed primarily by Swire Properties. The three hotels have had various equity partners, including Swire Properties. Financing for Conrad International Hong Kong started out with 40 percent equity from shareholders and 60 percent bank loan financing. The hotel's equity is currently held by Conrad International Hong Kong (30 percent), Swire (20 percent), and Pacific Electric Wire and Cable (50 percent).

Conrad International Hong Kong has established a reputation as Hong Kong's preferred business address. The hotel has achieved brand recognition as a distinctly unostentatious, five-star address that is both conservative and can-do in its attitude toward product and guest services. The design of the building, the functionality of public areas, and the range of services and facilities offered to discerning business guests reflect this hotel philosophy. The hotel's core business traveler segment is supplemented by demand from upscale leisure travelers looking for a combination of luxury and locational convenience.

Its location and access to transport are key factors in Conrad International Hong Kong's success in positioning itself as a deluxe business address for visitors to Hong Kong. Many parts of the surrounding office district are accessible on foot by means of covered and, in most cases, air-conditioned walkways. The links provided between Pacific Place and nearby buildings make the mixed-use complex an outstand-

The hotel's lobby, function areas, and restaurants are all located on the mixed-use tower's lower levels.

The Garden Cafe restaurant.

A view of Hong Kong Harbour from a guest room.

ing example of the efficient (and stylish) integration of a new development into an existing business environment.

The positioning of Conrad International Hong Kong as a deluxe corporate hotel means that the hotel must stay ahead of the curve in terms of product. This has resulted in the continuous enhancement and upgrading of guest rooms, public areas, and restaurants.

In Perspective

Since opening, Conrad International Hong Kong has made some notable design changes, especially to the business center and the access to the grand ballroom. The 24-hour business center, which is located on the seventh floor of the hotel, was doubled in size to accommodate a boardroom, private offices with computers, and a back-of-house area for handling requests for photocopies, faxes, and the like. This expansion was brought about by high demand from guests for well-equipped and comfortable working space apart from the guest rooms. A solid core of guests needed meeting rooms on demand around the clock for conducting conference calls to Europe or the United States and otherwise staying in contact with their headquarters operations.

After a few years of operation, a growing demand for upscale corporate and social parties, including wedding parties, convinced the hotel to renovate the grand ballroom and its access in order to better accommodate these high-profile and profitable functions. The grand ballroom is located in the lower lobby, and it was originally accessed by escalators from the main lobby. The facility was well designed for meetings and conventions, which were usually split into small groups and distributed throughout. However, the escalators cut into the available space in the prefunction areas and caused congestion problems when large parties were held. The renovation of the grand ballroom provided the opportunity also to make major changes in its access. The escalators were removed and a sweeping grand staircase was provided from the main lobby to the lower lobby. The new design effectively doubled the amount of available prefunction space, which now can much better accommodate cocktail parties and other events preceding functions in the ballroom. Removal of the escalator also increased the main lobby's floor space. The lobby and ballroom redesigns reflected and complemented the hotel's original decor.

Walt Disney World Dolphin and Swan Hotels

Lake Buena Vista, Florida

Dolphin.

Swan.

"Entertainment architecture" is the descriptor frequently attached to recent Walt Disney Company resort designs, and architect Michael Graves's two hotels that opened in 1990 at Walt Disney World—the 1,514-room Walt Disney World Dolphin and the 758-room Walt Disney World Swan—certainly fit in that category. The two hotels were developed by a joint venture of Metropolitan Life Insurance Company (50 percent), Aoki Corporation (25 percent), and, as managing partner, Tishman Realty & Construction Company (25 percent), with Disney as a design partner. Together, the hotels comprise the largest convention and resort hotel complex in the southeastern United States.

The hotels are situated on 86.4 acres of the 42-square-mile Disney property in Lake Buena Vista, Florida, 20 miles southwest of Orlando. The hotel sites are owned by Disney and are leased to the development partnership for 99 years. The terms of the ground leases entitle Disney to a percentage of hotel revenues from room occupancy and food and beverage sales.

The partnership has a 15+10-year management agreement with ITT Sheraton Corporation for the Dolphin and a 20+5+5-year management agreement with Westin Hotels & Resorts for the Swan. Coincidentally, Westin gained an indirect equity stake in the project when the company was acquired by Aoki.

The hotels are connected by a canopied pedestrian bridge across a crescent-shaped lagoon. Landscaped surface parking areas for up to 3,100 cars are located on site. Hotel guests have access to four swimming pools, a themed grotto waterpark, a sand beach, eight tennis courts, and the Disney golf courses. Nearby Epcot Center is a short walk or tram ride away; the Disney-MGM Studios Theme Park and the Magic Kingdom are within 10 minutes by boat and bus, respectively.

Planning and Design

The distinctive architecture of the hotels has provided them with much publicity. Particularly when viewed from afar, the buildings have proved to be something of a curiosity,

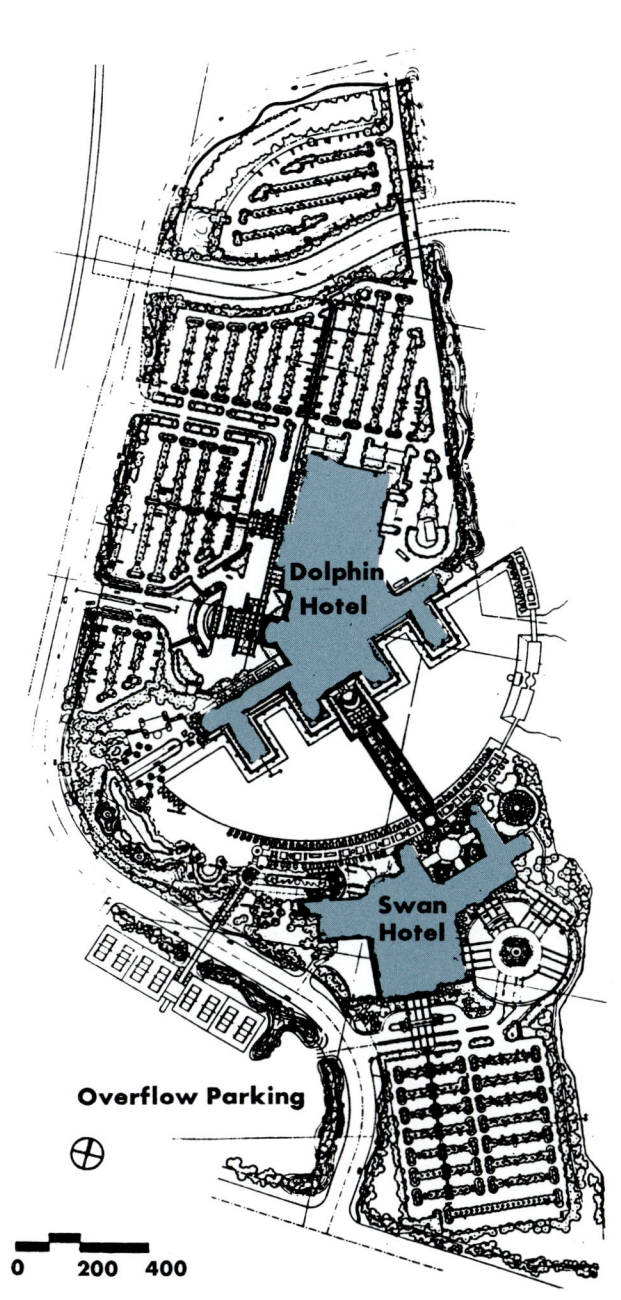

Site plan.

Dolphin.

Swan.

Key
- Public Areas
- Convention
- Guest Rooms
- Back-of-House

compelling park visitors to stop in and wander around to get a closeup look.

Columns—functional and decorative—dominate the scene at both hotels. From huge, boxy columns at the entrances to two-dimensional palm-tree columns scattered throughout, they play a principal role in breaking up long corridors or adding to the whimsy of the decor. The Dolphin's huge lobby is bedecked with a circus-canopy type of structure with a dolphin statue fountain in the middle. The lobby columns mimic trellises with flowering vines, giving the room the feel of an enormous gazebo. The corridors and some eating areas are enclosed by a sea of blue wallpapers with playful fish swimming. The Swan's lobby, decorated by a swan fountain, opens up to interiors that incorporate a profusion of water motifs.

Graves's attention to ornament and detail may be the reason the imaginative design works. From the three pineapples stenciled onto bed headboards to the beach scenes lining the corridors leading to the cabana doors of the guest rooms, to the cloud-shaped light sconces and brightly colored tables and chairs, Graves's design is meant to be playful and delightful.

Disney retained final approval of all planning and design decisions. Major decisions were made by a design committee that met almost biweekly while planning and design were underway. The committee was composed of representatives from Disney, the development partnership, the hotel operators, and the architects and designers. Graves was given authority for most of the design details, including even the silverware used in the restaurants and the ice buckets placed in each hotel room.

The project's landscape architecture also was subject to final approval by Disney. An Orlando firm, Herbert/Halback, Inc., was retained to implement Disney's general landscape

■ Walt Disney World Dolphin and Swan Hotels Project Data

	Dolphin	Swan
Land Use Information		
Site Area (Acres)	61.8	24.6
Gross Building Area (Square Feet)	1,400,000	617,000
Building Site Coverage	15.7%	18.7%
Floor/Area Ratio	0.52	0.58
Parking Spaces	2,450[1]	650
Building Use Information		
Total Floor Area (Square Feet)	1,400,000	617,000
Lobby/Reception Areas	30,000	10,000
Guest Rooms	718,600	329,000
Meeting Space	38,000	15,300
Restaurants/Lounges	40,000	21,000
Convention/Meeting/ Banquet Space	172,000	36,000
Retail	7,400	3,300
Health Center	3,000	3,400
Administrative Offices	20,000	17,200
Back-of-House Areas	226,000	108,300
Circulation	145,000	73,500
Guest Room Information		
Total Rooms	1,509	758
Rooms 325 to 375 Square Feet	1,358	625
Rooms over 450 Square Feet	151	133
Daily Room Rates		
Rooms	$179 to $350	$185 to $325
Suites	$425 to $1,850	$425 to $1,300

	Dolphin	Swan
Development Cost Information		
Site Improvement Costs	$12,100,000	$5,314,000
Excavation/Infrastructure	8,428,000	3,227,000
Landscaping/Irrigation	2,200,000	1,440,000
Fees/General Conditions	1,472,000	647,000
DolphinSwan		
Construction Costs	$128,282,000	$64,621,400
Superstructure	32,020,000	16,966,000
HVAC	10,400,000	5,234,000
Electrical	8,850,000	6,873,000
Plumbing/Sprinklers	10,200,000	4,437,000
Elevators	4,950,000	1,775,000
Finishes	26,265,000	13,347,000
Graphics/Specialties[2]	19,993,000	8,129,000
Fees/General Conditions	15,604,000	7,860,400
Furniture, Fixtures, and Equipment[3]	$25,695,000	$13,590,000
Soft Costs	$88,283,000	$35,364,600
Architecture/Engineering	8,991,000	5,235,413
Legal/Accounting	2,120,000	1,202,000
Taxes/Insurance	1,450,000	883,000
Title Fees	472,000	228,000
Preopening Costs[4]	11,860,000	6,673,000
Other	63,390,000	21,143,187
Total Development Costs[5]	$254,360,000	$118,890,000
Total Development Cost per Room	$168,000	$157,000

Notes
1. Includes 700 unpaved overflow spaces.
2. Includes site structures, pools, canopies, etc.
3. Excludes kitchens.
4. Includes sales, marketing, staffing, training, etc.
5. Excludes cost of special ornamentation, such as the swans, dolphins, cascades, and so forth, for which Disney was responsible.

Project Team

Developer/Owner
A joint venture of:
Tishman Realty & Construction Company, Inc.
Aoki Corporation
Metropolitan Life Insurance Company

Architects
Michael Graves Associates
Alan Lapidus Architect

Landscape Architect
Herbert/Halback, Inc.

Asset Manager
Tishman Hotel Corporation

Hotel Managers
ITT Sheraton Corporation (Dolphin)
Westin Hotels & Resorts (Swan)

guidelines, which were prepared by Edward D. Stone Jr. and Associates. Herbert/Halback collaborated with Graves on the areas closest to the hotels. Near the crescent lagoon, for example, Graves suggested a formal landscape, with palm trees evenly spaced and of similar height.

Disney was responsible for the fabrication of the large dolphin and swan statues. After consultation with the developer, Graves created the basic design. Disney made maquettes that were reviewed by the design committee. Then a final maquette was produced and ultimately approved. The statues were constructed primarily of structural steel and plywood with an exterior of "C" fiberglass, a type that Disney uses throughout the Magic Kingdom and Epcot Center because of its durability and the minimal maintenance required.

Construction

Site work began concurrently for the two hotels, in May 1988. Construction for each hotel took less than two years. The successful completion of the aggressive, tightly choreographed fast-track construction schedule was the result of a disciplined construction team managed by Tishman Construction Corporation with Aoki Corporation serving as general contractor. Construction began while many of the design issues were being hashed out.

The site itself was fairly level with scrub oak and palms as the predominant vegetation. The soil was distinguished by an extensive muck area where the Swan stands, loosely compressed subsurface sands, and a high water table that was somewhat depressed during the construction period as a result of two years of drought.

To prepare the site, the muck was removed and the excavated areas were filled with materials to support the foundations. Surcharges—a 40-foot-high mound of sand at the Swan site that approximated the weight of the future structure and a 75-foot mound on the Dolphin site—were installed for 90 days and 120 days, respectively, in order to stabilize the substrata. This process allowed the hotels to be built with spread footings instead of piles.

Regular meetings were held with officials of Reedy Creek Improvement District, the public authority responsible for land use, building, fire protection, zoning, pollution control, utilities, and other services on Disney property. The developer sought and the District granted a parking variance because market studies had shown that the parking lot of the Hilton at Walt Disney World Village was, at maximum levels, only 70 percent occupied, even when the hotel had a 95 percent occupancy. The variance allowed the Dolphin to build a ballroom where parking would have been.

During construction, an 18,000-square-foot preopening sales center was built consisting of 29 trailers opening up into one building. The center included models of three Dolphin and three Swan hotel rooms. Meeting planners could visit the site and see construction in action, as well as get a glimpse of the anticipated final product.

Dolphin lobby.

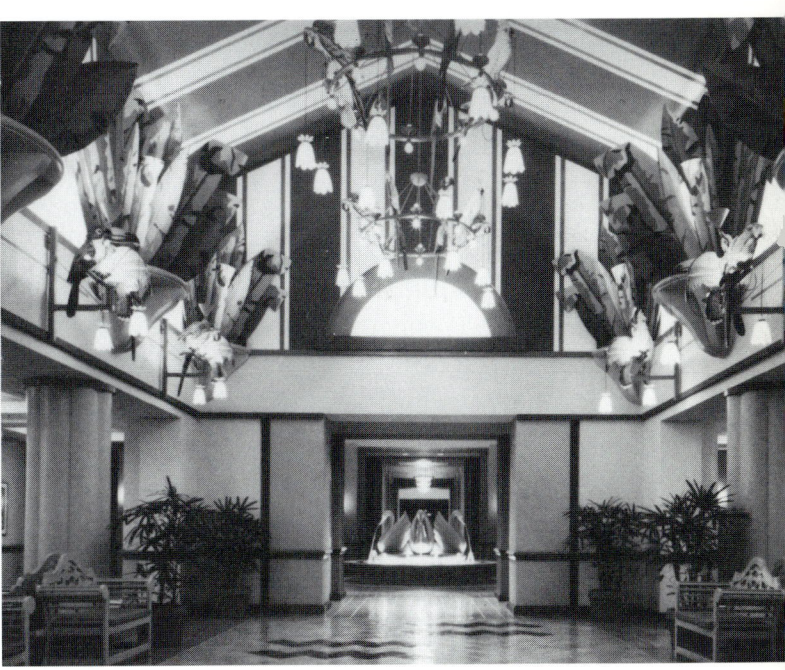

Swan lobby.

Marketing

The developer chose to have two separate hotel operators because of the marketing advantages. Many convention and meeting planners maintain loyalties to hotel chains; having two operators potentially doubles the exposure to meeting planners. For the first year of operations, the convention and meeting markets were a stronger force than

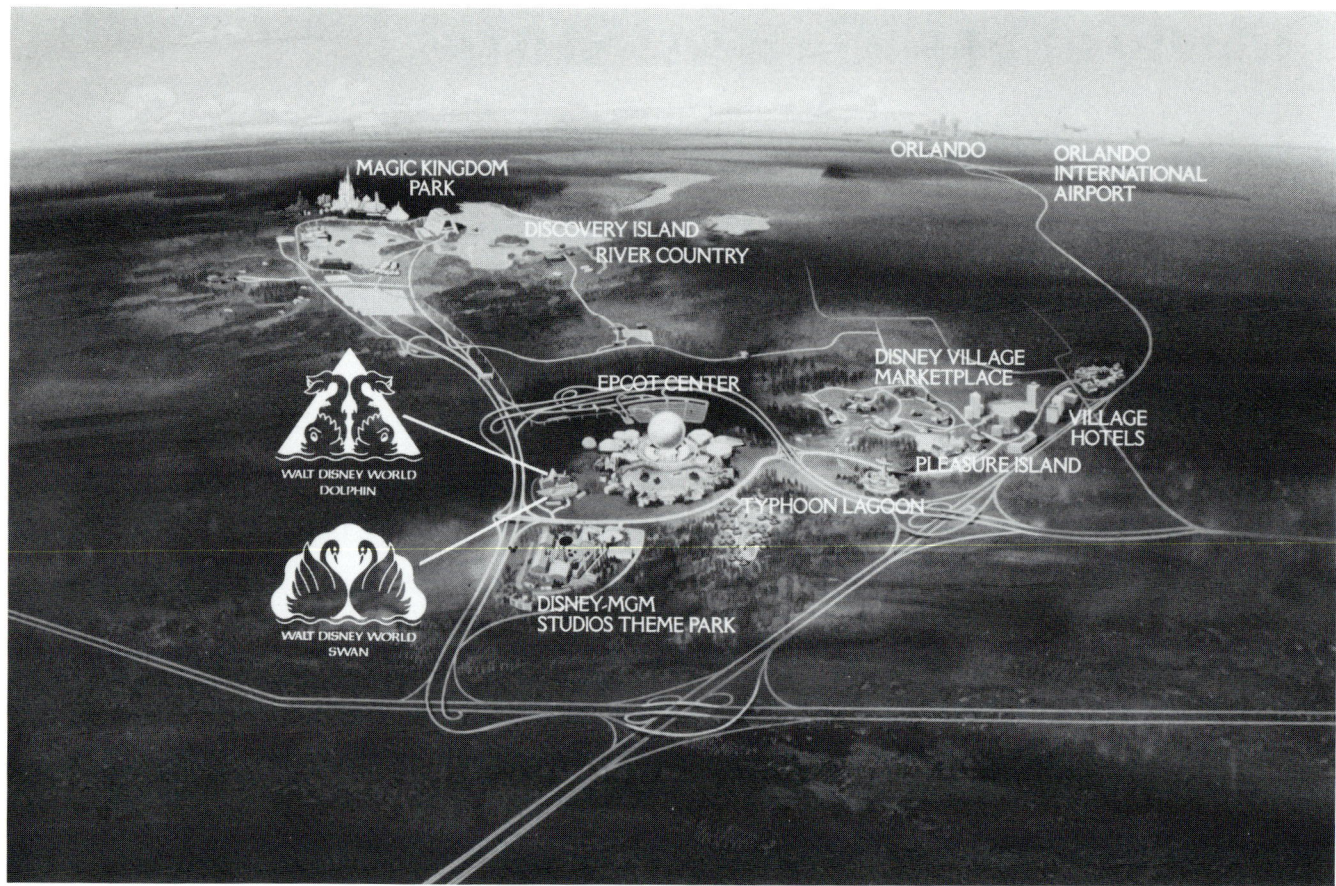

Location of the Dolphin and Swan hotels in Walt Disney World.

originally anticipated, making up 50 percent of the Swan's business and 60 to 65 percent of the Dolphin's. The top four markets for such business were Chicago, New York, Philadelphia, and Boston.

Through negotiation with the Walt Disney Company, rights to use "Walt Disney World" before the hotel names were obtained to give the hotels greater name recognition and association with the theme parks. Having two adjacent hotels under separate operational management but bearing the Walt Disney World name presents unusual marketing opportunities. The hotels advertise both separately and together. They purchase space in Disney advertising supplements and pay to be represented by a central Walt Disney World reservation system that serves the theme parks and hotels. Each hotel maintains a separate sales and marketing force in addition to jointly employing a marketing "ambassador."

In Perspective

- Because first guests are an important source of referrals, it would have been ideal for the two hotels to have opened at the same time. The first guests at the Swan, which opened in January 1990, six months before the Dolphin, had a completely different experience than guests do now.
- Retaining an on-site asset management group to monitor expenditures and operations facilitates involvement of the institutional owners in the capital budgeting process for each hotel as well as in the hiring of top management and marketing personnel.
- Careful siting of recreational amenities is very important. For example, Swan guests often do not discover the shared grotto waterpark, because it is not connected to the hotel's pool area.

DOUBLETREE GUEST SUITES/ NEW YORK CITY

New York, New York

All-Suite Hotels

Robert Wooley, founder of Granada Royale Homotels beginning in the late 1960s, and George Kaufman, founder of Guest Quarters beginning in 1972, pioneered the concept of the all-suite hotel. Today, the successors of these early all-suite chains—Embassy Suites (which bought Granada Royale Homotels in 1984) and Doubletree Guest Suites (formerly Guest Quarters)—are still the predominant players in the full-service, all-suite hotel segment.

The first all-suite hotels were an adaptation of the old apartment hotels that served as home to affluent individuals, as well as their servants, for extended periods of time. Before he moved into the hotel business, Kaufman operated a garden apartment with maid service catering to individuals who were relocating. Both Wooley and Kaufman focused on creating a residential ambiance by enhancing the guest room rather than on emphasizing the hotel's public areas. Thus, the guest room became the guest suite.

Today's all-suite segment of the hotel business includes many variations on the theme, ranging from independent luxury properties to limited-service, extended-stay facilities.

All-suite hotels provide separate spaces for sleeping and sitting. In some hotels, two adjacent guest rooms (typically 12 by 26 feet) make up the suite, with one being the bedroom and the other the living room. A more common layout is a single room of approximately 13 by 36 feet, with the sleeping area set up farthest from the entrance. Both suite layouts average 400 to 500 square feet. Suites usually offer such amenities as a wet bar, a refrigerator, and a microwave oven.

Although these traditional layouts are designed to maximize space and operating efficiency, variations on them are not uncommon. For example, well-located apartment buildings and other hotels are available on a limited basis for conversions to all-suite properties, and conversions typically result in a nontraditional suite layout.

As a counterpart to its larger and more flexible guest rooms, the typical all-suite hotel allocates less space to meet-

A Times Square location attracts business and leisure travelers.

Figure 12-1
Operating Results of Upscale All-Suite Hotels and Other Upscale Hotels, 1990–1996

	All-Suite Hotels			Other Hotels			Variance in Revenue per Available Room
	Occupancy (Percent)	Average Daily Rate	Revenue per Available Room	Occupancy (Percent)	Average Daily Rate	Revenue per Available Room	
1990	68.3%	$79.20	$54.05	64.1%	$70.17	$45.49	18.8%
1991	69.1	78.19	54.06	63.9	70.55	45.05	20.0
1992	71.3	78.66	56.11	65.3	71.12	46.42	20.8
1993	73.1	81.64	59.71	66.5	73.74	49.05	21.7
1994	74.4	84.40	62.82	67.7	76.92	52.06	20.7
1995	74.5	88.30	65.79	67.8	80.27	54.39	21.0
1996[1]	76.9	93.72	71.09	68.6	84.51	57.95	22.7

[1]Through July 1996.
Source: Smith Travel Research.

ing and banquet facilities, the lobby and other public areas, and food and beverage operations. Total space is generally divided as follows: guest suites, 75 to 80 percent; public areas, 5 to 10 percent; administrative areas, 1 to 3 percent; and service areas, 5 to 7 percent. Providing smaller and less elaborate common areas saves on development costs, so that the typical all-suite hotel can be built for approximately the same cost per key as a standard luxury hotel. Typical construction costs per suite (which typically involves two rooms, one bathroom, and one air-conditioning unit) exceed construction costs per guest room in conventional hotels by only 40 percent.

The suite product can appeal to business and pleasure travelers alike, offering the business traveler a separate space for working or meeting and other travelers extra living space and the flexibility of two rooms. The higher price for better value that is associated with all-suite hotels is the key demand factor. A study of hotel markets in 1995 (*Hotel & Motel Management,* June 1996) found that all-suite hotels attracted more corporate guests than leisure guests, except at resort destinations. Within both the corporate segment and the leisure segment, all-suite hotels tended to attract younger guests than did other hotels. Forty-one percent of corporate guests at all-suite hotels were aged 18 to 34; at other hotels, 37 percent of corporate guests were in this age group. Thirty-five percent of the leisure guests at all-suite hotels were in the 18 to 34 age range, compared with 30 percent at other hotels. All-suite hotels attracted a higher percent of families and a higher percent of affluent travelers (both corporate and leisure) than did other hotels.

Upscale all-suite hotels have historically outperformed other upscale hotels (see Figure 12-1). In the period from 1990 to 1995, upscale all-suite hotels achieved a revenue per available room (revPAR) that was 20.8 percent higher than revPAR for other upscale hotels. Among the factors accounting for this segment's high occupancy rates and room rates are the following:

- As a nonstandard room product, suites tend to be more immune to discounting as a method of attracting business.
- Guests are generally willing to pay higher rates for two rooms.
- Average stays at all-suite hotels are longer and these hotels appeal to weekend travelers—two factors that contribute to higher occupancy rates.

Side-by-side design.

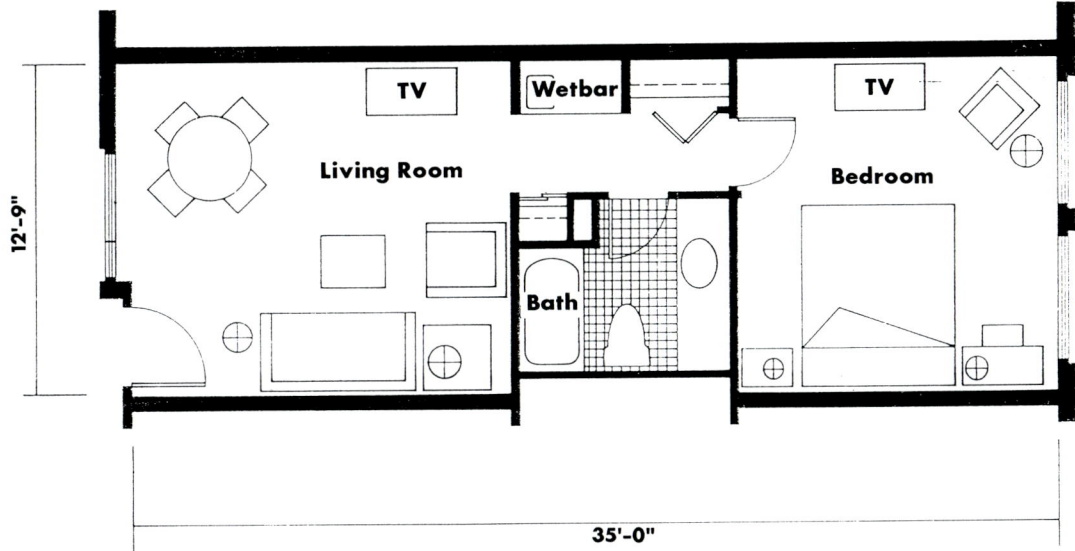

Atrium single-loaded corridor design.

- All-suite hotels are perceived to offer a high value for the price and their guest rooms can be flexibly used, so that all-suite hotels are able to target a broader demand base.
- The demand/supply ratio is favorable; all-suite properties provide only 5 percent of total available hotel guest accommodations in the United States.

Additionally, the all-suite hotel's smaller food and beverage operations, meeting spaces, and public areas provide savings in maintenance, labor, and energy costs—enabling these hotels to achieve high profit margins. While the all-suite hotel segment has achieved impressive operating results, the success of a particular all-suite hotel, as for all other hotel products, still depends on basic factors like location, brand affiliation, and management.

Doubletree Guest Suites/ New York City

Doubletree Guest Suites/New York City (DTGS/NYC) has undergone a number of major changes since its opening in 1991, but it has always relied on its all-suite product offering to maintain a competitive edge in one of the most competitive hotel markets in the United States—Manhattan. The hotel was developed by a partnership of Promus Hotels, General Electric Investments (G.E.I.), and a local investor, and it was operated as an Embassy Suites by Promus. Like many hotels developed during that period, it suffered financial distress. Unable to deliver debt payments, the hotel filed for bankruptcy in 1992.

In the financial workout, G.E.I. purchased the hotel and appointed Guest Quarters to manage it under the Embassy Suites flag. In September 1994, the hotel was rebranded as a Guest Quarters Hotel and in February 1995 it became a Doubletree Guest Suites when Guest Quarters and Doubletree Hotels Corporation merged.

Doubletree Guest Suites/New York City is a 43-story hotel located in the heart of Times Square at 47th Street and 7th Avenue. It has 460 two-room suites, as follows: 274 king-bed suites, 28 queen-bed suites, 144 double/double suites, 12 executive suites, and two presidential suites. The suite mix includes 12 family suites, 28 accessible suites, and 230 nonsmoking suites.

Each suite consists of a private bedroom and separate living room with a sofa bed, well-lighted dining and work table, wet bar, microwave oven, coffee maker, refrigerator, refreshment center, two remote-control televisions with cable and on-demand movies, and three telephones with call waiting and voice mail. Public and function spaces, other than the lobbies and registration area, are limited. The main dining room, Center Stage Cafe, is located on the fifth floor and seats 72 people. An adjacent room can seat an additional 80 people. The hotel offers only 3,600 square feet of meet-

A two-room layout and well-lighted work/dining area make the guest suites ideal for small business meetings.

■ Figure 12-2

Market Share Analysis for Doubletree Guest Suites/New York City, 1994, 1995, and 1996

	Fair Share	Market Share	Penetration Index	Occupancy Rate	Average Daily Rate	Revenue per Available Room
1994						
DTGS/NYC	7.0%	5.4%	94.0%	77.4%	$169.28	$130.97
Competitive Set	100.0	81.9	100.0	81.9	141.74	116.09
1995						
DTGS/NYC	7.0	6.3	90.0	75.0	165.74	124.25
Competitive Set	100.0	83.3	100.0	83.3	154.85	128.99
1996[1]						
DTGS/NYC	7.0	7.0	99.5	82.0	167.75	137.59
Competitive Set	100.0	82.4	100.0	82.4	164.37	135.44

[1]Through July 1996.

ing and banquet accommodations, with the largest single room able to hold 250 people with auditorium seating.

Doubletree Guest Suites/New York City is the only all-suite hotel in its competitive set. It has been positioned as family-friendly, a hotel that provides the comforts of home, personable staff, and a quieter atmosphere than the competition. This positioning has been effective in capturing both corporate and leisure business. Corporate travelers appreciate the hotel's location, the two-room suites equipped for conducting business and relaxing, the small size and quiet compared with convention hotels, and the availability of meeting space. Leisure travelers are drawn by the hotel's proximity to theaters and other local attractions, the value of a two-room suite for the price, and certain amenities for families—such as the Kids Club and family floors, which contain childproof suites.

The hotel competes directly against five first-class, full-service hotels in Manhattan: Sheraton New York Hotel and Towers (1,871 rooms); New York Marriott Marquis (1,911 rooms); New York Renaissance Hotel (305 rooms); Crowne Plaza Manhattan (779 rooms); and Millennium Broadway (629 rooms). DTGS/NYC's 460 guest suites represent 7 percent of the available rooms in this competitive set of hotels. A market share analysis for 1994, 1995, and the first half of 1996 is shown in Figure 12-2.

In Perspective

In its short life, Doubletree Guest Suites/New York City has experienced several changes in ownership, management, and brand affiliation—causing confusion and negative attitudes among guests and thus making the task of maintaining market share, rates, and customer loyalty more challenging. Furthermore, in 1995, the hotel completed a $3 million renovation of the first- and third-floor lobby areas and, while the renovation work was in progress, the hotel could not operate at its full potential.

The hotel's performance in 1994 reflects the typical challenges associated with a change in brand name. Nonetheless, the hotel was able to achieve a $27.54 rate premium, which produced revenue per available room that was 12.8 percent above the competition. In 1995, construction activity and yet another change in brand affected both the occupancy rate and the average daily rate. Occupancy fell substantially short of market occupancy, but the hotel still achieved a 7 percent rate premium, so that its revPAR was only 3.8 percent below market. Despite these challenges, the hotel's gross operating profit averaged an impressive 41 percent in 1994 and 1995, and its bottom-line profit averaged 22.7 percent.

Performance for the first seven months of 1996 was greatly improved, reflecting the completion of the initial renovation and no further brand change. Occupancy improved by 20 percent and average daily rate by 4.6 percent, for a 25.6 percent growth in revPAR over 1995. Doubletree Guest Suites/New York City penetrated its market at 99.5 percent and exceeded the market average daily rate by 2.1 percent, thus achieving a revPAR that was 1.6 percent above market revPAR. The hotel will be in good competitive position as it begins guest suite renovations in January 1997. Occupancy is projected to remain static over the next few years, and the hotel will rely on these suite renovations, along with aggressive marketing, to boost room rates. Competition and the pressure to increase rates are both strong, and the Doubletree Guest Suites/New York City is well positioned to realize the benefits of having an all-suite product.

Hilton Garden Inns
Prototype Design

The Hilton Inn is Hilton's existing product in the mid-price hotel segment, a market niche that was defined by Holiday Inn in the 1960s, refined by Ramada Inns and Quality Inns in the 1980s, and then redefined by Marriott in the 1980s. The Hilton Inn product line was developed in the 1960s and 1970s. But 90 Hilton Inns were eliminated from the system between 1987 and 1995 due to their age, leaving approximately 30 Hilton Inns. Rates throughout the mid-market segment are increasing, along with the average age of its hotels.

While demand for mid-price lodging has been growing, supply has failed to keep pace as other chains as well have been removing older hotels from their inventories. Thus, the mid-market segment over the past five years has been losing market share to new economy lodging products, such as Hampton Inns and Fairfield Inns by Marriott, and to first-class hotels that lowered their rates in order to maintain market share during the 1991 real estate and economic recession.

But by 1996, room rates in economy hotels had increased beyond the value that many of them offered in terms of services provided. In addition, first-class, full-service hotels were back in demand, and most had been able to recapture their higher rates. These factors restored demand for mid-

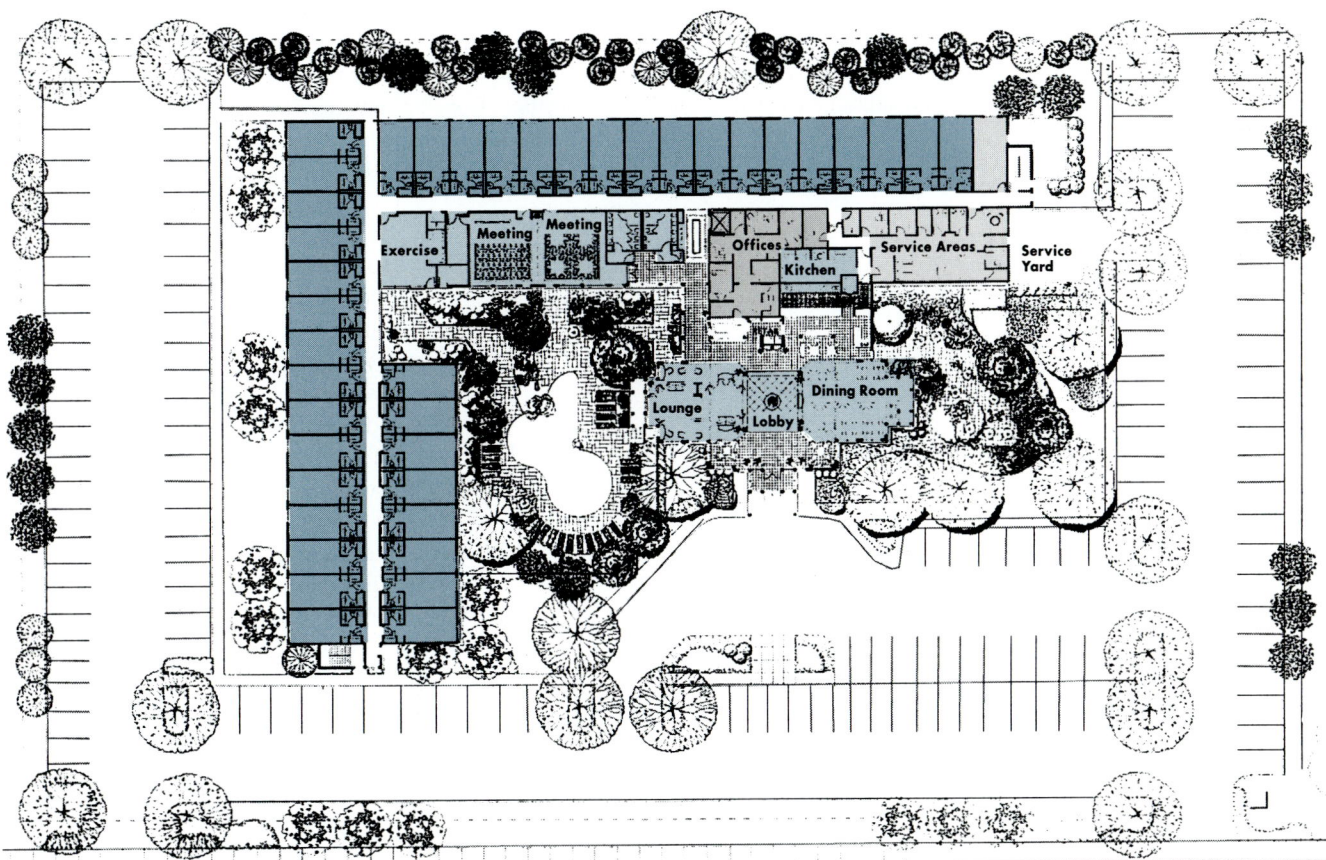

A separate pavilion housing the hotel's registration, lobby, and food and beverage functions is located in front of the guest room wing.

For the guest room wing, Hilton has designed both a low-rise prototype . . .

. . . and a mid-rise prototype.

price hotels, which currently constitute the fastest-growing hotel segment.

This is the context for the new Hilton Garden Inn. The Hilton Garden Inn targets value-conscious travelers and is designed for markets that cannot support a full-service Hilton. Positioned to be best in class within the mid–price market, Hilton Garden Inns feature state-of-the-art systems that offer operating economies without compromising on the level of services and amenities.

Its centerpiece is a structure called the pavilion. Located in front of the guest room portion of the hotel, the pavilion houses the registration area, the lobby, the business center, and the hotel's food and beverage facilities. It is designed—according to Hilton specifications—to be warmly welcoming and residential in atmosphere, while still functioning efficiently to minimize operating costs.

The goal has been to keep development and operational costs low, while delivering profit margins that exceed industry standards. The Hilton Garden Inn product is narrowly defined to distinguish it from upscale Hilton products.

The pavilion must be a distinct structure that is connected to the hotel—except in downtown locations, where the separation of guest room and other structures is not possible.

Low-rise and mid-rise prototypes for guest room wings have been designed. Each guest room is configured to combine business functionality with a residential atmosphere. The standard guest room is 12 by 26 feet, and it contains a hospitality center (microwave, refrigerator, and coffee brewer), an oversized work area (with a halogen lamp and task chair), two two-line telephones and a dataport, a 25-inch television with on–demand movies, a hair dryer, an iron and ironing board, and an easy chair with an ottoman or a sleep sofa. The number of rooms ranges from 80 to 250.

To justify charging higher rates than charged by limited-service hotels, Hilton Garden Inns offer many of the services that are found in full-service hotels. Employees are cross-trained to perform multiple tasks and trained to provide "focused service," which means service tailored to the traveler, whether an individual businessperson or a vacationer. Cross-training keeps service levels high and labor costs low.

Staffing levels, staff functions, and services are specified by department in order to make the Hilton Garden Inn easy to manage and operationally cost-effective, as follows:

- *Front Office.* The front desk provides guest registration, PBX service, and reservation services.
- *Food and Beverage.* Hotels must offer hot-breakfast service—at a charge to guests who use it. In hotels with 125 or fewer rooms, lunch and dinner service is optional, but if such service is not provided, a good-quality restaurant must be located next to the property. The menus are standardized—and engineered to offer a wide variety of selections that require a minimum of preparation time, kitchen space, and kitchen equipment. Restaurants do not have hosts/greeters or cashiers, so one or two servers per shift can handle the floor, bartending, and room service; one steward per shift can handle busing, dishwashing, and meeting-room setups; and one or two cooks can handle food preparation and service on the buffet line. This menu engineering for low staff requirements also provides a high level of guest satisfaction and strong profit ratios.
- *Housekeeping and Laundry.* Housepersons are cross-trained and minimally supervised, which, again, allows for low staffing levels. One supervisor manages a small staff and, after a training period, no inspections take place.
- *Maintenance.* One supervisor and a two-person staff manage the maintenance of the building. Maintenance staff members are extensively cross-trained to be able to accomplish a wide variety of interior maintenance and groundskeeping tasks.

The pavilion is designed for operational efficiency as well as to make guests feel comfortable and at home.

- *Marketing.* A sales director and, if the size of the hotel and the amount of meeting space warrant, a sales manager run the marketing operation. The focus is on individual business travelers. Small groups needing meeting space are accommodated only if the meetings entail guest room sales.
- *Management.* A general manager and an assistant manager handle management tasks. Accounting is centralized, but an on-site human resources administrator performs daily accounting, handles human resources and training functions, and oversees the administrative work flow of the hotel.

Hilton will provide equity investment and financial support from 1996 through 1997 to launch this franchise product line. Development cost per key will be the most critical element in financial performance as measured by cash-on-cash returns. Since room rates in the mid-price hotel market range generally from $65 to $85, the cost per key, including land and all development costs, will have to be at or below $60,000 to $65,000. Hotels within this rate range enjoy a strong stabilized occupancy potential in most markets. Together with low operating costs, such hotels should produce a high rate of return.

By the end of 1996, approximately 20 Hilton Garden Inns will be under construction. By mid-1998, it is expected that 80 additional properties will be operational or under construction.

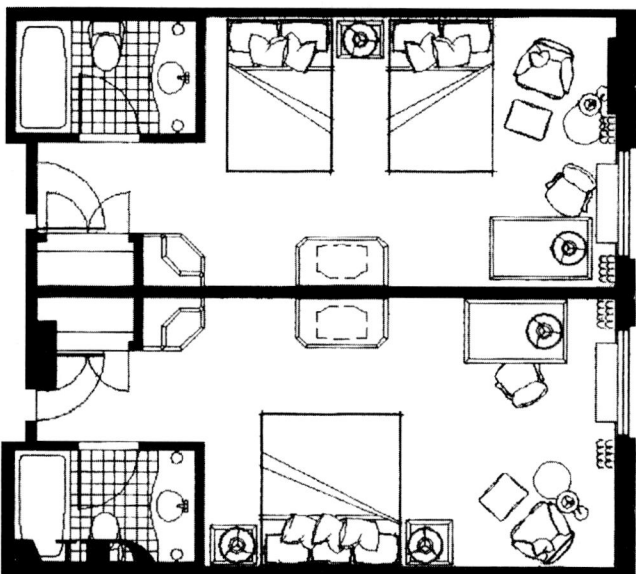

The hotel focuses investment dollars in the guest rooms, which are furnished to appeal to business and leisure travelers.

Holiday Inn Express/ Strathclyde Country Park
Strathclyde, Scotland

Holiday Inn Worldwide, the hotel business of Bass PLC (United Kingdom), launched Holiday Inn Express in Europe in early 1994. This initiative attracted interest from a number of potential franchisees. However, the U.K. lending community was reluctant to invest in a product that was as yet locally untested—without a demonstrable financial commitment by the franchiser. Bass decided to invest in the ownership and management of a number of Express hotels in the United Kingdom in order to demonstrate the concept and profitability of the product.

Holiday Inn Express/Strathclyde Country Park is the brand's debut in the United Kingdom. The 80-room hotel opened in April 1996. Targeted at price-conscious business and leisure travelers, the hotel is owned and operated by Holiday Inn Worldwide and is the hotel chain's 36th flag in the United Kingdom. The hotel was constructed on three acres that are leased from the Strathclyde Regional Council for a term of 125 years. The site is approximately ten miles south of the center of Glasgow and 12 miles from Glasgow International Airport, and is adjacent to an intersection on the M74 highway from Carlisle to Glasgow. Strathclyde Country Park, the United Kingdom's third most visited park, surrounds the hotel. It incorporates an Olympic-standard rowing lake, which hosts major international events.

■ Holiday Inn Express/Strathclyde Project Data

General Information
Site Area: 3 acres
Guest Rooms: 80

Development Cost Information

	U.K.£	U.S.$[1]
Design and Build Contract	£1,762,755	$2,813,000
Services	25,000	40,000
Suspended Floors (Provision)	30,000	48,000
Furniture, Fixtures, and Equipment	432,000	689,000
Professional/Statutory Fees	63,380	101,000
Contingency on Development	80,000	128,000
Pilings[2]	70,000	112,000
Capitalized Interest	148,000	236,000
Preopening Expenses	100,000	160,000
Working Capital	25,000	40,000
Total Development Costs	**£2,737,135**	**$4,367,000**

Total Development Cost per Room

Notes
1. At an October 1996 exchange rate of £1 = $1.5956.
2. Not a normal expense.

Another example of a Holiday Inn Express, this one located in Springfield, Virginia.

Guest room at Strathclyde.

The design of this Holiday Inn Express sets it apart from the standard corporate design. The facade gives the hotel a homelike appeal and fits in with the country surroundings. Distinctive landscaping helps blend the yellow brickwork into the background.

Smoking and nonsmoking rooms are offered, as well as accessible rooms for disabled guests. In addition to traditional guest room amenities such as hairdryer, remote-control color television, and direct-dial phones with voice mail, all rooms have a spacious and well-lighted working desk, computer/modem outlets for laptops, and an innovative, well-finished bathroom.

To support the business needs of guests, the hotel provides fax and photocopying facilities and makes computers and other business equipment available on request. Meetings for up to 15 persons can be accommodated.

A central feature of the Holiday Inn Express/Strathclyde is the great room, a multipurpose lobby and lounge in which guests can simply relax, enjoy a drink in the evening, or eat breakfast in the morning. A complimentary breakfast bar and a vending machine for hot and cold drinks and snacks are located in the great room.

Next to the hotel is a family restaurant and tavern that is not owned or operated by the hotel. Location near such a restaurant is an important site selection criterion for Holiday Inn Express hotels, although it is not a requirement.

Development financing was provided from Holiday Inn Worldwide's internal cash flow. Total development costs were $4.4 million (£2.7 million, or $55,000 per guest room. Furniture, fixtures, and equipment represented 15.8 percent of the total development cost.

The strategy of demonstrating this new hotel product by developing and operating a local prototype has proved its worth. The Holiday Inn Express/Strathclyde has attracted interest from potential franchisees. Stories in the press have prompted officials of the National Westminster Bank and the Bank of Scotland to arrange appointments with Bass to discuss the advantages of the Holiday Inn Express product for potential investors and ways in which the banks might participate in the development program.

The Hotel Roanoke and Conference Center

Roanoke Virginia

For more than a century, the Hotel Roanoke, known affectionately as the Grand Old Lady on the Hill, served as a symbol of grace and vitality for the Roanoke, Virginia, community, weathering major depressions and two fires. Over the years, however, time took its toll and, in November 1989, the antiquated and deteriorating hotel closed, laid to rest after 107 years.

But not for long. A redeveloped Hotel Roanoke reopened in April 1995, with $28 million in renovations and a $13 million conference center. The story behind the Hotel Roanoke involves more than bricks and mortar.

The Hotel's History

Built in 1882 by the Norfolk and Western Railroad Company, the Hotel Roanoke, like many of its contemporaries—including the Greenbrier in West Virginia, the Breakers in Palm Beach, Florida, and the Banff Springs Hotel in Alberta, Canada—was a resort destination built by a railroad to attract passengers.

Located on a hill overlooking the growing town's railroad passenger station, the Queen Anne style hotel, with 38 elegantly decorated guest rooms, was constructed at a cost of $60,000 and it quickly became the center of Roanoke's social and business scene. The hotel boasted some amenities that were considered quite luxurious, including an elevator that ran from the basement to the third floor, on-call chambermaids and bellmen, and a sewer line—the first in the town.

Over the next century, the Hotel Roanoke established itself as a premier resort destination, hosting such notables as John D. Rockefeller, Amelia Earhart, Joe DiMaggio, and Dwight D. Eisenhower. Although the hotel's classiness remained essentially the same, the facility increased in size tenfold and modernized in a number of renovations and expansions through the years.

In 1981, Norfolk and Western merged with Southern Railroad, creating the Norfolk Southern Corporation. The new company immediately moved its corporate headquarters to Norfolk, stripping Roanoke of its century-old railroad industry. Eight years later, Norfolk Southern decided to concentrate its resources on rail service, not room service. The Grand Old Lady on the Hill was closed and donated to the Virginia Polytechnic Institute and State University (known as Virginia Tech) in nearby Blacksburg.

Development Process

As a land grant institution, Virginia Tech's mission is to serve the needs of the people of Virginia. Within this mission, the university decided to renovate and restore the hotel to house a management/executive development and continuing education facility.

At the same time, the city of Roanoke was considering erecting a $20 million to $25 million convention center near the hotel, to attract business to its stagnant down-

Hotel Roanoke and Conference Center Project Data

Building Use Information

Guest Rooms: 332, including 19 suites
Conference Center: 63,000 square feet

Development Cost Information

Hotel Construction Costs	$21,893,100
Construction	16,000,000
Asbestos Abatement	1,305,000
Furniture, Fixtures, and Equipment	4,588,100
Hotel Soft Costs	$5,996,900
Architecture/Engineering/Other	2,216,900
Reserves for Operations and Debt Service	2,100,000
Preopening Operating Expenses	1,000,000
Taxes/Insurance/Other	430,000
Construction Interest	250,000
Total Hotel Development Costs	$27,890,000
Conference Center Development Costs	$12,800,000

Total Hotel Development Cost per Room: $84,000

Project Team

Project Managers
Hotel Roanoke Conference Center Commission
Wishneff & Associates

Developer
Faison Associates

Architect
TBA Architects

Interior Designer
CWB Design

Hotel/Conference Center Management
Doubletree Hotels

Purchasing Agents
INNCO Corporation
City of Roanoke

Scope, Funding, and Ownership

	Hotel Roanoke	Conference Center
Scope:	■ Renovation of a historic hotel, restaurant, pub, and public spaces	■ Construction of a state-of-the-art conference center, including a ballroom and meeting rooms
Funding:	■ $6.5 million bank loan ■ $6 million HUD loan ■ $7 million equity from Renew Roanoke ■ $4 million donation from Virginia Tech Real Estate Foundation ■ $3 million from land sales ■ $1.3 million loan from Doubletree Hotel	■ $12.8 million from city of Roanoke general obligation bonds
Ownership:	■ Virginia Tech Real Estate Foundation, 67 percent ■ Renew Roanoke, 33 percent	■ Hotel Roanoke Conference Center Commission

Sponsorship Goals

	Hotel Roanoke	Conference Center
Virginia Tech:	■ Provide practical experiences for students in hospitality, tourism, and management programs ■ No state or university funds involved	■ Facility for continuing education and for hosting regional, national, and international programs ■ Operational expenses and revenue shared with city
City of Roanoke:	■ Economic stimulation ■ 300 new jobs (hotel and conference center)	■ $1.2 million in annual tax revenue (hotel and conference center) ■ Operational expenses and revenue shared with Virginia Tech
Renew Roanoke:	■ Local campaign to secure corporate and individual donations ■ Promote civic pride	

Main lobby.

town. In the summer of 1990, the city scaled back its plans and decided to join with Virginia Tech to build a $12.8 million conference center adjacent to the Hotel Roanoke. All operational revenues and expenses of the conference center would be shared equally between the city and the university.

Financing would be through general obligation bonds, issued by the Hotel Roanoke Conference Center Commission, a body made up of city and university officials, that was created in 1991 by the state legislature to oversee the operation of the conference center.

Ownership rights to the Hotel Roanoke were given to the H.R. Foundation, a for-profit subsidiary of the Virginia Tech Real Estate Foundation. The $30 million hotel renovation would be financed by a $4 million donation from the real estate foundation and funds raised by the university through bank loans and other sources.

In March of 1992, Faison Associates was hired to design and build/refurbish the conference center and hotel. The firm, based in Charlotte, North Carolina, had developed two projects in Roanoke—Valley View Mall and First Union Tower—and thus was well known to city and university officials. As developer, Faison also assisted in securing capital and was responsible for recommending the hotel and conference center manager.

After a two-year search, Doubletree Hotels Corporation was selected as manager. Doubletree had experience in managing hotels for academic institutions, most notably at Harvard University in Cambridge Massachusetts, where it developed and operated the Inn at Harvard. Additionally, the company was able to provide crucial financing for the project.

Securing the financing for the hotel renovation became a greater challenge than had been anticipated, as depression gripped the hotel industry and the banking crisis of the early 1990s unfolded. A $6 million loan from the federal Department of Housing and Urban Development was secured, but a $10 million commitment that had been expected from area banks failed to materialize.

The city helped the cause by purchasing the conference center site from the Virginia Tech Real Estate Foundation— for $3 million. However, the project was still $17 million short, and Virginia Tech was compelled to set a financing deadline of December 31, 1992. If the financing was not secured by this time, the project would cease and the donation from Norfolk Southern would have to be declined.

With both city and university resources exhausted, the citizens of Roanoke rose to the challenge. In the fall of 1992, 300 community and civic volunteers joined together and formed Renew Roanoke, a foundation seeking tax-free donations for the renovation of the hotel. The campaign was a success. In just six weeks, more than 3,000 citizens and businesses donated $7 million. This included a $2 million contribution from Norfolk Southern.

This effort together with $7.8 million in loans and a $3 million scaleback saved the project. Renew Roanoke's contribution earned the group a one-third ownership right in the hotel it had worked to save.

Design

The operator consulted on all aspects of design, from the number of restaurants to the size, furnishings, and layout of the guest rooms.

However, there was little leeway in the renovation budget for design extravagance. Furthermore, under city and Virginia Tech guidelines, a majority of the products and services used in the construction had to be of local origin. Doubletree was able to marry the needs of the hotel with the requirements of the city and the university. The project came in on budget, with 80 percent of the construction products and services provided by local vendors.

The goal of the renovation was to retain the hotel's old southern charm while adding modern comforts and amenities. Many of the public areas were left intact. The lobby's mahogany paneled walls, marble floors, and historical murals were carefully restored. The Shenandoah and Pocahontas ballrooms were also restored. While the original Crystal Ballroom was razed, its chandeliers, sconces, wood paneling, and mirrored Palladian windows were incorporated into the design of the new Crystal Ballroom, which is located in the conference center.

The old hotel's popular Regency Room restaurant retains its legendary charm and style, and still serves its famous peanut soup and spoonbread. A meeting room was converted to a pub—the Pine Room. The kitchen was converted to meeting space, and a new kitchen was built in the conference center.

The guest rooms component was most extensively renovated. All the rooms were razed to the slab and reframed.

Asbestos was discovered and had to be removed at a cost of over $1 million. New plumbing, electrical, and heating systems were installed. Considerations of comfort prevailed over nostalgia in the decision to replace the original heating system, which was central steam supplied from the railroad.

The guest rooms were enlarged, which reduced the room supply from 400 to 332, including 19 suites, three of which have their own fireplaces. The rooms are decorated to reflect the hotel's history, but designed to accommodate the modern business traveler. They include desks with low platforms for laptop computers, two-line telephones, and speakerphones.

The renovated 19th century hotel boasts a 21st century, 63,000-square-foot conference center, with such features as ergonomically designed seats and workstations, video-conferencing, and high-speed computers that connect to the Internet. With more than 29 meeting rooms, including a 14,400-square-foot ballroom, the center can accommodate up to 4,500 people.

Two noteworthy projects funded by the Virginia Department of Transportation and the city of Roanoke are associated with the hotel and conference center. A pedestrian bridge, a $5.3 million glass-enclosed catwalk that connects the hotel to downtown Roanoke, permits guests and residents to avoid an at grade six-track crossing. The second of these projects—the Wells Avenue realignment—involved relocating the street to align with the main entrance of the hotel and converting it to a tree-lined boulevard with period streetlamps.

Marketing

Doubletree markets the Hotel Roanoke and Conference Center as a destination meeting facility specializing in educational meetings and learning programs. In the first year, group business represented 62 percent of the guest room

Conference center lecture hall.

Regency Room.

sales, with educational organizations and associations being the primary groups. The education market encompasses various forms of university and medical training, meetings, continuing education, and conferences. Virginia Tech is one of the primary clients in this segment. The association market consists of meetings hosted by regional and state associations, and some of this segment's meetings involve a number of properties.

The hotel aggressively markets to corporations and associations throughout the mid-Atlantic region. The marketing efforts are supported by Doubletree's national hotel network and its database of group-business contracts.

In capturing the group market, the Hotel Roanoke and Conference Center goes up against several formidable competitors located throughout the state. These competitors are some of Virginia's most prestigious hotels and conference centers, including the Lansdowne Conference Resort, a 305-room Frank Lloyd Wright–inspired complex in Leesburg; The Kingsmill Resort, a 405-room luxury hotel and conference center on the James River near Williamsburg; and the 335-room Westfields International Conference Center in Northern Virginia.

In Perspective

- Had numerous public and private organizations not collaborated and persevered, the Grand Old Lady on the Hill would not now be smiling down on the town that had fought so hard to save her.
- The early involvement of the hotel and conference center operator was critical. Doubletree's operational and development experience helped to create a hotel that would meet both functional and aesthetic needs.

Hyatt Regency Hill Country Resort
San Antonio, Texas

For generations, Texans have considered the Hill Country an ideal vacation destination. Likewise, people from all over the world want to visit San Antonio. Capitalizing on the popularity of both destinations, Woodbine Development Corporation of Dallas developed San Antonio's first full-scale destination resort on 200 acres of tree-covered ranch property. Hyatt Regency Hill Country Resort includes a 500-room, two- to four-story luxury hotel; an 18-hole, championship golf course; tennis courts; a nature trail for walking and jogging; a health club; and a four-acre, tree-shaded water area with a variety of recreational options. The hotel's traditional Hill Country architecture complements the site's thousands of native live oaks, limestone-banked creeks, and other natural features.

The Development Process

This was a project of firsts: in 1993, it was the first major hotel built in Texas in five years, and it is San Antonio's first destination resort, and Woodbine's first attempt to put together an international partnership for financing.

Woodbine's initial interest was in acquiring a hotel on San Antonio's historic River Walk. When the developer could not come to terms on the price or financing of such a venture, it reset its sights on land 20 minutes from the River Walk.

Prices for existing hotel properties in 1989 and 1990 had fallen to as little as half of their construction costs, so whatever transactions that were occurring in the hospitality industry were in acquisitions, not development.

Nonetheless, in September 1990, Woodbine and Hyatt announced that capitalization for the project had been negotiated. Affiliates of Shimizu Corporation, Kawasaki Steel Corporation, Woodbine, and Hyatt would provide equity. The Long-Term Credit Bank of Japan would provide debt financing. At the same time, the team purchased the 200-acre site from the Rogers/Wiseman family of San Antonio.

About four months later, as Woodbine was about to announce the project design team, the crisis in the Texas banking industry worsened. Bexar Savings & Loan, a financial partner on the underlying note on the property that had been purchased from the Rogers/Wiseman family, was put in receivership by the Resolution Trust Corporation. The RTC stopped making payments on the notes to the family, which was forced to foreclose on the property. While the banking crisis did not directly affect the resort project, it fueled the growing uncertainty facing real estate projects. In spite of the hurdles, the development team was able to close project financing on June 30, 1991. Dirt started flying on July 1, when the notice to proceed was given to the general contractor.

Design

The developers knew that their financial success depended on careful controls on both design and construction to ensure adherence to the $100 million budget as well as to the design team's vision of a four-star hotel. The extravagance of resort development of the 1980s was to be avoided.

The design team was led by a crew of Texans. Texans know Hill Country and they know that big live oak trees, craggy mesquite trees, and prickly pear cactuses are important parts of it. The designers researched the area's historical architecture and ranch style interiors and hired a local landscape architect to make sure that the landscaping was in character.

The project's interior designer, Wilson & Associates of Dallas, brought an understanding of hotel design as well as an understanding of themed design. To satisfy a conservative budget, local woodcrafters were hired to create replicas of 18th-century Texas wooden furniture, a solution that gave interiors a hand-crafted look as well as saved money. Some of the savings were used to buy lavish upholsteries, such as leather on sofas and wool tapestries on chairs.

After almost three years of operation, very few design changes have been needed. Exceptions include a larger health club and a larger poolside food and beverage outlet. In the design, poolside food service was minimized, with the thought that the nearby general store would compensate. After opening, however, Hyatt's cost-benefit analysis revealed the need for a larger facility at poolside. The added space paid for itself in added revenue in its opening summer.

The resort's entry road meanders through the rolling landscape, allowing travelers occasional glimpses of golf fairways as they proceed to the hotel's Town Square, the heart of the resort and the site of a century-old live oak tree.

The hotel's 500 guest rooms, which include 57 suites, are strategically located within nine wings that form scenic courtyards. The decor is relaxed. Country-quilt style coverlets and maple furniture with a washed-pine finish furnish the guest rooms. A themed decor is used in the suites.

Entering the hotel lobby, guests are reminded of a Texas ranch house, complete with a shady back porch. The homey ambiance is further conveyed by two massive, open-hearth stone fireplaces and small groupings of comfortable, overstuffed chairs and sofas. The pure pleasure of arrival is separated from the business activities—the front

Ramblin' River as it passes one of the nine guest room wings.

The Log Cabin suite.

desk and concierge services, which are situated to the left of the lobby.

Across from the front entrance is Aunt Mary's Porch, an area with an inspiring view, cherry decor, and comfortable wicker furniture where visitors can relax with a refreshment. An adjoining porch and deck overlook a 5,490-square-foot outdoor function space—The Lawn—that opens to the resort's water park and golf course fairways.

Two other public spaces—the Springhouse Cafe, a three-meal restaurant with tall windows overlooking the garden and pool areas, and Charlie's Long Bar, a traditional Texas style saloon with a masterfully crafted, 56-foot-long, copper-top bar—offer inspiring views.

A wide corridor leads from the lobby to more than 27,000 square feet of meeting space, which comprises a 13,590-square-foot ballroom and a 5,712-square-foot ballroom (the

Main lobby.

ballrooms have 22-foot ceilings and each can be divided into seven meeting rooms); 6,120 square feet of space that can be divided into as many as ten meeting rooms; a 1,050-square-foot private dining room; and a 450-square-foot boardroom. This configuration accommodates large meetings with smaller breakout sessions. Parking for 800 cars is adjacent to the conference facilities.

Outdoor functions can be held on a 3,808-square-foot deck outside the ballrooms, a 1,380-square-foot porch adjacent to the lobby bar and overlooking The Lawn, and a 3,600-square-foot covered pavilion with a large stone-front fireplace.

The resort offers a variety of on-site recreation, from fast paced to relaxed. A four-acre water park includes a 950-foot-long Ramblin' River designed for floating, two swimming pools separated by a cascading waterfall, an outdoor spa, a fire pit area suited for evening storytelling, and a poolhouse that offers towels, snacks, and beverages.

Floaters can take a side stream into a shallow pond designed for wading or journey along the river into the aquatic garden, which includes towering bald cypress trees and horsetails, to its exit at a sundeck lined with chaise longues.

The Ramblin' River gardens are part of a network of special gardens located around the 30-acre hotel site and along walking/jogging paths that offer guests a closeup view of local flora and fauna.

The Hill Country Golf Club, an 18-hole championship golf course designed by Arthur Hills and Associates of Toledo, Ohio, carefully preserves the area's natural landscape. The course was named one of the top ten new public courses in the United States by *Golf* magazine in February 1994 and received *Corporate Meetings & Incentives* magazine's Golden Links award in April 1995.

The clubhouse, which serves hotel, golf, and tennis patrons, is accessed by a dedicated approach from the hotel entry road. It offers men's and women's locker rooms, a 100-square-foot attended bag storage area, and a golf/tennis pro shop. The clubhouse also features the Cactus Oak Tavern and Antlers Lodge, a destination restaurant with Hill Country and southwestern decor and cuisine.

■ Hyatt Regency Hill Country Resort Project Data

Land Use Information

Site Area: 200 acres

Hotel
Guest Rooms: 500
Meeting Space: 27,000 square feet

Parking: 800 spaces

Water Park: 4 acres

Guest Room Information

	Average Occupancy	Average Room Rate
1993[1]	55%	$124.23
1994	68%	$138.07
1995[2]	72%	$152.02

Development Cost and Financing Information (Hotel)

Total Investment: $75,500,000
Total Investment per Guest Room: $151,000
Equity Investment: 31%
Financing: 69%

Project Team

Developer
Woodbine Development Corporation

Interior Designer
Wilson & Associates

Hotel Manager
Hyatt Hotels Corporation

Notes
1. Hotel opened in late February 1993.
2. Estimated as of October 1995.

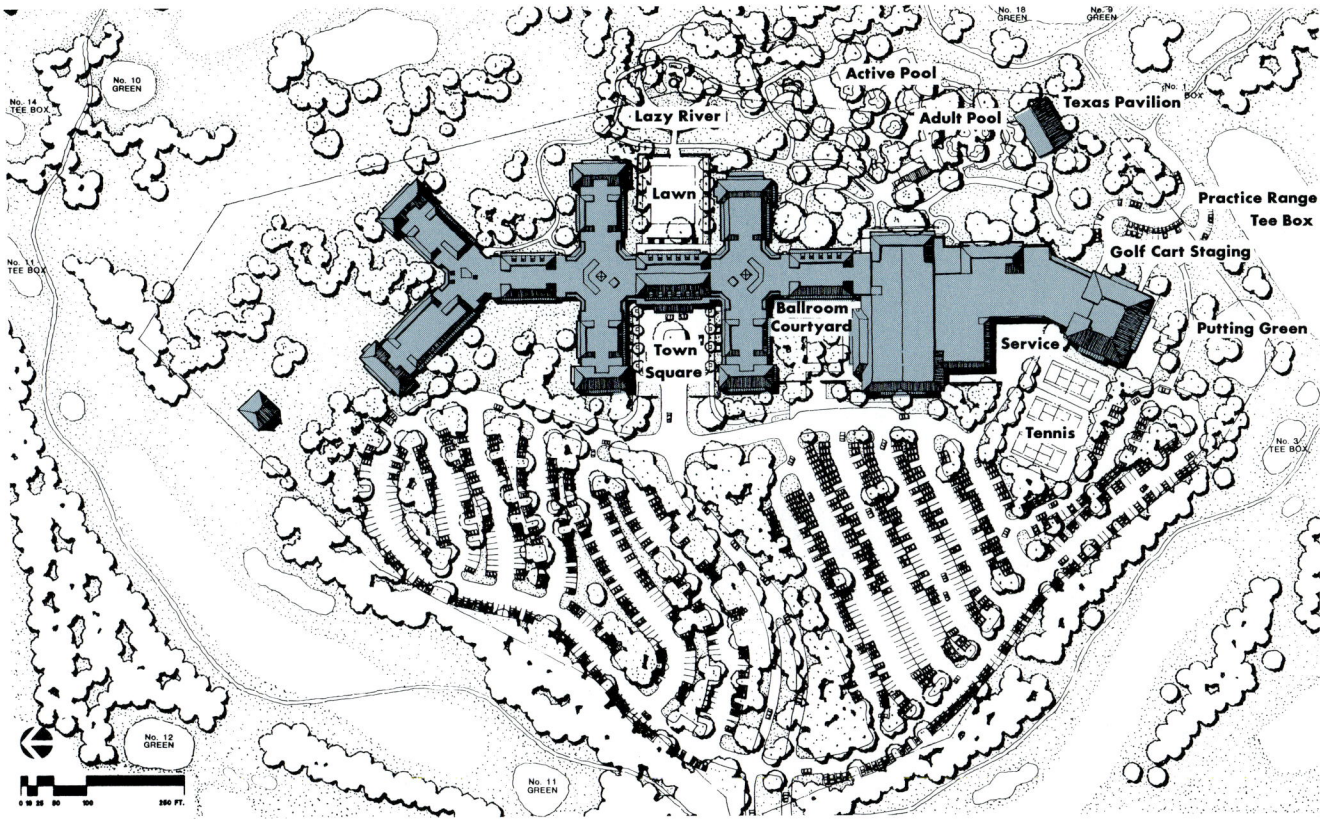

Site plan.

Marketing

The Hyatt Regency Hill Country Resort offers a combination of seclusion, exclusiveness, and self-containment. Its seclusion, however, presents a marketing challenge. Even locals cannot find the hotel. The developer hired a San Antonio public relations firm to ensure that the resort receives steady play in the San Antonio media. This firm meets regularly with the resort's marketing committee and is an integral part of the marketing team. The resort continues to be featured in regional and national travel publications, minimizing the need for promotional advertising.

The facility is geared to both the group and tourist markets. The developer believed the resort would attract tourists within the region seeking short getaways—especially working couples and families without the time or resources to visit East Coast, West Coast, or international resorts. They also sought group meetings and convention business to fill the rooms on weekdays. While San Antonio had been strong in the group market for years, it was not known as a resort destination. To complicate matters, the Hill Country was not an identifiable place concept outside of Texas.

"To the rest of the world, Texas Hill Country is difficult to explain. In our minds, this resort had to be more than a Disney-themed hotel, because Texans just wouldn't buy into that. It had to be real. It had to be positioned as natural and comfortable and casually elegant. So in trusting our intuition and marrying ourselves to the Hill Country concept, we took on a real marketing challenge," says John Scovell, president and CEO of Woodbine. "Needing to constantly explain, 'No, it's not on the River Walk or within walking distance of the Alamo,' the Hyatt sales staff found

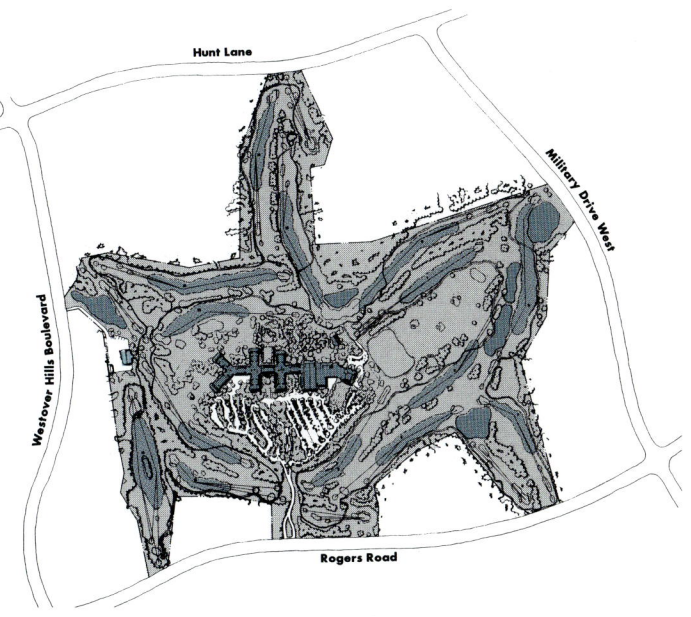

Golf course site plan.

141

A windmill evokes the history of the Texas Hill Country.

that FAM [familiarity] trips were the best marketing tools for group meeting planners, because once they got them on site, the sale was easy."

Thus far, the team is comfortable with the design and positioning decisions. With an average annual occupancy approaching 74 percent, the resort currently has an annualized market split of approximately 65 percent group, which is heavily corporate, and 35 percent frequent individual travelers. During the peak spring and summer travel periods, the share of individual travelers is higher, indicative of San Antonio's appeal as a vacation destination. Guests in both categories come mainly from Texas (Houston, Dallas, and San Antonio), the Northeast, Midwest, and California. They pay an average daily rate of about $152 (1995 dollars).

In Perspective

- Never assume that the so-called experts know everything. Do not be afraid to ask questions and challenge responses from consultants, the operator, and the contractor.
- Thoroughly evaluate environmental issues and the potential economic impact of mitigation efforts. At this development, the seemingly simple removal of an underground storage tank for fuel for agricultural equipment became a major undertaking when it was discovered that it had once leaked.
- Allow ample time for negotiations that involve a number of equity partners. Keeping the involvement of costly legal counsel to a minimum is highly desirable, although also difficult to accomplish.
- Do not underestimate legal fees in the project budget. Control of the legal process is critical. The business issues, to the extent possible, must be controlled by the principals more than by legal counsel.
- This project validates the developer's strategic philosophy of securing a local partner and using local consultants in venturing into new markets. They provide knowledge of the local political and regulatory environment.
- The preservation of water rights and water resources was a critical consideration in keeping golf course costs reasonable. An underground water source provides irrigation water and protection of the rights to that water will be a continuing need.
- It is imperative to bring the proposed hotel operator into the process early to contribute technical expertise to the project's design. However, it is also very important to challenge the operator's insights on proposed design changes from a cost-benefit perspective. Determine what the operator really needs, not just what it wants.
- A resort project can be designed and marketed to appeal to both the group and individual traveler market sectors.

Loews Miami Beach Hotel

Miami Beach, Florida

When the Loews Miami Beach Hotel opens in spring 1998, it will be the city's first major hotel to be built in 30 years. Located on Collins Avenue and 16th Street, the hotel occupies a prime oceanfront site in the historic Art Deco District of Miami Beach. Construction began in the summer of 1996, thanks to a seven-year effort led by the Miami Beach City Commission and several South Florida business and civic leaders, who sought a hotel to help the city's convention center reach its potential. Although Miami Beach had spent more than $92 million renovating and expanding the convention center, the shortage of nearby first-class hotel rooms had made marketing the facility to larger groups and trade shows difficult. The new hotel would focus on the group segment, while still appealing to vacation travelers.

Following a highly competitive selection process, the $135 million project was awarded in 1994 to Loews Hotels and its development partners—the Coral Gables–based Codina Group and the Forest City Ratner Companies.

The city's redevelopment agency is providing $29 million in financing, as well as $20.6 million for the land. In addition, the city has agreed to build an 800-space public garage across Collins Avenue and to reopen 16th Street to help alleviate parking problems.

Loews Hotels is providing $40 million and helping to assemble a group of banks to secure $66 million in first mortgage debt financing. Given the economic climate of the time, financing a project of this magnitude would have been nearly impossible without such a financing entity. Ini-

Loews Miami Beach Hotel Project Data

Building Use Information

Guest Rooms: 800
In Remodeled St. Moritz: 100
In New 17-Story Tower: 700

	Square Feet
Meeting Space	85,000
Grand Ballroom	28,000
Junior Ballroom	7,000
Other Function Rooms and Areas	50,000

Financing

City of Miami Beach[1]	
For the Hotel	$29,000,000
For the Land	$20,600,000
Loews	$40,000,000
Bank Consortium First Mortgage	$66,000,000

Note
1. The city also is building an 800-car garage that will serve the hotel.

Typical guest room.

tial studies have projected that the project will create 2,900 jobs, directly and indirectly.

The hotel features 800 guest rooms and suites—700 rooms in a new 17-story tower and 100 rooms in the landmark St. Moritz Hotel, which will be completely renovated to return it to its art deco splendor.

Miami-based architects Nichols, Brosch, Sandoval & Associates and Zyskovich, Inc. handled the design, which melds classic Florida architecture with the spirit of South Beach. The interiors are by Hirsch Bedner & Associates and the landscape architecture by Savino & Miller Design and Bradshaw, Gill & Associates. The decor emphasizes the romance of the 1930s and 1940s, but offers the amenities of the 1990s. The interior design blends Latin American, Caribbean, and South Florida styles.

Complementing the nearby Miami Beach Convention Center, Loews Miami Beach Hotel offers 85,000 square feet of meeting and function space, including a 28,000-square-foot grand ballroom, with opera balconies and sweeping views of the ocean, and a 7,000-square-foot junior ballroom. The hotel's 18 meeting and function rooms range from 600 to 4,000 square feet.

Catering to both the group market and the individual traveler, the hotel offers an array of recreational amenities. These include a 4,500-square-foot fitness center, swimming facilities, and a comprehensive children's activities camp (part of the "Loews Loves Kids" program). Among the dining options are four restaurants and lounges, including a casual bistro for all-day dining, a specialty restaurant in the lobby of the St. Moritz, and a poolside/oceanfront café.

With an anticipated market mix of 70 percent group business and 30 percent individual travel, the hotel is geared to offer products and services matching those in the best convention hotels in the world, and the range of activities and amenities that upscale travelers expect from a world-class resort.

Lobby.

RED ROOF INN/ALAMO DOWNS
SAN ANTONIO, TEXAS

Red Roof Inns is the third largest owner/operator of economy hotels in the United States. Its 248 properties containing more than 27,000 rooms are located in 33 states, primarily in the Midwest, East, South, and Gulf Coast regions. Founded in 1972, the company opened its first property in Columbus, Ohio, with rooms costing $8.50 a night.

Red Roof's hotels are designed to attract business and leisure travelers who are seeking good-quality rooms in locations that are generally comparable to those of mid-market hotels but with lower rates. The chain's targeted typical customer does not value in-house restaurants or cocktail lounges, banquet centers, conference rooms, room service, recreational facilities, or other management-intensive services and facilities. By not providing full services, Red Roof is able to deliver a product that meets customers' price expectations.

In general, Red Roof's guests are evenly divided between business and leisure travelers. The firm typically seeks locations near suburban freeways or adjacent to business parks, universities, hospitals, major recreational facilities, and other demand generators that would be complemented by limited-service lodging accommodations.

The typical Red Roof Inn has approximately 123 rooms of about 300 square feet each. Rooms contain full baths and are carpeted and well furnished and lighted. Rooms have dataport modems, desks, premium television channels, and television remote control to serve the needs of many business travelers.

The Site

Expected to open in late 1996, the Red Roof Inn/Alamo Downs is the company's second hotel in San Antonio and will allow Red Roof to increase its brand awareness in the third largest city in Texas. The inn is located in a densely developed corridor of retail, restaurant, and commercial office space and is convenient to Sea World, one of the city's major tourist attractions. It is near several major employers,

including Southwest Research Institute, U.S. West Telemarketing, and World Savings.

The 3.37-acre site is fully visible and accessible from the western portion of the I-410 beltway. The hotel occupies a 2.58 acre L-shaped parcel. The remaining area will be marketed to a restaurant operator. The location is on the east side of the highway and at the north entrance to Alamo Downs Business Park. A 195-room La Quinta Inn and a 72-room Holiday Inn Express are in the immediate area. These hotels have room rates that are typically $15 to $20 higher than Red Roof's.

Planning and Development Process

At the time the site was purchased in February 1996, all Red Roof Inn properties were company owned and operated. Each new construction project goes through a two-phase process: design management and project management. In the design phase, Red Roof's design and construction department prepares a preliminary site plan to determine if the company's prototype hotel will fit within the site and to identify any unusual site characteristics that may have to be dealt with. In the project phase, the site is fully studied.

The decision to build and operate a Red Roof Inn is based on a feasibility study that assesses current and future market conditions and determines the initial investment that will be required to construct the inn.

The market assessment was performed in-house, using information from Smith Travel Research trend reports and from representatives of competitive properties in the market; various local generators of commercial and leisure demand; and local convention and visitors bureaus, chambers of commerce, and economic development commissions.

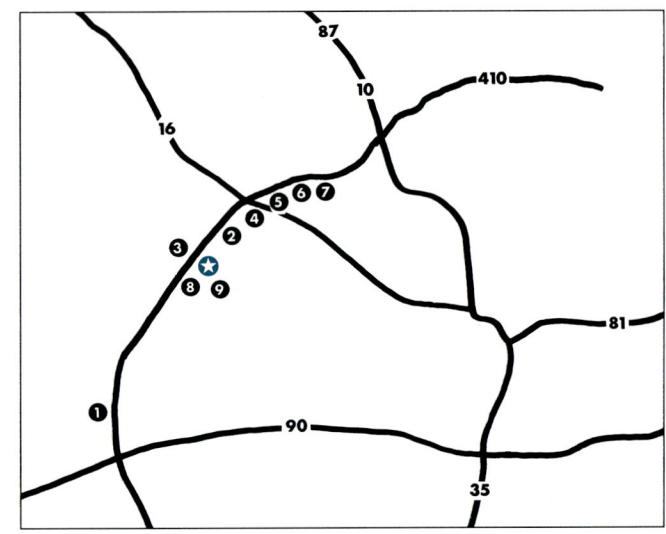

Competition
1 Motel 6
2 Stratford House
3 Best Western
4 Days Inn
5 Comfort Inn
6 Lexington Suites
7 Hampton Inn
8 La Quinta
9 Holiday Express
✪ Red Roof Inn/ Alamo Downs

The historical performance of the market was carefully analyzed to determine trends that may affect the hotel's future performance.

Concurrently, Red Roof's operations department evaluated factors relating to the day-to-day operations, including ingress/egress, signage, visibility, security, and local wage rates and other staffing issues. The firm's construction people assessed the condition of the site, looking for unusual circumstances, and they worked with local jurisdictions on zoning and permitting issues.

■ Red Roof Inn/Alamo Downs Project Data

Land Use Information

Site Area: 3.38 acres
Hotel: 2.58 acres
Residual Land and Restaurant Pad: .79 acres

Guest Rooms: 123
Parking: 133 spaces

Guest Room Information

Type of Room	Size (Square Feet)	Number
Single	28	288
Double	52	312
King	36	312
Handicapped Accessible	7	312

Development Cost Information

	Total	Per Room
Site Costs	$1,007,436	$8,191
Land Acquisition	772,035	
Residual Land	(350,000)	
Site Improvement	585,401	
Construction and Soft Costs	$3,986,100	$32,407
Building Construction	2,609,475	21,215
Furniture, Fixtures, and Equipment	522,578	4,249
Professional Fees	131,000	1,065
Construction Loan Interest	159,343	1,295
Development Fees	55,000	447
General Requirements	452,704	3,681
Startup Expense	56,000	455
Total Development Costs	$4,993,536	$40,597

Expansive soils, a typical condition in south Texas, raised site costs for the project above what is average. Other than soils, there were no particular problems associated with the development of the site.

The purchase price for the land was $5.25 per square foot, or $772,035. Financing for the development of all new Red Roof Inns comes from internally generated funds or from draws on the company's unsecured-credit facility. Typically, at the time that Red Roof enters into a binding contract for the purchase of ground, the company secures a five- to six-month feasibility period during which time several studies are undertaken.

Economy property occupancies in the Alamo Downs market range range from 74 percent to 84 percent. Projections for continued growth in demand suggest that occupancy at this inn will stabilize in the third full year at 78 percent. A $39 single-room rack rate in the first year, which equates to a $46 average daily rate, is projected to increase each year at a rate of 1 percent over inflation, or 4 percent.

Revenue projections, cost factors, and operating expenses were combined into a financial model that showed a favorable return. Hence, the project received approval. Construction commenced in April 1996.

Design

Red Roof Inns has designed a new prototype building based on input from customers and operational concerns. In particular, the design seeks to improve labor efficiency. The profile of the typical customer—including age, sex, income level, education, and reason for travel—was considered. Industry trends and the need to contain costs were other factors that were considered in the new design.

The Alamo Downs hotel is a three-story, L-shaped, 51,116-square-foot building. It has 123 guest rooms and 133 parking spaces and no food or beverage services or meeting space. The exterior finish is a combination of stone and stucco in earth tones. The building has a traditional, signature Red Roof Inn hood. To satisfy different preferences, the ground floor has an exterior corridor while the second and third floors have interior corridors.

The one-story lobby is centrally located. It measures approximately 4,200 square feet and contains elevators and a vending area.

The central core also contains the back-of-house areas—the laundry and maintenance operations. Locating all operations centrally enhances employee security. Red Roof operates a night laundry so that the hotels have both an auditor and a laundry person on duty during the night hours. Additionally, a central core equalizes the distances between the guest rooms and housekeeping operations, thereby lowering the labor costs associated with room maintenance.

Rooms sizes range from 288 square feet for single rooms to 312 square feet for double and king-size rooms. Room mix, which is determined through an analysis of business and leisure demand generators in the market, is as follows:

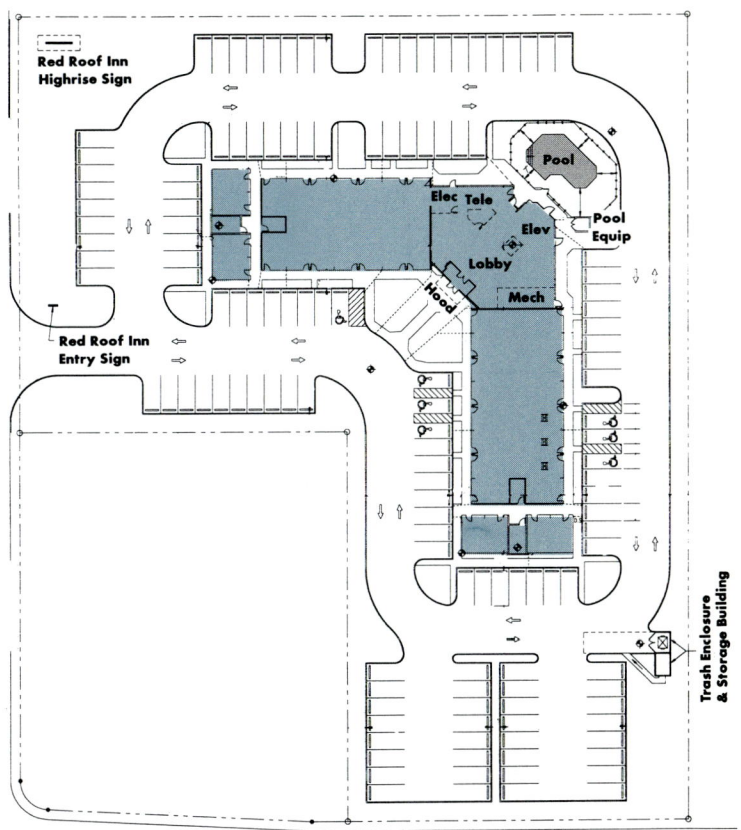

Site plan.

singles (22 percent), doubles (42 percent), king-size rooms (29 percent), and accessible (6 percent). All guest rooms have a full bathroom with a full-size vanity. All are furnished with a remote-control color television, a direct-dial telephone, and individually controlled heating and air-conditioning units. Business king-size rooms have a computer modem hookup. Rates range from $38.99 for a single room up to $53.99 for a business king-size room.

Marketing

The marketing strategy for a particular property is based on Red Roof's customer profile and the specific demand generators at the property. The average Red Roof customer is 43.3 years old with an income of $48,700. Fifty-four percent are college educated, and 86 percent are employed (42 percent are in management or professional positions; 29 percent are in technical, sales, or administrative positions; and 5 percent are in service occupations). Their reason for travel is business (53 percent) or leisure (47 percent).

Red Roof Inn's reservation system and 800 number deliver a high number of room nights and significantly outperform the economy lodging segment. At Red Roof Inns, 81 percent of the guests arrive with reservations (compared with 71 percent for the economy segment as a whole). At Red Roof, 45 percent of the guests make their reservations

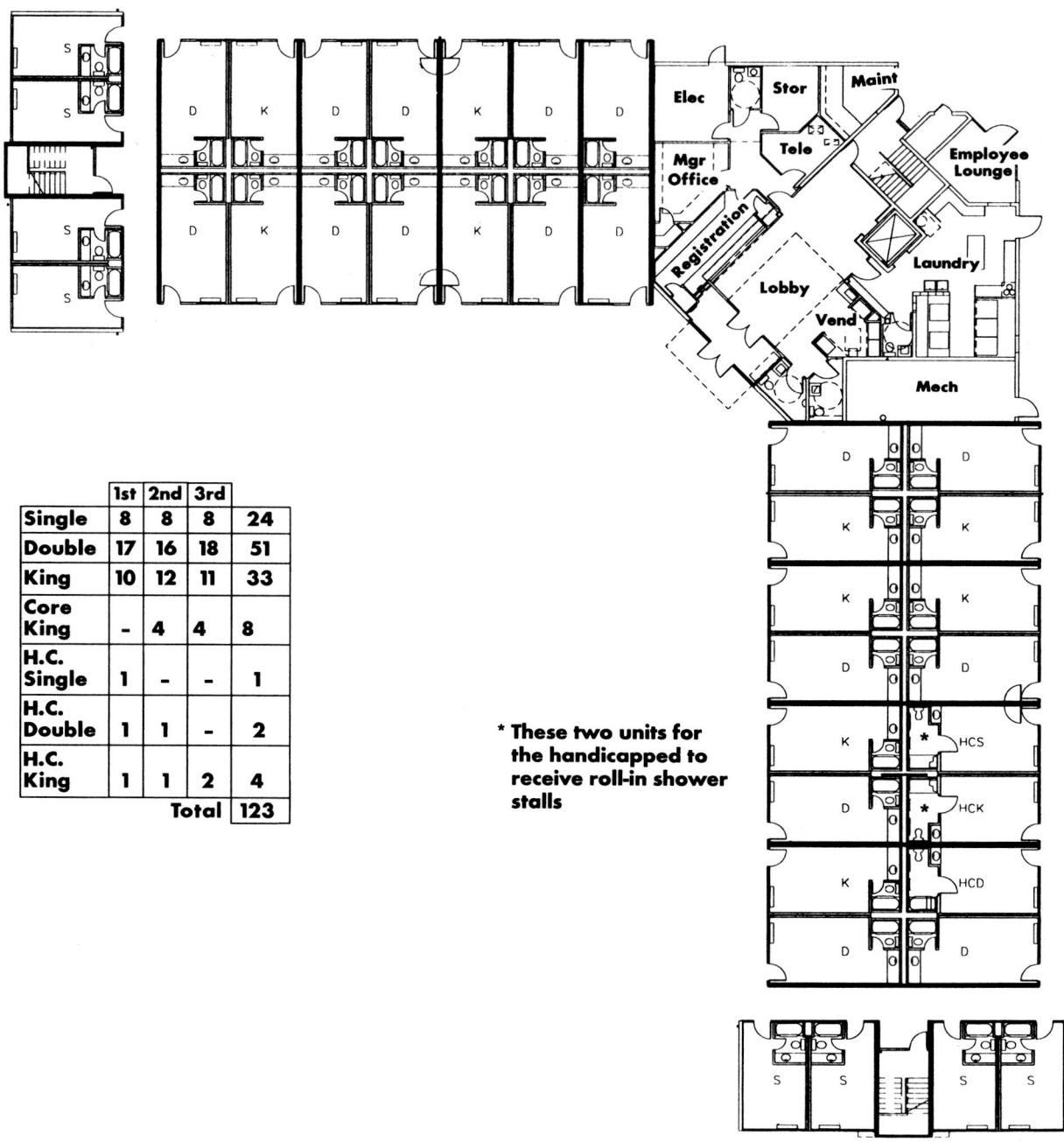

	1st	2nd	3rd	
Single	8	8	8	24
Double	17	16	18	51
King	10	12	11	33
Core King	–	4	4	8
H.C. Single	1	–	–	1
H.C. Double	1	1	–	2
H.C. King	1	1	2	4
			Total	123

* These two units for the handicapped to receive roll-in shower stalls

First-floor plan.

through the 800 number (versus 24 percent for all economy hotels); 20 percent make them directly with the hotel (versus 27 percent); and 3 percent make reservations through a travel agent (versus 5 percent for the economy segment as a whole).

Red Roof is relatively new in south Texas and specifically in the city of San Antonio. The Alamo Downs hotel, therefore, initially will not receive a Red Roof Inn's customary high number of reserved room nights through the central reservation system. Red Roof will aggressively market the property via traditional media outlets, which include regional *USA Today* advertising and spot radio and television ads.

A grand opening public relations effort and marketing support from other Red Roof Inn properties are planned. A blitz marketing effort will be made to the commercial demand generators in the area. Direct mail and reservation center marketing will help kick off the property. Roadside billboards visible from cars traveling in both directions along I-410 will be placed near the property.

Sheraton Great Valley Hotel

Chester County, Pennsylvania

Located in the western suburbs of Philadelphia at the southern limit of the Great Valley/U.S. Route 202 corridor, the 154-room, full-service Sheraton Great Valley Hotel opened in July 1990, a difficult time for hotels in the recessionary northeastern United States.

The project had its beginnings in the mid-1980s, with the assemblage of the site. However, because of numerous delays in the zoning approval process and in the extension of a sewer main, the hotel missed out on the boom years of the late 1980s. Nonetheless, it has been a success. Its performance has consistently improved since it opened. In the fourth quarter 1994, the hotel was recognized by Sheraton as having one of the most improved levels of service in its division, earning it membership in the chain's Chairman's Club. The hotel is consistently rated by its guests among the top 10 percent of Sheratons worldwide.

The Site and Development Process

The Sheraton Great Valley is situated at the interchange of U.S. Route 202 and U.S. Route 30. During the 1980s, numerous business/corporate parks and an abundance of retail facilities developed along Route 202, a limited-access highway with links to the Pennsylvania Turnpike and the Schuylkill Expressway to Philadelphia. The business parks provide the bulk of demand for area hotels. The location is also convenient to tourist and visitor attractions, including Valley Forge National Park, and accessible via Route 30 to the attractions of Lancaster County to the west. The Sheraton competes with a number of other hotels along the Route 202 corridor for marketwide demand. All built in the mid- to late 1980s, the competitors include a 230-room Doubletree Guest Suites, a 150-room Marriott Courtyard, and the 201-room Desmond Hotel & Conference Center (formerly a Hilton).

The development entity, Glen Lincoln, Inc., was formed for the sole purpose of developing the hotel. It is made up of eight local investors engaged in a variety of businesses. The president, Michael S. Lehnkering, operates a design and development firm, MSL Associates, Ltd. With no specific development plans in mind, he began assembling the site on a speculative basis in the mid-1980s. Rather quickly, however, development trends pointed to a hotel as the highest and best use for the site.

White Horse Restaurant.

Indoor pool.

Glen Lincoln obtained a miniperm construction loan in the amount of $9 million from Meridian Bank. Total project costs approximated $10 million, including site acquisition costs of $632,000.

Design

The hotel has a Chester County theme, playing off the county's historic setting and sense of place. A six-story hotel tower containing the guest rooms, main lobby, a 75-seat lounge (Chesterfield's), and an indoor pool is connected by means of a single-story structure to two fully renovated historic buildings: a circa 1874 tavern that now houses five meeting rooms making up most of the hotel's 6,500 square feet of meeting and function space and a circa 1825 residence that now houses the 125-seat White Horse Restaurant. In 1990, the hotel won Sheraton's award for "Best Interior Atmosphere—New Construction."

Guest rooms are attractively furnished in a traditional motif—including poster beds in the king-bed units—in keeping with the Chester County theme. Modern conveniences include two telephones, fully stocked minibars, and coffee makers. Most rooms are equipped with telefax or computer access. Standard guest rooms are approximately 324 square feet. The two Parlor Suites are 473 square feet and have a wet bar and whirlpool bath. The Ambassador Suite and the Presidential Suite, which are each approximately 1,200 square feet, have two baths and a dining room.

The White Horse Restaurant's seven dining rooms—all with fireplaces—occupy two levels. The restaurant features oriental rugs and original hand-carved wooden mantelpieces. Chesterfield's, the lounge, is located in the connecting structure adjacent to the restaurant and elevated above the lobby. It features stuffed armchairs, a cathedral ceiling, and a wood-burning fireplace. The lower level of the hotel tower contains the 1,950-square-foot Regency Ballroom (capacity 200) and the tower's indoor pool area offers an unusual reception area.

Within its defined market, the Sheraton Great Valley thus offers a lodging alternative with an ambiance that distinguishes it from its competition.

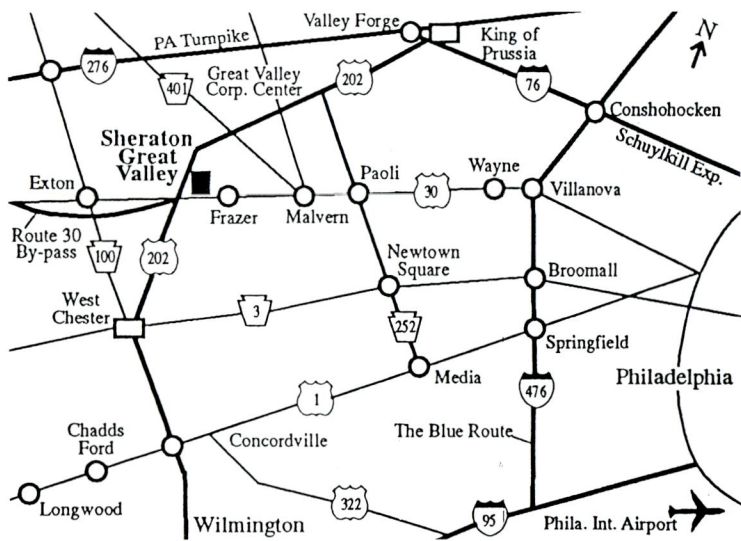
Location map.

Marketing

Since its opening in the depths of a regional recession, the Sheraton Great Valley has shown consistent improvement in occupancy and rate levels. While the Sheraton affiliation contributes to occupancy, the hotel has succeeded primarily through word of mouth and referrals. It has achieved a substantial amount of repeat business.

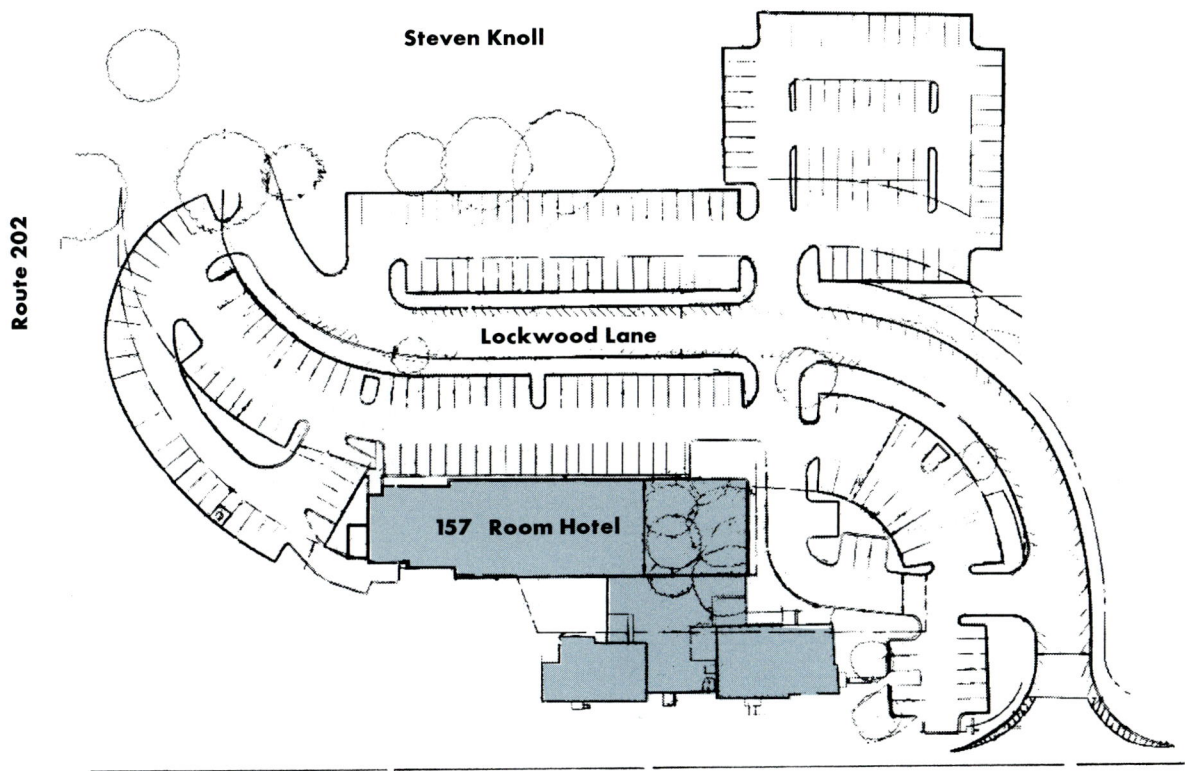

Site plan.

■ Sheraton Great Valley Hotel Project Data

Land Use Information

Site Area: 4.5 acres
Guest Rooms: 154
Restaurant: 125 seats
Lounge: 75 seats
Meeting and Function Space: 6,500 square feet
Parking: 252 spaces

Guest Room Information

Type of Room	Number	Size (Square Feet)
Double/Double	74	324
King-Bed Double	76	324
Parlor Suites	2	473
Suites	2	1,200

Meeting Space Information

	Size (Square Feet)	Maximum Seating Theater	Maximum Seating Banquet
Regency Ballroom	1,950	216	200
Astoria	1,128	127	100
Cambridge/Windsor	1,250	130	80
Westminster	651	73	50
Small Rooms (4)		<20	18–28

Development Cost Information

Site Costs	$733,500
Land Acquisition	632,000
Site Preparation	101,500
Construction Costs	$6,366,620
Furniture, Fixtures, and Equipment	$1,306,435
Soft Costs	$1,587,650
Total Development Costs	$9,994.205

Total Development Cost per Room: $64,897

Project Team

Developer
Glen Lincoln, Inc.

Architect
MSL Associates, Ltd.

Hotel Manager
Meyer-Jabara Hotels

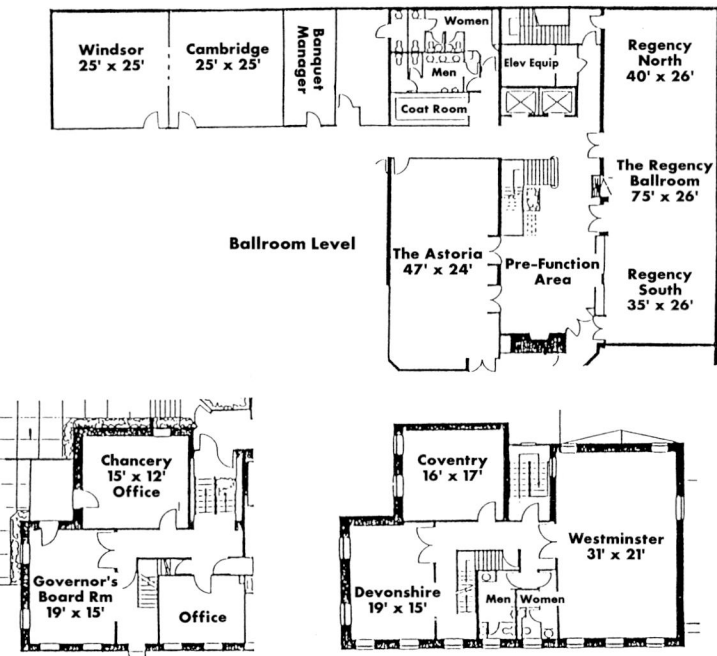

Floor plans.

Regency Ballroom.

QVC, a nearby home shopping TV network, began recommending the hotel shortly after its opening. The network's chairman, Barry Diller, rented the Presidential Suite for three months. The hotel numbers many celebrities among its regular patrons, including Joan Rivers, Susan Lucci, Victoria Principal, Bob Hope, and Mary Tyler Moore. Bell Atlantic's PGA tournament, held annually at the nearby Chester Valley Golf Club, has brought in such name guests as Arnold Palmer, Jack Nicklaus, Chi Chi Rodriguez, and Raymond Floyd, as well as ESPN executives. The hotel enjoys a large and loyal local patronage. It hosts about 60 weddings annually and a number of local meetings, including regularly scheduled Rotary and Kiwanis meetings. The restaurant and lounge achieve above-average revenue from local customers.

The Sheraton Great Valley's market is approximately 51 percent corporate, with major accounts including Shared Medical Systems, QVC, Smith Kline Beecham (now Phizer), and the Vanguard Group. The remainder of the market mix is 31 percent group—made up of both corporate meetings and local social events—and 17 percent leisure. The leisure guests are attracted by the nearby King of Prussia retail complex, Valley Forge National Park, and various Chester County visitor and tourist attractions.

Appendices

Appendix 1
Leading Hotel Chains, 1996

	U.S. Properties		Status of U.S. Properties				Foreign Properties	
	Number of Rooms	Number of Properties	Company Owned	Franchised/ Licensed	Management Contract	Other	Number of Rooms	Number of Properties
Hospitality Franchise Systems								
339 Jefferson Road								
P.O. Box 278								
Parsippany, New Jersey 07054-0278								
Days Inn of America	151,754	1,590	0	1,590	0	0	4,964	50
Howard Johnson	57,739	540	0	540	0	0	6,525	52
Ramada	120,853	813	0	813	0	0	0	0
Super 8 Motels	76,725	1,254	0	1,254	0	0	1,753	28
Park Inn International	6,790	53	0	53	0	0	0	0
Villager Lodge	2,567	23	0	23	0	0	0	0
Travelodge	28,400	354	116	237	1	0	8,520	76
Thriftlodge	1,620	31	13	18	0	0	180	2
Knights Court	892	10	0	10	0	0	0	0
Knights Inn	15,702	173	0	173	0	0	144	2
TOTAL	**463,041**	**4,841**	**129**	**4,711**	**1**	**0**	**22,086**	**210**
Holiday Inn Worldwide								
3 Ravinia Drive								
Paranta, Georgia 30338								
Holiday Inn Hotels	241,839	1,366	39	11,310	11	6	41,653	271
Holiday Inn Suites/Hotel & Suites	468	2	0	2	0	0	557	4
Crowne Plaza Hotel & Resorts	12,310	35	3	27	0	0	21,030	67
Holiday Inn Express	25,199	288	1	287	0	0	1,930	19
Holiday Resort/Sunspree	3,224	14	0	14	0	0	920	7
Holiday Inn Garden Court	0	0	0	0	0	0	9,292	61
Holiday Inn Select	2,788	10	5	5	0	0	220	1
TOTAL	**285,828**	**1,715**	**48**	**1,645**	**11**	**6**	**75,575**	**430**
Choice Hotels International								
10750 Columbia Pike								
Silver Spring, Maryland 20901								
Clarion Hotels/Suites/Resorts	10,420	63	5	58	0	0	2,423	20
Comfort Inns/Suites	87,551	1,015	23	992	0	0	18,891	279
Econo Lodges	42,801	633	1	632	0	0	493	9
Friendship Inns	3,528	80	0	80	0	0	222	5
Quality Inns/Hotels/Suites	43,281	341	14	327	0	0	22,512	20
Rodeway Inns	9,539	128	1	127	0	0	263	3
Sleep Inns	3,672	51	1	50	0	0	218	2
TOTAL	**200,792**	**2,311**	**45**	**2,266**	**0**	**0**	**45,022**	**519**

	U.S. Properties		Status of U.S. Properties				Foreign Properties	
	Number of Rooms	Number of Properties	Company Owned	Franchised/ Licensed	Management Contract	Other	Number of Rooms	Number of Properties

Marriott International
Marriott Drive
Washington, D.C. 20058

Courtyard by Marriott	34,873	239	198	41	0	0	400	4
Fairfield Inn	20,078	202	50	152	0	0	0	0
Marriott Hotels/Resorts/Suites	109,000	274	1	76	197	0	10,684	44
Residence Inn	23,478	193	144	85	107	0	120	1
TOTAL	187,429	908	393	354	304	0	11,204	49

Best Western International
P.O. Box 10203
Phoenix, Arizona 85064-0203

Best Western	175,682	1,890	0	0	0	1,890	102,046	1,509
TOTAL	175,682	1,890	0	0	0	1,890	102,046	1,509

Hilton Hotels Corporation
9336 Civic Center Drive
Beverly Hills, California 90210

Conrad Hotels	0	0	0	0	0	0	2,493	7
Hilton Garden Inns	657	4	1	3	0	0	0	0
Hilton Hotels	47,178	49	17	0	21	11	0	0
Hilton Inns	40,545	157	0	157	0	0	0	0
Hilton Suites	1,246	6	5	1	0	0	0	0
TOTAL	89,626	216	23	161	21	11	2,493	7

IBL Limited, Inc.
2 Overhill Road
Suite 420
Scarsdale, New York 10583-5325

Motel 6	86,717	769	692	0	77	0	0	0
TOTAL	86,717	769	692	0	77	0	0	0

Promus Companies Incorporated
1023 Cherry Road
Memphis, Tennessee 38117

Embassy Suites	26,018	110	9	52	27	22	460	2
Hampton Inn	53,787	482	15	444	23	0	397	3
Homewood Suites	3,891	26	8	18	0	0	0	0
TOTAL	83,696	618	32	514	50	22	857	5

ITT Sheraton Corporation
60 State Street
Boston, Massachusetts 02109

Sheraton Hotels/Resorts/Casinos	57,550	150	13	99	20	18	42,473	152
Sheraton Inns/Four Points Hotels	16,448	84	0	84	0	0	1,180	6
The Luxury Collection	2,819	8	3	0	4	1	9,384	17
TOTAL	76,817	242	16	183	24	19	53,037	175

Carlson Hospitality Worldwide
Carlson Parkway
P.O. Box 59159
Minneapolis, Minnesota 55459-8212

Country Hospitality	3,016	39	0	37	2	0	914	13
Radisson Hotels	52,596	210	0	191	19	0	25,156	97
TOTAL	55,612	249	0	228	21	0	26,070	110

	U.S. Properties		Status of U.S. Properties				Foreign Properties	
	Number of Rooms	Number of Properties	Company Owned	Franchised/ Licensed	Management Contract	Other	Number of Rooms	Number of Properties
Hyatt Hotels Corporation								
Madison Plaza								
200 West Madison								
Chicago, Illinois 60606								
Hyatt Hotels	52,775	103	0	2	101	0	0	0
Hyatt International	0	0	0	0	0	0	24,242	67
TOTAL	52,775	103	0	2	101	0	24,242	67
La Quinta Motor Inns, Inc.								
112 East Pecan Street								
P.O. Box 2636								
San Antonio, Texas 78299-2636								
La Quinta Inns	30,356	236	234	1	1	0	0	0
TOTAL	30,356	236	234	1	1	0	0	0
Doubletree Hotels Corporation								
410 North 44th Street								
Suite 700								
Phoenix, Arizona 85008-6572								
Doubletree Club Hotel	2,573	14	0	9	5	0	0	0
Doubletree Hotel	16,269	49	0	9	40	0	0	0
Doubletree Guest Suites	7,378	34	1	6	27	0	0	0
TOTAL	26,220	97	1	24	72	0	0	0
Red Roof Inns								
4355 Davidson Road								
Hilliard, Ohio 43026								
Red Roof Inns	24,552	220	220	0	0	0	0	0
Trueman Club Hotel	182	1	1	0	0	0	0	0
TOTAL	24,734	221	221	0	0	0	0	0
Westin Hotels & Resorts								
The Westin Building								
Seattle, Washington 98121								
Westin Hotels & Resorts	21,471	37	16	4	13	4	14,144	32
Caesar Park Hotels	0	0	0	0	0	0	2,012	8
Camino Real	0	0	0	0	0	0	476	2
TOTAL	21,471	37	16	4	13	4	16,632	42
Hospitality International, Inc.								
1726 Montreal Circle								
Tucker, Georgia 30084-6809								
Passport Inns	1,166	22	0	22	0	0	0	0
Master Hosts Inns	1,959	18	0	18	0	0	0	0
Red Carpet Inns	8,742	147	0	147	0	0	0	0
Scottish Inns	8176	159	0	159	0	0	0	0
TOTAL	20,043	346	0	346	0	0	0	0
R&B Realty Group								
1054 31st Street NW								
Suite 1000								
Washington, D.C. 20007								
Oakwood Corporate Apartments	19,620	35	27	0	8	0	0	0
TOTAL	19,620	35	27	0	8	0	0	0

	U.S. Properties		Status of U.S. Properties				Foreign Properties	
	Number of Rooms	Number of Properties	Company Owned	Franchised/ Licensed	Management Contract	Other	Number of Rooms	Number of Properties
Renaissance Hotels International								
17th Floor New World Tower II 16–18 Queen's Road Hong Kong								
Stouffer Hotels & Resorts	11,519	13	2	1	4	6	297	1
Renaissance Hotels/Resorts	5,103	27	0	0	27	0	11,032	34
Ramada International Hotel & Resorts	0	0	0	0	0	0	12,051	52
TOTAL	16,662	40	2	1	31	6	23,380	87
Preferred Hotels								
1901 South Meyers Road Suite 220 Oakbrook Terrace, Illinois 60181								
Preferred Hotels	15,294	62	0	0	0	62	8,446	48
TOTAL	15,294	62	0	0	0	62	8,446	48
Circus Circus Enterprises								
P.O. Box 14967 Las Vegas, Nevada 89114-4967								
Various Hotels	14,653	9	9	0	0	0	0	0
TOTAL	14,653	9	9	0	0	0	0	0
Red Lion Hotels & Inns								
4001 Main Street P.O. Box 1027 Vancouver, Washington 98666								
Red Lion Hotels & Inns	13,881	53	38	0	15	0	0	0
TOTAL	13,881	53	38	0	15	0	0	0
Wyndham Hotels & Resorts								
2001 Bryan Street 23rd Floor Dallas, Texas 75201								
Wyndham Hotels & Resorts	13,132	49	30	2	17	0	1,325	4
TOTAL	13,132	49	30	2	17	0	1,325	4
Omni Hotels								
Hampton, New Hampshire 03842								
Omni Hotels	12,962	36	9	16	11	0	2,352	5
TOTAL	12,962	36	9	16	11	0	2,352	5
National 9 Motels, Inc.								
2285 South Main Suite 9 Salt Lake City, Utah 84115								
National 9 Inns	10,110	152	5	147	0	0	0	0
National 9 Motels	802	14	0	14	0	0	0	0
National 9 Suites	1,125	13	1	12	0	0	0	0
TOTAL	12,037	179	6	173	0	0	0	0
Budgetel Inns, Inc.								
250 East Wisconsin Avenue Suite 1750 Milwaukee, Wisconsin 53202								
Budgetel Inns	11,229	106	82	24	0	0	0	0
Woodfield Suites	339	3	3	0	0	0	0	0
TOTAL	11,568	109	85	24	0	0	0	0

	U.S. Properties		Status of U.S. Properties				Foreign Properties	
	Number of Rooms	Number of Properties	Company Owned	Franchised/ Licensed	Management Contract	Other	Number of Rooms	Number of Properties

Outrigger Hotels Hawaii
16000 Ventura Boulevard
Suite 1010
Encino, California 91436

Outrigger Hotels Hawaii	8,773	28	13	0	15	0	0	0
TOTAL	**8,773**	**28**	**13**	**0**	**15**	**0**	**0**	**0**

Ritz-Carlton Hotel Company
3414 Peachtree Road, NE
Atlanta, Georgia 30326

Ritz-Carlton	8,621	25	0	0	25	10	1,690	6
TOTAL	**8,621**	**25**	**0**	**0**	**25**	**10**	**1,690**	**6**

ShoLodge, Inc.
217 West Main
Gallatin, Tennessee 37066

Shoney's Inn	8,194	76	28	45	3	0	0	0
TOTAL	**8,194**	**76**	**28**	**45**	**3**	**0**	**0**	**0**

Budget Host International
P.O. Box 14341
Arlington, Texas 76094

Budget Host Inns	7,442	176	0	176	0	0	96	2
TOTAL	**7,442**	**176**	**0**	**176**	**0**	**0**	**96**	**2**

Drury Inns, Inc.
10801 Pear Tree Lane
St. Louis, Missouri 63074

Drury Inn	5,754	48	48	0	0	0	0	0
TOTAL	**5,754**	**48**	**48**	**0**	**0**	**0**	**0**	**0**

Aston Hotels & Resorts
2255 Kuhio Avenue
Honolulu, Hawaii 96815-2658

Aston Condominiums	3,063	18	0	0	18	0	0	0
Aston Hotels	2,337	15	2	0	13	0	0	0
TOTAL	**5,400**	**33**	**2**	**0**	**31**	**0**	**0**	**0**

Four Seasons/Regent Hotels & Resorts
1165 Leslie Street
Toronto, Ontario, M3C 2K8
Canada

Four Seasons/Regent Hotels & Resorts	5,384	17	6	0	9	8	7,588	22
TOTAL	**5,384**	**17**	**6**	**0**	**9**	**8**	**7,588**	**22**

Harrah's Entertainment
219 North Center Street
Reno, Nevada 89501

Harrah's Casinos	5,345	6	6	0	0	0	0	0
TOTAL	**5,345**	**6**	**6**	**0**	**0**	**0**	**0**	**0**

	U.S. Properties		Status of U.S. Properties				Foreign Properties	
	Number of Rooms	Number of Properties	Company Owned	Franchised/ Licensed	Management Contract	Other	Number of Rooms	Number of Properties

Doral Hotels & Resorts
122 East 42nd Street
Suite 1601
New York, New York 10168-1694

Doral Hotels & Resorts	4,656	13	10	3	0	0	689	4
Other	600	2	0	0	2	0	0	0
TOTAL	5,256	15	10	3	2	0	689	4

Independent Motels of America, Inc.
West Highway 18
Winner, South Dakota 57580

Independent Motels of America	4,800	127	0	0	0	127	0	0
TOTAL	4,800	127	0	0	0	127	0	0

Shilo Inn and Hotels
11600 SW Barnes Road
Portland, Oregon 97225

Shilo Inns	4,766	47	47	0	0	0	0	0
TOTAL	4,766	47	47	0	0	0	0	0

Loews Corporation
667 Madison Avenue
New York, New York 10021-8087

Loews Hotels	4,104	11	7	0	4	0	1,205	3
TOTAL	4,104	11	7	0	4	0	1,205	3

U.F. Franchise Systems
One Airport Way
Suite 200
Rochester, New York 14624

Microtel	1,976	20	0	20	0	6	0	0
Hawthorn Suites Hotels	2,023	16	4	12	0	0	0	0
TOTAL	3,999	36	4	32	0	6	0	0

HLC Hotels, Inc.
P.O. Box 13069
Savannah, Georgia 31416-0069

Masters Economy Inn	3,594	29	23	5	1	0	0	0
TOTAL	3,594	29	23	5	1	0	0	0

Chalet Suisse International, Inc.
Chalet Drive
Wilton, New Hampshire 03086

Suisse Chalet	3,535	34	25	8	1	0	0	0
TOTAL	3,535	34	25	8	1	0	0	0

Grande Hotels and Resorts
1859 Northgate Boulevard
Sarasota, Florida 34234

Grande Hotels and Resorts	2,813	18	0	18	0	0	1,682	18
TOTAL	2,813	18	0	18	0	0	1,682	18

	U.S. Properties		Status of U.S. Properties				Foreign Properties	
	Number of Rooms	Number of Properties	Company Owned	Franchised/ Licensed	Management Contract	Other	Number of Rooms	Number of Properties

Signature Inns, Inc.
One Parkwood Crossing
250 East 96th Street
Suite 450
Indianapolis, Indiana 46240

Signature Inn	2,749	23	0	23	23	0	0	0
TOTAL	**2,749**	**23**	**0**	**23**	**23**	**0**	**0**	**0**

Wilson Hotel Management Company
1629 Winchester Road
Memphis, Tennessee 38116

Wilson Inns	1,196	11	0	11	0	0	0	0
Wilson World	1,293	5	0	5	0	0	0	0
TOTAL	**2,489**	**16**	**0**	**16**	**0**	**0**	**0**	**0**

Lexington Hotel Suites & Inns
2120 Walnut Hill Lane
Suite 106
Irving, Texas 75038

Lexington Hotel Suites & Inns	2,482	15	5	10	0	0	0	0
TOTAL	**2,482**	**15**	**5**	**10**	**0**	**0**	**0**	**0**

ClubHouse Inns of America
11230 College Boulevard
Suite 130
Overland Park, Kansas 66210-1891

ClubHouse Inn	2,177	15	8	1	6	0	0	0
TOTAL	**2,177**	**15**	**8**	**1**	**6**	**0**	**0**	**0**

InnSuites Hotels
P.O. Box 26907
Phoenix, Arizona 85068-6907

InnSuites Hotels	1,470	12	8	4	0	0	105	1
TOTAL	**1,470**	**12**	**8**	**4**	**0**	**0**	**105**	**1**

Sources: Lodging Hospitality; and PKF Consulting.

APPENDIX 2

GLOSSARY OF HOTEL TERMS

actual market share, see **market share.**

all-suite hotel, a hotel in which all guest rooms have a sleeping area and a living area, which are not necessarily physically divided.

amenities, in general, the services and facilities offered by a hotel or in a hotel's market area.

anchor tenant, a major tenant in a commercial or retail space, such as a department store in a shopping center.

appraisal, an analysis, opinion, or conclusion relating to the nature, quality, value, or utility of specified interests in, or aspects of, identified real estate (as defined in the *Code of Professional Ethics* of the Appraisal Institute). In this usage, appraisal covers a variety of assignments, including valuation, consulting, and review.

average daily rate per occupied room, total guest room revenue for a given period divided by the total number of rooms occupied (room nights) during the same period.

average daily room rate per guest, total guest room revenue for a given period divided by the total number of guests accommodated during the same time period.

back-of-house, the work areas of a hotel that are not accessible to the public, including the kitchen, laundry, storage areas, machinery rooms, and shops.

base year, the year that serves as a benchmark for projections of a hotel's performance.

cash flow, the net spendable income, determined by deducting all operating and interest expenses from the gross income. If expenses exceed income, cash flow is negative.

central reservations system (CRS), a toll free number maintained by a hotel chain or group to take reservations.

commission, an amount, usually a percentage, paid to travel agents for the sales of products or services.

condominium, the fee simple ownership of a unit, generally in a multiunit building, plus an undivided interest in the common elements. The concept is extended to timeshare hotels and resorts.

construction loan, an open-end mortgage, usually for a short term, used to finance the construction of buildings.

convention hotel, a hotel that provides facilities and services geared to meet the needs of large meetings and trade shows. Typically, such hotels contain more than 400 guest rooms and substantial function and banquet space that is flexibly designed for various uses. A convention hotel often works in concert with other convention hotels and convention centers to provide facilities for citywide conventions and trade shows.

cost approach, a method of estimating a property's market value based on its current reproduction or replacement cost, deducting accrued depreciation, and adding land value and entrepreneurial profit.

demand generator, any entity that creates or attracts demand for hotel rooms. Examples include office parks, convention centers, natural attractions, shopping malls, hospitals, sporting arenas or events, universities, military bases, and airports.

double occupancy rate, the room rate for a double or twin room when it is occupied by two people. See also **single occupancy rate.**

equity, the interest or value that an owner has in real estate over and above any mortgage against it.

fair market share, a hotel's percentage share of the total number of competitive rooms in the market. Fair share is compared with actual market share to determine a property's capture rate or penetration. See also **market share.**

fixed expenses, costs that are more or less permanent and vary little from year to year, such as real estate taxes and insurance for fire, theft, and hazards.

full-service hotel, a hotel that provides a wide range of facilities, including food and beverage outlets, meeting rooms, and recreational amenities.

franchise, a private contractual agreement under which the franchisee operates a business using a designated trademark and operating procedures.

gross revenue, all revenues of any kind derived directly or indirectly from the property, including rentals or other payments from tenants and concessionaires.

gross operating profit, see **income before fixed charges.**

hotel, see **lodging property.**

hotel management company, a company that uses its own trademark and reservations system in providing management and operating services for lodging properties, which it owns, leases, or manages. See also **independent operating company.**

incentive fee, see **management fee.**

income before fixed charges (gross operating profit), income after management fees, property taxes, and insurance. Does not include deductions for depreciation, rent, interest, amortization, management fees, property taxes and insurance. Comparisons beyond income after management fees, property taxes, and insurance are virtually meaningless due to wide variances in ownership, depreciation methods, financing bases, income taxes, and so forth.

income capitalization approach, a method of estimating a property's market value by dividing its anticipated benefits (cash flows and reversion) by investors' required rate of return (market capitalization rate).

independent operating company, a hotel company providing management and operating services for lodging properties that it owns, leases, or manages, but without the use of a trademark or reservations system of its own. It may operate a franchise property that carries a lodging chain's trademark and reservations system. See also **hotel management company.**

induced demand, room night demand that has been attracted to a market by some new attraction or other demand generator.

limited-service hotel, a hotel that provides only some of the facilities and amenities of a full-service property. This category includes properties occasionally referred to as motels or motor hotels.

lodging property, any commercial lodging accommodation available for transient guests, including hotels, motels, inns, and resorts. The word "hotel" used in this text carries the same meaning.

management contract, a written agreement between the owner and the operator of a lodging facility by which the owner employs the operator as an agent to assume full responsibility for operating and managing the property.

management fee, the basic fee and/or the incentive fee paid to the operator. The **basic fee** is the remuneration that the hotel owner agrees to pay the operator for performing the duties specified in the management contract. The fee is usually an agreed percentage of gross revenues, but is sometimes a fixed amount independent of the volume of revenue realized. The **incentive fee** is the remuneration that the owner agrees to pay the operator for achieving a certain profit, income, or level of cash flow from the operation. The fee is usually an agreed percentage of gross operating profit, or a percentage of cash flow after debt service and other ownership obligations. An incentive fee may be paid in addition to or in lieu of the basic fee, depending upon the provisions of the contract.

market share, the percentage share of the total room nights in the market that is actually captured by a particular hotel. See also **fair market share.**

market value, the highest price for which a property would sell, assuming a reasonable period of time within which the sale can occur, a knowledgeable buyer, and a seller not acting under duress.

net rooms revenue, the revenue from rooms that remains after expenses such as sales taxes, room taxes, and other occupancy taxes are deducted.

operating expenses, the expenses necessary for the continuous operation and maintenance of an income property.

operator, an affiliated independent operating company responsible for the professional management of a hotel property. See also **hotel management company and independent operating company.**

owner-in-foreclosure, an entity—usually a commercial bank, savings and loan association, real estate investment trust, or savings bank—that has assumed ownership of the property as a result of the original developer/owner's inability to honor its loan commitments.

penetration, the percentage relationship between a hotel's market share and its fair market share. If a hotel is capturing more than its fair market share, its penetration is greater than 100 percent.

percentage of occupancy, the percentage of available rooms that are occupied during a given period.

property, a hotel, motel, or restaurant building, including its furniture, fixtures, and equipment, and the land it occupies.

published rate, the room rate listed in hotel directories and on rate cards. Generally, the published rate is the hotel's highest room rate. Also called the rack rate.

rack rate, see **published rate.**

real estate investment trust (REIT), mutual real estate funds enjoying special tax benefits. REITs raise funds through the sales of shares to the public, and make mortgage or equity real estate investments.

reservations system, see **central reservations system (CRS).**

resort hotel, a hotel, usually in a suburban or isolated rural location, with special recreational facilities to attract pleasure-seeking guests.

room night, one hotel room occupied by one or more people for one night, used as a unit of hotel demand.

sales comparison approach, a method of estimating a property's market value based on a comparison of the property's price to the prices of similar properties that have been sold recently.

single occupancy rate, the discounted room rate for a double or twin room when it is occupied by one person. The discount rate is usually less than 50 percent.

suite hotel, see **all-suite hotel.**

variable cost ratio, operating expenses, including taxes, insurance, maintenance, management, and utilities, expressed as a percentage of gross revenue.

working capital, funds provided from the operation's cash flow (and from the owner as required) to cover operating expenses.

yield, income or profit earned on an investment.

Appendix 3
Sample Hotel Project Brief

Summary

Number of Keys	350
Number of Modules	394
Suites as a Percent of Keys	12.2%
Square Meters/Feet per Key (Categories 1.00–18.00)	118.2/1,271.69
Square Meters/Feet per Module (Categories 1.00–18.00)	105.0/1,129.67
Guest Rooms as a Percent of Building	60.4%
Public Space and Back-of-House as a Percent of Building	39.6%

1.00–22.00 Total Project

		Square Meters	Square Feet
1.00	Guest Rooms and Circulation Areas	24,965	268,623
2.00	Public Areas	485	5,218
3.00	Retail	260	2,797
4.00	FrontDesk	183	1,970
5.00	Guest Amenities/Recreation	937	10,082
6.00	Food and Beverage Areas	1,162	12,503
7.00	Function Areas	2,777	29,880
8.00	Function Support	1,693	18,218
9.00	Executive Offices	93	1,002
10.00	General Offices	232	2,496
11.00	Accounting Offices	160	1,722
12.00	Food Service Areas	1,417	15,249
13.00	Housekeeping/Laundry	370	3,983
14.00	Maintenance	195	2099
15.00	Employee Facilities	580	6,240
16.00	Mechanical/Electrical	2,460	26,470
17.00	Receiving and Purchasing	296	3,185
18.00	Circulation	3,100	33,356
Subtotal		**41,365**	**445,093**
19.00	Pool Facility	75	808
20.00	Water Treatment	400	4,304
21.00	Waste Water Treatment	600	6,456
22.00	Landscape Maintenance Facility	114	1,227
Subtotal		**1,189**	**12,795**
Project Total		**42,554**	**457,888**

1.00 Guest Rooms and Circulation Areas

		Square Meters	Square Feet
1.01	Rooms (1 Module = 47.5 square meters)		
185	King Rooms (1 Module)	8,788	94,559
122	Double Rooms (1 Module)	5,795	62,354
20	Parlor Suites (1.5 Modules)	1,425	15,333
21	Executive Suites (2 Modules)	1,995	21,466
2	Presidential Suites (5 Modules)	475	5,111
1	Club Lounge (5 Modules)	237	2,550
Subtotal Guest Rooms		**18,715**	**201,373**
1.02	Corridors	2,500	26,900
1.03	Vertical Transportation	1,400	15,064
1.04	Service	1,350	14,526
1.05	Balconies	1,000	10,760
Subtotal Circulation Area		**6,250**	**67,250**
Total Guest Rooms and Circulation Area		**24,965**	**268,623**

2.00 Public Areas

		Square Meters	Square Feet
2.01	Porte-Cochere (Outside)	–	–
2.02	Entry Vestibule	19	205
2.03	Reception Lobby	186	2,000
2.04	Grand Stair	85	915
2.05	Toilets	175	1,883
2.06	Telephone	20	215
Total Public Areas		**485**	**5,218**

3.00 Retail Space

		Square Meters	Square Feet
3.01	Sundry	50	538
3.02	Gift Shop	50	538
3.03	Logo Shop	80	861
3.04	Travel	20	215
3.05	Beauty Salon at Fitness Center	60	645
Total Retail Area		**260**	**2,797**

	Square Meters	Square Feet
4.00 Front Desk		
4.01 Registration/Cashier	19	205
4.02 Work Counter	9	97
4.03 Safety Deposit Boxes (SDB)	5	54
4.04 SDB Viewing Area	5	54
4.05 Front Office Manager (Office)	9	97
4.06 Credit Manager	9	97
4.07 Reservations/Telephone Operators	60	645
4.08 Concierge	15	161
4.09 Bell Captain/Baggage Storage	23	248
4.10 Valet Parking	9	97
4.11 Circulation	20	215
Total Front Desk Area	**183**	**1,970**
5.00 Guest Amenities and Recreation		
5.01 Business Center	47	506
5.02 Executive Fitness Club	700	7,532
5.03 Pool (Outdoor)	–	–
5.04 Tennis Courts (4) (Outdoor)	–	–
5.05 Squash Courts (2)	190	2,044
5.06 Children's Facility (Outdoor)	–	–
Total Guest Amenities and Recreation Area	**937**	**10,082**
6.00 Food and Beverage Areas (Number of Seats)		
6.01 Fine Dining Restaurant		
Dining (80)	250	2,690
Private Dining (14)	37	398
6.02 Three-Meal Restaurant		
Dining (140)	350	3,767
Bar (5)	–	–
Cafe Terrace (75) (Outside)	–	–
6.03 Lobby Lounge (100)	280	3,012
6.04 Specialty Restaurant		
Dining (64)	170	1,829
Private Dining (36) (3 Rooms)	75	807
6.05 Pool Facilities (Outside)		
Bar (5)	–	–
Covered Dining (35)	–	–
Covered Terrace (20)	–	–
Total Food and Beverage Area	**1,162**	**12,503**
7.00 Function Areas		
7.01 Main Ballroom	1,400	15,064
7.02 Junior Ballroom	500	5,380
7.03 Boardroom No. 1	75	807
7.04 Boardroom No. 2	37	398
7.05 Meeting Room No. 1	50	538
7.06 Meeting Room No. 2	80	861
7.07 Meeting Room No. 3	80	861
7.08 Meeting Room No. 4	80	861
7.09 Meeting Room No. 5	95	1,022
7.10 Meeting Room No. 6	95	1,022
7.11 Meeting Room No. 7	95	1,022
7.12 Meeting Room No. 8	95	1,022
7.13 Meeting Room No. 9	95	1,022
Total Function Area	**2,777**	**29,880**

	Square Meters	Square Feet
8.00 Function Support Areas		
8.01 Prefunction Area	985	10,599
8.02 Grand Stair	100	1,076
8.03 Toilets	325	3,497
8.04 Storage	170	1,829
8.05 Public Phones	50	538
8.06 Audiovisual Storage	19	205
8.07 Banquet Service Manager	19	205
8.08 Control Booth	10	108
8.09 Coatroom	15	161
Total Function Support Area	**1,693**	**18,218**
9.00 Executive Offices		
9.01 General Manager	14	151
9.02 Administrative Assistant	9	97
9.03 Food and Beverage Executive	9	97
9.04 Secretary	9	97
9.05 Rooms Executive	9	97
9.06 Secretary	9	97
9.07 Storage	9	97
9.08 Reception	9	97
9.09 Circulation	16	172
Total Executive Offices Area	**93**	**1,002**
10.00 General Offices		
10.01 Catering and Conference Services Director	10	108
10.02 Catering and Conference Service Managers	49	527
10.03 Administrative Assistants	28	301
10.04 Sales and Marketing Director	9	97
10.05 Sales Managers	56	603
10.06 Administrative Assistants	33	355
10.07 Market Research Analysts and Guest History	11	118
10.08 Public Relations	7	75
10.09 Copying, Mail, and Coffee	9	97
10.10 Circulation	20	215
Total General Offices Area	**232**	**2,496**
11.00 Accounting Offices		
11.01 Controller	9	97
11.02 Assistant	7	75
11.03 Administrative Assistant	7	75
11.04 General Cashier/Safes	14	151
11.05 Counting Room	16	172
11.06 Clerks	50	538
11.07 Computer Room.	23	248
11.08 Storage, Mail, and Copying	15	161
11.09 Circulation	19	205
Total Accounting Offices Area	**160**	**1,722**

		Square Meters	Square Feet
12.00 Food Service Operations			
12.01	Kitchen and Dishware Washing	372	4,003
12.02	Second Kitchen	232	2,496
12.03	Specialty Restaurant Kitchen	232	2,496
12.04	Butcher Shop and Garden Manager	65	699
12.05	Bake Shop, Chocolates, and Pastry Dish-Up	65	699
12.06	Pastry Dish-Up	9	97
12.07	Chef Office	15	161
12.08	Room Service	19	205
12.09	Dry Storage	19	205
12.10	Chemical Storage and Toilets	9	97
12.11	Refrigerated Storage	19	205
12.12	Freezer Storage	19	205
12.13	Liquor Storage	28	301
12.14	Main Service Bar	50	538
12.15	Wines and Beer	9	97
12.16	Soda	9	97
12.17	Steward Office	9	97
12.18	Silver Storage	19	205
12.19	Silver Burnishing	9	97
12.20	China and Glass Storage	9	97
12.21	Function Pantry	200	2,152
Total Food Service Area		**1,417**	**15,249**
13.00 Housekeeping and Laundry Operations			
13.01	Linen Storage	19	205
13.02	Secured Storage	9	97
13.03	Housekeeping Storage	13	140
13.04	Sewing	9	97
13.05	Lost and Found	7	75
13.06	Director (Office)	9	97
13.07	Assistant Manager and Secretary	9	97
13.08	Laundry	165	1,775
13.09	Uniform Issue	19	205
13.10	Mechanical	9	97
13.11	Sorting	19	205
13.12	Detergent Storage	9	97
13.13	Valet	65	699
13.14	Supervisor	9	97
Total Housekeeping and Laundry Area		**370**	**3,983**
14.00 Maintenance Operations			
14.01	Director	9	97
14.02	Assistant	9	97
14.03	Key Room	9	97
14.04	Parts	9	97
14.05	TV Room	9	97
14.06	Paint Shop	19	205
14.07	General	93	1,001
14.08	Yard Storage	38	408
Total Maintenance Area		**195**	**2,099**
15.00 Employee Facilities			
15.01	Men's Locker Room	140	1,506
15.02	Women's Locker Room	140	1,506
15.03	Cafeteria	160	1,722
15.04	Training Room	95	1,022
15.05	Restrooms	45	484
Total Employee Facilities Area		**580**	**6,240**
16.00 Mechanical and Electrical Equipment			
16.01	Transformer Vault	50	538
16.02	Generator	600	6,456
16.03	Switch Gear	300	3,228
16.04	Panel Room	60	646
16.05	Mechanical	750	8,070
16.06	Boiler	300	3,228
16.07	Telephone, Computer, and PBX	25	269
16.08	Chases	25	269
16.09	Elevator Machine Room	350	3,766
Total Mechanical and Electrical Area		**2,460**	**26,470**
17.00 Receiving and Purchasing			
17.01	Truck Dock	40	430
17.02	Compactor	9	97
17.03	Receiving	9	97
17.04	Temporary Storage	19	205
17.05	Refrigerated Garbage	9	97
17.06	Can Wash	5	54
17.07	Dry Wash	5	54
17.08	Security and Fire Control	40	430
17.09	Purchasing	15	161
17.10	Personnel	9	97
17.11	Assistant	40	430
17.12	Waiting	9	97
17.13	Storage	40	430
17.14	Food Washing and Sorting	20	215
17.15	Benefits Office	8	86
17.16	Nurse	9	97
17.17	Flower Shop	10	108
Total Receiving and Purchasing Area		**296**	**3,185**
18.00 Circulation			
18.01	Public	1,300	13,988
18.02	Back-of-House	1,800	19,368
Total Circulation Area		**3,100**	**33,356**
19.00 Pool Facility			
19.01	Kitchen, Coolers, and Server Station	51	549
19.02	Towel Issue	5	54
19.03	Toilets, Janitor's Closet, and Mechanical	19	205
Total Pool Facility Area		**75**	**808**
20.00 Water Treatment			
20.01	Pump Room	85	915
20.02	Water Storage	315	3,389
Total Water Treatment Area		**400**	**4,304**
21.00 Wastewater Treatment			
21.01	Treatment Equipment	400	4,304
21.02	Wastewater Storage	200	2,152
Total Wastewater Treatment Area		**600**	**6,456**
22.00 Landscape Maintenance Facility			
22.01	Office	11	118
22.02	Secured Locker	14	151
22.03	Secured Locker	9	97
22.04	Uniform Issue Closet	7	75
22.05	Restrooms	5	54
22.06	Bays	58	624
22.07	Circulation	10	108
Total Landscape Maintenance Facility Area		**114**	**1,227**